INDIA IN BRITAIN

(*frontispiece*) Mahatma Gandhi, the leader in the
struggle for Independence, leaves 10 Downing Street.

Kusoom Vadgama

INDIA IN BRITAIN

The Indian contribution
to the British way of life

Robert Royce Limited

LONDON

This book is affectionately dedicated to my mother and to the memory of my father.

Published by Robert Royce Limited,
93 Bedwardine Road, London SE19

Editorial selection ©Kusoom Vadgama 1984
Design ©BLA Publishing Limited 1984.

First published 1984.

This book was designed and produced by
BLA Publishing Limited, Swan Court, London Road,
East Grinstead, Sussex, England

A member of the Ling Kee Group
LONDON HONG KONG TAIPEI SINGAPORE NEW YORK

Printed in England by Adlard & Son Limited,
Bartholomew Press, Dorking, Surrey
Bound by Norton Bridge Bookbinders Limited, Hitchin, Herts.

ISBN: 0 947728 03 1

Contents

Prologue   *page*   7

Foreword by H.R.H. The Prince of Wales   9

Foreword by Mrs Indira Gandhi   11

Note to the reader   12

INTRODUCTION: India in Britain   13

CHAPTER ONE: Victoria, Kaisar-i-Hind   17

CHAPTER TWO: Indian nobility: the nineteenth century   41

CHAPTER THREE: India on display   59

CHAPTER FOUR: The Coronations   73

CHAPTER FIVE: World War I   92

CHAPTER SIX: Indian nobility: the early twentieth century   107

CHAPTER SEVEN: Sporting encounters   122

CHAPTER EIGHT: Indians in Westminster   151

CHAPTER NINE: World War II   168

CHAPTER TEN: The Indian influence   177

CHAPTER ELEVEN: Indians and their British alma maters   195

CHAPTER TWELVE: Indian nobility – the years before
    independence   213

CHAPTER THIRTEEN: Gandhi and the Round Table
    Conferences   225

CHAPTER FOURTEEN: Towards Independence   241

A personal postscript   251

Index   254

Acknowledgements

IT IS WITH GREAT PERSONAL PLEASURE and national pride that I publish this first ever book on the dignity and influence of India in Britain during the years of the Raj, 1852 to 1947. A long-cherished dream now becomes a reality as I present this permanent pictorial record of Indian contribution in Britain with a hope that it will also, in some measure, counterbalance books about the British in India during the corresponding years.

It would be impossible to compile a book such as this, without the help and understanding of the individual members of the staff of libraries, photographic archives and private collectors, patiently dealing with my requests and endless inquiries. I have gratefully leant on their readiness to assist me in my research.

I am grateful to Her Majesty the Queen for graciously allowing me to select photographs and historical data from the Royal Archives. In particular I thank Miss Frances Dimond for help. I am especially indebted to Mr Terence Pepper of the National Portrait Gallery for sharing with me his extensive knowledge and offering invaluable assistance at all times in the selection of pictures. I would also like to say a special thank you to Miss Elaine Baird of Brighton Central Library for looking up pictures and text on the First World War. My sincere thanks to Miss Pauline Adams of Somerville College, Mrs Margaret Gaskell of Girton College, Mr Patrick Strong of Eton College, Mr George Matthews of the Communist Party Library and Archives, and to Miss Barbara Mason of The Religious Society of Friends.

I am most grateful to Mr David Grayston for providing important additional material and vital research; I have benefited greatly by his expertise and shared enthusiasm for the subject. I am equally grateful to Mr Iqbal Singh for his valued comments on the Introduction. I am also happy to acknowledge the assistance so generously given by Mr Ian Jack. I owe an overwhelming debt of gratitude to Mr Jon Wynne-Tyson, Centaur Press Ltd. I am extremely happy that Mr Elwyn Blacker of BLA Publishing Ltd has made such an excellent job of the design of the book. With his editor, Ms Margaret Hickey, who also researched and added valuable additions to the text, he has mastered the complicated task of learning Indian names, titles and places! My thanks also to the staff of Adlard and Son, Dorking for the care and attention they have given to the printing of this book.

I am deeply saddened by the sudden death of Mr Harsukh Pandit who was closely involved with the book. For all his wonderful support and guidance I convey my thanks to his wife Sarlaben.

And finally my thanks to my uncle Chimanlal Gajjar, in Amreli, for providing the history of my maternal ancestors and for the use of the gold medal from the family collection.

PICTURE CREDITS

The author and publishers wish to acknowledge permission to reproduce the illustrations as follows:
By gracious permission of H.M. the Queen 19, 25, 27, 28, 29, 30, 31, 32, 33, 34, 35, 36b, 38t, 42, 48, 49, 50, 51, 53, 65, 79, 91b, 106, 108, 119, 184, 195, 196.
BBC Hulton Picture Library *Frontispiece*, 15, 88, 93, 114, 115, 117, 118b, 120, 132t, 135, 137, 138, 140, 141, 151, 161, 191, 203, 204, 211, 214, 223t, 235b, 239t, 240, 247, 249.
George A. Beldam Collection 124.
Bodleian Library 200.
Camera Press 8, 10, 222.
Central Press 135b, 168, 216/7, 220, 221t, 222.
Communist Party Archives 159.
East Sussex County Library 98, 99, 100, 102.
Fasal Collection 220.
Lord Ferrier 39.
Fox Photos 86, 87, 89, 129, 146b, 150, 187, 219, 221b, 230.
Mistress and Fellows of Girton College 199, 206, 207, 208, 209.
Illustrated London News Picture Library 36t, 37, 40, 44, 45, 46, 47, 52, 64, 66, 68, 69, 71, 72, 74, 75, 79b, 80, 82, 83, 85, 90, 112, 118t, 127, 128, 131, 133, 139, 142, 143, 144, 145b, 146t, 147b, 148, 149, 183, 189, 205, 241, 244.
Imperial War Museum 92, 169, 170, 173b, 174.
India Office Library 96, 97, 100b, 225, 231, 237, 248.
Keystone Press 171, 172, 173t, 175, 176, 212, 215, 223b, 224, 226, 236, 248b.
Mansell Collection 59, 60, 61, 62, 63, 81, 177, 238, 239b.
Marylebone Cricket Club 122, 123, 125, 134, 145.
National Army Museum 38b, 78, 103.
National Portrait Gallery 18, 76, 77, 84, 95, 107, 110, 157, 188, 192, 227, 235t, 237b.
Popperfoto 91t, 111, 113, 121, 130, 147t, 153, 193, 197, 213, 218.
Private collection 39, 164.
Punch 17, 21, 23, 228, 229.
Religious Society of Friends 16, 234.
Somerville College 210.
Sunday Times 186.
The Times 132b, 242, 245, 250.
The Walker Art Gallery, Liverpool 54, 55.
Dr. Williams's Trust 180.

Prologue

A PURELY PRIVATE VENTURE of three ships that sailed from Britain in 1591, established the first trading contact with India. Captain Lancaster brought back with him information that gave rise to subsequent commercial voyages to India, and the formation of a trading company in 1600. So successful was this overseas enterprise that its charter was renewed in 1609, 1657, 1661, 1693 and 1744. By 1683, £100 Indian Stocks were selling for £500.

In 1698 the 'London' Company was suspended for three years and a new company, the 'English' Company, was chartered; the two were merged in 1702. The new East India Company was established two years later in 1704. The affairs of the Company were brought before the Parliament in London in 1772, after accusations had been brought against it of gross irregularities in its running, including serious crimes. By way of correcting the situation, two acts of Parliament were passed; one authorised a loan of £1,000,000 to the Company and the other introduced the India Bill that brought about the change in the constitution of the Company and its relationship with India.

Warren Hastings was appointed the first Governor-General with a fixed £25,000 annual salary. Other presidencies were then made subordinate and a supreme court of judicature was instituted in Calcutta. The affairs of the Company came under one control which recognised its different departments. All their territorial correspondence passed through the British Ministry and a new bill was passed in London that appointed the Board of Control. The Company's charter was again renewed in 1793 for another 20 years and in 1813 trade with India was opened to everyone.

The Indian Mutiny of 1857 changed everything. With the disappearance of the Company's own army, the Government of India was transferred to the Crown and, by Royal assent, the Board of Control was duly replaced by the Council of State for India. On 1st September 1858, the East India Company's power came to an end and, on 1st November 1858, Queen Victoria was solemnly proclaimed as Empress of India.

By an interesting coincidence, Lord Attlee, the British Prime Minister responsible for India being granted Independence in 1947, was educated at Haileybury College. This college was founded in 1862 and the main building was originally built in 1806 for the East India College where students of the East India Company received their education and training.

BUCKINGHAM PALACE

A book such as this, which relies chiefly on photographs, has the ability to convey atmosphere and impressions in a way that words very often fail to do. The photographs that the author has collected are indeed fascinating and make the reader aware of the impact India had on the life and culture of Britain during the days of the Empire. Today, 35 years after Independence, India still has a considerable influence on the life of Britain, albeit in a somewhat different way, with many people from the sub-continent determined to succeed in their various endeavours in the country of their adoption. There may be no more princes or Indian orderly officers, but the culture of India can still enrich and expand our lives in many different ways, despite the problems that are bound to exist during what, I suspect, will be a transitional phase.

Charles.

2nd August, 1982

PRIME MINISTER

MESSAGE

Countless books have been written on the years of British rule in India. The Company and the Raj were served by a large number of articulate recorders. Less well known is the story of Indians in Britain – not only those who showed off their wealth but those who battled for large causes, intellectual and political.

"India in Britain" is a timely book. It should help the good work of bringing about closer understanding between our two peoples.

(Indira Gandhi)

New Delhi,
May 4, 1982

Note to the reader

A GREAT PART of this book consists of extracts from contemporary reports, principally commentaries from *The Times, The Illustrated London News* and *The Graphic*, as well as a number of other periodicals of the day. The texts of these extracts have been reproduced exactly as they appeared, although there are several inconsistencies of spelling, particularly with reference to the names of places in India and the titles of the Indian nobility. The reader is asked to understand the editor's desire to respect the integrity of the pieces, and to accept that, for example, the Victorian 'Maharajah of Kuch Behar' was the same person as the Edwardian 'Maharajah of Cooch Behar'. Where more than one version of a name is recorded, that which is accepted by modern scholars will be included in the index.

It is also worth noting that the Victorian practice of referring to followers of Islam as 'Mohammedans' is no longer acceptable, since Muhammad was no more than a prophet of God; believers are correctly referred to as Muslims.

I am grateful to Mr Krishna Kripalani for his permission to quote from his biography *Rabindranath Tagore,* published by Oxford University Press. My grateful thanks also to George Allen & Unwin for their permission to use extracts from *Mahatma Gandhi* by C. F. Andrews; quotations by Jawaharlal Nehru are reprinted with permission of The Bodley Head from his autobiography.

The Prologue has been adapted with the permission of Macmillan Publishing Company from *The Dictionary of Dates* (Vol. I) by Helen Rex Keller. In Chapter Seven the score cards for the 1932, 1936 and 1946 Test matches are reproduced, with kind permission, from *Wisden Cricketers' Almanac.*

I am also grateful to Debrett for providing me with biographical details of Sir Jamsetjee Jejeebhoy.

India at the 1937 Coronation and 1947 Independence ceremony extracts reprinted with the permission of *Times* Newspapers Limited.

India in Britain

THE WORLD has been so preoccupied with the British in India during the Raj that it has found little or no time to either appreciate or even acknowledge the Indian contribution to Britain during that period. Volumes have been written about the lives and achievements of sahibs and civil servants in India but hardly a word exists about the princes and philanthropists who served Britain, in peacetime as well as in war. This one-sided view of Imperial history cannot be allowed to go uncorrected. The tide of anti-immigration and racial feelings must be checked by a considered reappraisal of the services rendered to Britain by noble, if unremembered, men and women of India.

In publishing this book, a mainly pictorial account of the activities of Indians in Britain between 1852 and 1947, my purpose is to put the record straight and thus provide a corrective to arrogance and to the delusion that one race is superior to another.

Indians who came to these shores brought with them something of their rich and variegated culture, which made an impact on British life, high and low. The Establishment of the day, the politics of the time, the society of the period, the sports of the season were all enriched by the Indian connexion: India was, and remained, the brightest jewel in the crown that helped Britain project its image as a super-power and a great world leader. India mattered enormously at every occasion – state or official, ceremonial or commemorative. Every class of Indian, from the maharajah to the humble servant in the royal household, was looked upon with respect. The British revelled in, and acclaimed, the pomp of the princes, the courage of the soldiers, and even boasted of the loyalty of the common man to the Raj. The tendency to play down or even denigrate India and its importance in British affairs is of relatively recent origin and is connected with the surfacing of racist strains in British society.

Since the subject of Indians and their impact on British life during the period of the Raj has been greatly neglected, I have tried to relate events and represent personalities in exactly the way they first appeared in the British newspapers and periodicals of the time. The period begins during the reign of Queen Vicoria, and ends with the celebrations of the birth of Independent India, outside India House, London. In preparing this book I have examined the files of *The Times* and the many contemporary periodicals and consulted reference libraries and archives all over the country. The wealth of the material available is staggering, as the extracts published here will, I hope, show. Every detail, from the singing of the 'God Save the Queen' in Sanskrit to the selling of Indian shawls in a Regent Street shop, is authentic and verifiable.

The Court and Social pages of *The Times* are full of announcements of the arrival and departure of visiting maharajahs, most notable among them the Gaekwar of Baroda, the Maharajahs of Cooch Behar, the Maharajah of Gwalior, the Maharajah of Bikaner, the Thakore of Morvi, the Thakore of Gondal and the Rao of Cutch. In her diaries, Queen Victoria describes in detail what she thought of some of them. The Rao of Cutch was 'handsome' and he and his brother were like a 'dream': the Maharajah of Cooch Behar was 'tall and good-looking'. Her Majesty, who seems to have been spellbound with the glamorous notion of being the Empress of India, though she never visited the country, often wrote letters to some of the princes and maharajahs in India. On 15th August 1893 for instance, she wrote to the Maharajah of Bhavnagar:

My Dear Maharajah – I waited before thanking your Highness for your very kind letter, and for the beautiful cup made in your country, till my long-promised gift was ready. It is, however, now finished, and I hasten to forward it to you hoping that it may remind you of a true friend who will every pray for your health and prosperity.
Pray also accept my sincere thanks for your photographs which are extremely like, and I greatly value.
I truly appreciate all your kind and loyal expresions to myself and my Empire, and ask you to be assured that no one takes a warmer interest in the welfare and happiness of India than your Highness's sincere and faithful friend VICTORIA*

Some of these princes were known for their diplomatic skills, some for their elegance, some for their wealth and some for the power they exercised, but none was as popular as the great 'Ranji', the cricketer and captain of Sussex from 1899 to 1904 and the Jam Saheb of Navanagar. These princes added colour to public as well as social life. State occasions and ceremonial processions were never without the presence of a mounted escort of turbaned princes and soldiers. At the Coronation of George V in 1911, *The Times* wrote: 'For the magnificence in Oriental dress and splendour of turn-out there was nothing to equal the Indian Procession.'

There was nothing to equal the loyalty and sacrifices of the Indian officers and soldiers in the two world wars either. The total casualties for the 1914–1918 war alone was 121,598. Significantly, to the British these soldiers were 'their' soldiers, with whom they often shared jokes and cigarettes at their convalescence home in Brighton. Comradeship ruled the day.

Like the maharajahs and the soldiers, the rest of the Indian community was also often in the news. They dominated the social and cultural scene; some of them making the headlines by donating enormous sums of money to various British institutes, obtaining professional qualifications from universities and some achieving fame by their active participation in British politics. To date, three Indians have been elected to Parliament and one raised to the peerage. One, whose contributions to Britain by any standards remains memorable, and who represented the culture, the intelligence and the public spirit of India at its best, was Dadabhai Naoroji, the first Indian member of Parliament, who was elected as a Liberal in 1892 to represent Finsbury Central, London, which surely deserves a suitable memorial in the House. The Grand Old Man of India, as he was later popularly known, had come to Britain in 1855.

*This signature also written in Hindustani characters.

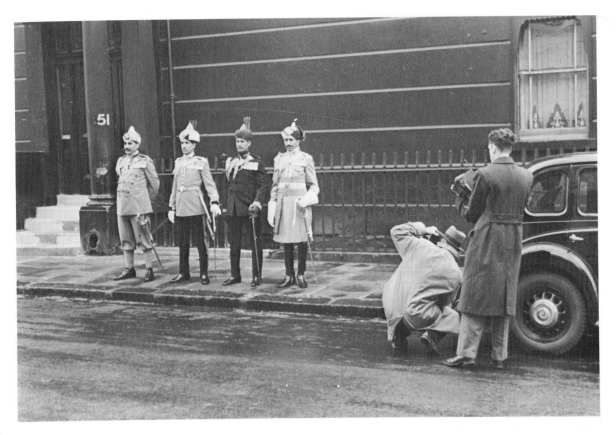

The King's Orderly Officers of 1939 make a magnificent sight as they stand at ease . . .

The man who followed Dadabhai Naoroji in the House of Commons in 1895, was Sir M.M. Bhownagree, a brilliant organiser and negotiator both inside and outside politics. He was one of the key men to put together the highly successful Colonial and Indian Exhibition of 1886 in South Kensington, London. As a national memorial to Queen Victoria's Golden Jubilee the following year, the exhibition was made permanent in the shape of the Imperial Institute – now the Commonwealth Institute.

Men like Rabindranath Tagore and Uday Shankar brought to prominence the literature and performing arts of India, while sportsmen like the great Ranjitsinhji (surprisingly still without any suitable memorial in Britain), and the Nawab of Pataudi provided thrills and excitement on the playing fields. India was never so characteristically represented and Britain was never so colourfully entertained.

Apart from this, there were those who made an intellectual, political and moral impact on this country. Men like the Rt. Hon. V.S. Srinivas Sastri, Privy Councillor, who was given the Freedom on the City of London in 1921 and was a member of the Round Table Conference, the Rt. Hon. Gopal Krishna Gokhale, Vallabh Bhai Patel, the industrialist and businessman Jamsetji Nasarwanji Tata, the Indian thinker and poet Sir Muhammad Iqbal, Sir Tej Bahadur Sapru, Swami Vivekananda, Baboo Keshu Chandra Sen, and the most recent of them all, V.K. Krishna Menon, who was given the Freedom of the Borough of St Pancras in London and who devoted a lifetime to the cause of India, becoming Independent India's first High Commissioner in London in 1947.

Pictorial material on most of these men and many others is not available for inclusion in the book; nevertheless their contribution cannot be underestimated.

Mahatma Gandhi, Laurence Housman and Krishna Menon with others leaving Friends House after a meeting on 12th September 1931.

No one nation can claim to have enriched Britain socially, culturally, financially, in manpower and in prestige, all at the same time and for so long, as India has. In present-day Britain these facts may not seem relevant, but the need to remind ourselves of them cannot be denied and must somehow be filled, especially when there is an inclination, mistaken I believe, to associate the Indian presence in this country with post-second world war immigration problems. In reviving public awareness of an often almost-forgotten era, I hope to be able to focus attention on a most significant aspect of British-Indian relations which is often neglected; there is enormous and abiding interest in the days of the Raj and the presence of the British in India, but a shift of perspective will show us the impact and tremendous contributions made by India in Britain.

CHAPTER ONE

Victoria, Kaisar-i-Hind

ALTHOUGH SHE NEVER LEFT EUROPE, the authority and presence of Queen Victoria so impressed itself on her subjects in even the furthest-flung reaches of Empire that many saw her as something supra-human – the Great White Mother across the waters.

In India, most particularly, she was regarded with such awe that even her Viceroy shone in reflected glory. Disraeli, ever flamboyant, conceived a plan to further consolidate what was already a strong bond between Britain and India, and, at the same time, afford some pleasure to his monarch. IIe had judged rightly; the Queen would be immensely gratified to add to her titles 'Kaisar-i-Hind', Empress of India, and a Durbar was organised to mark with due ceremony this momentous occasion. As was customary, His

Punch, then as now, summed up current events with fine drawing. This cartoon was published on 11th September 1858, marking the passing of the India Act.

Excellency the Viceroy represented Britain, but there were Indians present who were convinced in later years that the Queen had been there and that they had seen her.

The Durbar in 1887 marked a midway point in Victoria's relationship with this, her most beloved colony. From the earliest years she had shown a marked keenness of interest in India, an interest shared by Albert, which manifested itself, for example, in the Great Exhibition of 1851 at the Crystal Palace, where the Indian exhibits aroused excited comment.

At the end of the eighteenth century, Thomas and William Daniell, uncle and nephew, based themselves in Calcutta and produced hundreds of sketches and paintings of India. Their popularity in Calcutta among the Company families was exceeded by their popularity in fashionable society once back in England, and Victoria's images of India will have been formed by their work, as well as by the handsome gifts she received from visiting nobility.

Her sympathy for India, however, was not based simply on a romantic apprehension of its exotic splendours; she can be seen to have interested herself in the conditions of her people there, as when she lent her support to a campaign to reduce the numbers of deaths among Indian women during labour. Unusually perceptive, she urged that her Viceroy must show respect for the native people and govern with wisdom, these qualities being endangered by what she called 'Red-tapeism . . . our great misfortune.'

The genuineness of her sympathy for India was put to the test by the events surrounding the Indian Mutiny and its aftermath. The

The Queen is seen here working on her papers out of doors at Frogmore, attended by an Indian servant whose tunic is decorated with a crown.

Queen Victoria with Mustafa and
Chidda, 1896.

mutiny, most especially the massacre at Cawnpore where many
women and children were cut down, provoked a terrible revenge
from the British. Not only did they kill ruthlessly, they humiliated
and defiled the Hindus and Muslims by forcing them to break their
most sacred laws, such as by forcing beef and pork down the throat
of a Hindu before his death.

The reconciliation that followed these intense events was conducted by Lord Canning, with Victoria's wholehearted backing.
Very shortly after the mutiny she wrote to Canning to advise him
that 'the Indian people should know that there is no hatred to a
brown skin, none; but the greatest wish on their Queen's part is to
see them happy, contented and flourishing.' Not only did she wish
relations to return to a state of mutual respect, she wished to
emphasise that 'We do strictly charge and enjoin all those who may
be in authority under us that they abstain from all interference
with the religious belief or worship of any of our subjects on pain of
our highest displeasure.'

Following what proved to be a remarkably swift healing of the
wounds, Victoria drew a lesson from the tensions and ignorance

that gave rise to the massacres and made clear her wishes that Indians, according to their 'education, ability and integrity' should be promoted within the ranks of the civil service, the judiciary and all the machinery of government up to the highest levels, this to put an end to the restlessness and discontent that must arise if a people is kept always in humble stations. While the Queen never went to India, she arranged that India came to her. In all of her palaces, most especially at Windsor, which she increasingly favoured, many of her personal servants were Indians.

Her diaries recall that when two young men, newly arrived from India, were presented to her she thought they were very fine, and we know that she rebuked Salisbury, her Prime Minister, for referring to Indians as 'black men'. Several photographs show the Royal children being cared for by Indian attendants – the Queen showing no preference for Hindu, Sikh or Muslim – and towards the end of her life she appeared to grow ever more dependent on her faithful Indian manservants.

Around the time of her Golden Jubilee, a young groom of the chamber, Abdul Karim, was appointed. He rapidly gained the confidence and favour of the Queen, perhaps filling the place left empty after the death of John Brown, the ghillie whose candour and dependability had been appreciated by a monarch surrounded by advisers either timorous or bombastic.

From his appointment, Abdul Karim, or the Munshi, as he was soon called, began to give Hindustani lessons to the Queen, who appears to have studied assiduously and who was able to show some of her knowledge in letters to certain of the native princes. Her protegé frequently accompanied her on visits to Scotland and she visited him at Frogmore, where he had one of his homes. His portrait in oils was commissioned by her and she occasionally dined with him, when he would present some of his native dishes. In short, the Queen had found someone whose company gave her pleasure, and she rounded on those who would belittle his humble background or his race.

Pressure was eventually put upon Victoria to restrict the free-dom she had given him to deal with confidential papers relating to India. Although she acquiesced, she flashed her claws by promptly giving him the title of Indian Secretary and let it be known that she wished him to have a place of honour in her funeral procession.

Even after a wedge had been driven between her and her Indian confidant, Victoria's concern for India persisted. She was in constant communication with Curzon from the time when he was appointed Viceroy in 1899 until her death in 1901. Like her, he was determined to defend the native Indians where lesser men might have fallen in with a prevailing attitude of hauteur and superiority.

From her accession to the throne in 1837 to her death in 1901, Britain's monarch influenced generations of her subjects. Her enthusiasm and support for India and Indians quickened a similar response in the British public and it became fashionable to invite well-born Indians to one's social occasions and to employ Indian servants, not only for their diligence, but for their exotic and rather splendid looks.

Even after her death, India retained its special relationship with Britain: Victoria had left behind a legacy of affection and fasci-nation for the land she never saw.

The India Act of 1858

THIS ACT gave an assurance to the Princes of India, that there would be no further encroachment on their lands and rights, and it marked the transfer of authority from the East India Company to the Crown.

A few weeks earlier, on 24th June, Chancellor Benjamin Disraeli revealed in a letter to Victoria that his thinking had already left the Act behind:

> It is, the Chancellor of the Exchequer really thinks, a wise and well-digested measure, ripe with the experience of the last five months of discussion; but it is only the ante-chamber of an imperial palace; and your Majesty would do well to deign to consider the steps which are now necessary to influence the opinions and affect the imagination of the Indian populations. The name of your Majesty ought to be impressed upon their native life. Royal Proclamations, Courts of Appeal in their own land, and other institutions, forms and ceremonies, will tend to this great result.

Queen Victoria proclaimed Empress of India. Disraeli finally got his way with the passing of the Royal Titles Bill in 1876, which conferred the title on her. *Punch* was once more on hand to record the event which took place on 15th April 1876, and the cartoonist gave Disraeli the treatment that his flamboyance always seemed to demand, this time casting him as a character from Aladdin and entitling the cartoon 'New Crowns for Old'.

THE TIMES (Second Edition): *27th June 1857*

The Indian mutiny, 1857

India (By submarine and British Telegraph)

WE HAVE RECEIVED the following telegraphic message from Marseilles, dated Friday night:

'By the Vectis Capt. W. Hochte, from Alexandria, we have dates from Bombay to the 27th of May.

'Some native regiments have mutinied at Meerut, Ferozepore and Delhi. At Delhi they secured 15 lacs and proclaimed a king.

'A force is marching sufficient to overwhelm the mutineers in every quarter

'Oude is tranquil

'Troops from Cylone have reached Calcutta and the native Princes are offering their contingent.

THE TIMES: *29th June 1857*

Money market and City intelligence

THE NEWS from India this morning caused the funds to open at a decline of a quarter per cent, which was soon followed by increased heaviness. The fortnight to elapse before the arrival of another mail will therefore be characterized by great anxiety and caution in all departments of business.

Bank Stock left off at 212½ to 214; India Bonds and Exchequer bills 10s to 5s discount.

Editorial: 29th June 1857

THE DETAILS of the Indian Mutiny, as given by our correspondents at Bombay and Calcutta, from the number of compensating incidents seem somewhat less alarming than was the bare telegraphic despatch. Meerut has been entirely delivered from the mutineers. The Lieutenant Governor of the North-West Province had placed the districts of Meerut and Delhi under martial law. In the meantime troops were advancing from Agra, and the Rajahs of Bhurtpore, Gwalior and Putteeallah, with their tributary Princes, were sending in their contingents. It is therefore probable that the next mail will bring news of the suppression of this dangerous outbreak and the condign punishment of the offenders. At Lucknow a tendency to revolt was checked by the firmness of Sir Henry Lawrence. At Benares and throughout Bengal all was quiet. So stand matters for the present.

The mutiny has not been confined to one body of troops or one locality. At Ferozepore, higher up in our north-west territory, a similar spirit showed itself. The disturbances beginning with the Hindoos have actually ended in placing on the throne of Delhi a Mahomedan Emperor, and the fever has gone on to seize the distant garrisons of what were lately the Sikh States. A movement so universal and so independent of conditions and circumstances must have its root in feelings which the prejudices of religion or the neglect of a proper supervision may indeed have strengthened. The

JUSTICE: The remorseless reprisals taken after the Indian Mutiny of 1857 received the endorsement of *Punch*, although the cartoonist seems to show some pity for the women and children.

fact seems to be that we have arrived at that point in our Indian career when the total subjection of the native element and the organization of all that we have conquered become a matter of necessity. We have gone so far in the conquest of the country that it is now necessary to complete the task. A hundred years ago, when the disaster of Fort William was avenged, a policy was begun which, excellently suited for the time, has been continued into an age when it is both meaningless and injurious. As England governed her Indian settlements anomalously through a Company, so the Company chose to govern anomalously through a vast, complex, and often unintelligible native organization. Indian rulers became our tributaries or our pensioners; Indian territory which our arms had conquered was mapped out among the native potentates who aided our cause or had been the instruments of our schemes. Up to within the last few years the habitual state of our Indian rule has always been war. We have always had before us the next country which it was our destiny to conquer. The best arrangement for the moment has always been made with dethroned, or conquered, or inefficient Princes; pensions have been granted, new sovereignties have been established, or old ones divided, without any purpose except the assurance of immediate tranquillity and the easy possession of what had been latest gained.

Whatever may have been the effect of the unclean cartridges at Barrackpore, there is one thing now evident – that we have an enormous empire, with 150,000,000 people, and an army of 200,000 native troops, and that this empire is in a state of profound peace, and this great army is to some extent reduced to the duties of a police force.

The first thing, of course, is to put down force by force. Justice, humanity, the safety of our countrymen, and the honour of the country demand that the slaughter of Delhi shall be punished with unsparing severity. Asiatics are not the people to whom rulers can safely grant impunity of crime. When the ancient capital of India falls into the hands of the rebel soldiery, and the descendant of a dethroned monarch is actually set up as a rival to British authority, it is too late to talk of mildness and negotiation.

Now that we have conquered India from the Indus to the frontiers of Siam, it is our interest to establish in it a homogeneity which it has never before possessed. There is no reason why the British Government should not attempt to fuse into a solid mass the conglomeration of provinces which is called India. Why, for instance, should there be a MOGUL at Delhi, whose very existence, as we see in the present case, preserves the memory of what we should endeavour to obliterate? We should even hope that the death of the NIZAM may be the occasion of the Deccan being brought more completely under British sovereignty. We cannot now refuse our part or change our destiny. To retain power in India we must sweep away every political establishment and every social usage which may prevent our influence from being universal and complete.

ADDRESS TO THE QUEEN BY INDIAN GENTLEMEN IN LONDON, DEPLORING THE MUTINIES IN INDIA, 1857. TO THE QUEEN'S MOST EXCELLENT MAJESTY

May it please your Majesty,

We, Indian noblemen and gentlemen, now in London approach the Throne in great humility; and crave permission to express to your Majesty our deep-felt sorrow for what has taken place at Delhi, Meerut, and other places. We do most deeply deplore these events. We deplore them on the score of humanity; we deplore them for the sake of an Army that a WELLESLEY, a HARDINGE, a GOUGH and a NAPIER have led to Victory. We deplore them as Men earnest in the social and political improvement of India. But we find some consolation in being allowed, this early, to assure your Majesty that the hearts of your Indian subjects (and we speak from a life-long knowledge of them) are essentially loyal and attached to your person and throne. Earnestly – most earnestly do we, therefore, hope that your Majesty will not allow these provocations, great as they are, to abate your love and affection for the rest of your Indian subjects whose allegiance never has been nor can be suspected.

We earnestly *pray* that Peace may be restored to our land; and that your Majesty may live many years to bless it with happiness and prosperity.

Signed in Urdu and in English by,
MEER JAFUR KHAN BAHADOOR OF SURAT
A. RUSTUMJEE, MIRZA MAHMED BAHADUR *and others.*

Queen Victoria's servants

DURING HER SIXTY-FOUR YEAR REIGN, the Queen met but a tiny fraction of the millions she ruled. Yet if they knew little of her, she knew almost nothing of them, at least not at first hand. The first Empress of all India never visited the jewel in the crown of her Empire, and her experience of its people came exclusively through the Indians she met in Britain. Most of course, were rulers just as she, and such came and went. But her Indian servants were fixtures, and Victoria depended on them both for knowledge of their homeland and often for advice on matters of policy.

It may be difficult for the modern mind to conceive of a servant influencing a monarch, but for the Victorians there was no doubt.

There were many amongst her British subjects who took great exception to her practice of discussing Imperial affairs, and often studying state papers, with Indian servants.

Prince Edward, Prince Albert and Princess Mary with Abdullah, at Balmoral in 1898.

Most prominent amongst them was Abdul Karim, the Munshi. After her accession as Empress of India, she developed a passion for all things Indian. In 1888 he was appointed Munshi and Indian clerk to the Queen. *Black and White* magazine commented:

> The duties of the Munshi consist chiefly in assisting Her Majesty with her Indian correspondence and State documents, and generally acting as the Queen's private secretary in all Indian affairs, and the post is one requiring great ability and integrity. Abdul Karim has also been the Queen's teacher in Hindustani. Since Her Majesty has taken up this study she has made excellent progress, both in the writing and reading of this important language, which speaks well for the qualifications of the Munshi as a teacher.

But this proximity to the Queen and influence with her caused resentment at court. However, he was not to leave her side until her death in January 1901, and soon after returned to India bearing a present from her son and successor:

> Munshi Abdul Karim is returning to India after many years of faithful service as Queen Victoria's Indian secretary. King Edward has presented the Munshi with a silver pen and ink case
> – *Black and White* magazine, 27th April 1901.

THE ILLUSTRATED LONDON NEWS: *27th May 1893*

The Queen's Indian secretary

HER MAJESTY, being Empress of India as well as Queen of Great Britain and Ireland, wisely and graciously studies, as few English ladies have attempted to do, the history, condition, manners and ideas of her Asiatic subjects, who number, with the inhabitants of Native States under her Imperial protectorate, nearly three hundred millions of mankind. We can scarcely suppose, with the utmost researches and supports of those learned and laborious men, Indian civil servants, literary philologists, investigators of the laws, customs, religions, and social traditions of so vast a population, comprising some thirty different nations, Hindoo, Mohammedan, Sikh, Buddhist, and heathen, in the great Anglo-Oriental Empire, that any one mind knows all about them. But their Empress Victoria has the credit, which is much among Sovereigns, of having learnt enough of a language – Hindustani, the common speech of the most important provinces of British India – to understand and reply to phrases of courtesy in her interviews with princely visitors; and those who witnessed her cordial greeting of several at the recent opening of the Imperial Institute must be aware of her kindly feelings towards them. It would indeed be well that the educated classes of Englishmen and Englishwomen should take more interest than they do in acquiring information on the subject of Indian native life and character. With this sentiment we present the portrait of the Munshi or professor of languages and of polite writing, who has the honour of serving her Majesty as private secretary in her Indian correspondence.

Queen Victoria and Munshi Abdul Karim are seen here in the Garden Cottage, Balmoral, in October 1895.

The Munshi is a native of Agra and was born in 1863. Previous to coming to England, he was for several years in the service of the Nawab of Jawara. He has held his present secretarial post since 1888, and is said to have found his position as an instructor of royalty a particularly pleasant one, while the Queen is enthusiastic over his merits as a teacher.

Few there are who learn Hindustani from pure love of the study, but Her Majesty has shown a quite remarkable zest to acquire the language, and is, it need scarcely be said, the only British monarch who has attempted it.

Dining at Windsor Castle in 1895 with Prince and Princess Henry of Battenberg, and three of their children, Prince Alexander, Princess Victoria Eugénie and Prince Maurice, the Queen is attended by two handsomely uniformed Indian servants.

(*left*) Mohammed Baksh with Prince Alexander of Battenberg, in February 1888.

As this group photograph, taken at Darmstadt *c.* 1890, clearly shows, Queen Victoria was accompanied by her Indian attendants even while travelling abroad.

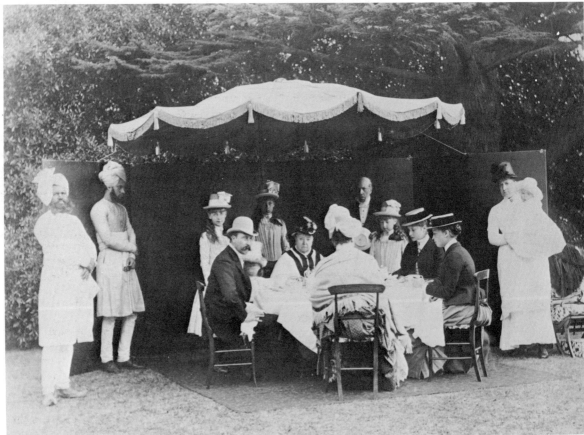

(*left*) Even a Queen Empress can't resist a little dog . . . here Victoria is seen at Balmoral in September 1897 with her dog Turi and Bella the pony. Accompanying her are the Duchess of Roxburgh and two servants, George Gordon and Mohamed Ismail.

The Queen's Hindustani

BEATRICE followed her mother's instructions and destroyed much of the Queen's journal, but an interesting passage survives which shows that the Hindustani taught to the Queen by her Indian servants was of more than academic interest to her.

In December of 1887 the Maharani and the Gaekwar of Baroda, together with the Maharani's sister, arrived to see their Empress, whose journal takes up the story: 'The Maharani bent low and shook hands. She is a pretty little thing and wore a close-fitting jacket and trousers, no petticoat, of pale blue satin, over the whole a long crimson and gold gauze veil, which passed over her head and covered her completely, excepting her face, which she uncovered as she came into the room.

She had splendid jewels on. She looks very gentle but is said to be very wilful and to wish to see everything without being seen. She regretted not having seen Bertie [the future Edward VII]. Both Princesses had a red spot painted in the centre of their foreheads. The Maharani understands a little English, and says a few words, but her sister does not.

'Excellent progress in the reading and writing of this important language . . .' So wrote the *Black and White* magazine. This page from the Queen's Hindustani exercise book was written on 20th June 1897 – the sixtieth anniversary of her accession.

I ventured upon a sentence in Hindustani which Abdul and Mohamed had helped to teach me. I also presented Beatrice in Hindustani. The Maharani said she wished to see the Castle and after she had sat a little while on the sofa next to me, she shook hands and took leave.'

The Queen not only practised the spoken language, but worked at writing out English and Urdu, as may be seen in the extract from her workbook, reproduced above.

(*left*) In this group photograph, taken at Osborne House in August 1887, may be seen two Indian servants whom Victoria mentions in her letters. Mohammed Baksh (*left*) she found '. . . very dark, with a very smiling expression.' Beside him is Abdul Karim, of whom the Queen wrote '. . . he is much lighter, tall and with a fine, serious countenance. His father is a doctor in Agra.' The letters also note, 'They both kissed my feet on arrival.'

Jubilee celebrations

IN MANY CASES Queen Victoria's two Jubilee celebrations in 1887 and 1897 were the highspots of a Golden Age. Never before had London seen such a gigantic affirmation of its place as the hub of a great Empire.

The Diamond Jubilee of 1897 was Britain's most glittering pageant of the century, the celebration of a people secure in their strength and their belief in themselves.

An essential part of that belief was given a physical form by the presence of many thousands of the Empire's leading subjects, for their diversity was seen as a source of strength rather than weakness.

The distant scions of that family – the Princes, Maharajahs, Nawabs and assorted aristocracy – gave the great Imperial occasions a distinct tinge of the romantic and the exotic in the eyes of the popular Press. India's rich variety of native royalty, coupled with their wealth and flamboyance, meant that their doings were always newsworthy.

What gave the occasions even greater weight and solemnity was the fact that, by her Silver Jubilee, Victoria was not only Queen, but, following a proposal put forward by Disraeli, an Empress. Her title, in Urdu, Kaisar-i-Hind, gave dignity and the final authority to the imperial ambitions of the British power.

(*top right*) Indian Officers, most of them wearing military decorations, photographed at Buckingham Palace *c.* 1887.

(*bottom right*) Queen Victoria's Indian escort for the Golden Jubilee in 1887, assembled at Windsor Castle.

Preceding Queen Victoria's carriage in the Golden Jubilee procession in 1887 are her Indian cavalrymen carrying drawn swords. The banner reads 'May children of our children say she brought her people lasting good'.

2

The Jubilee Garden Party and Reception

THE ROYAL GARDEN PARTY was as much of an institution in Queen Victoria's day as it is now, and an especially splendid one was held to celebrate her Golden Jubilee in June 1887. Fortunately the Queen's own record of that party and the equally glittering reception on the following day have survived to give us an insight into those days.

Buckingham Palace, 29th June 1887. People were spread all over the garden, and there were a number of tents, and a large one for me, in front of which were placed the Indian Escort. I walked right round the lawn in front of the Palace with Bertie, and I bowed right and left, talking to as many as I could, but I was dreadfully done up by it and could not speak to, or see, all those I wished. Marie of Belgium and a number of the Furstlichkeiten (those of Princely rank) came into my tent for tea, including Holkar and some of the other Indian Princes who came up to speak to me.

In spite of the sixty-eight-year-old Queen's exhaustion, she carried on with the State Ceremonial the following afternoon.

30th June. After luncheon at three, I had a great reception of Indian Princes and Deputations, in the Green Drawing-room, the Great Officers of State, Louisa Buccleuch, Gold Stick and Lord Cross being in attendance. Beatrice, Arthur, Louischen and Liko were with me. The Indian escort stood opposite and looked splendid. The whole was very imposing.

'Sir Partab Singh, who is an ADC to Bertie, stood behind me with the Great Officers. Holkar was the first to enter and offer his present, after which I gave him an enamel portrait of myself, and invested him with the Grand Cross of the Star of India, knighting him. He had great difficulty in kneeling down.

Then came the handsome young Rao of Kutch, most beautifully dressed; really he and his brother were like a dream. He had wonderful jewels on. He brought me an Address in a golden case, and said a few appropriate words so nicely and in such good English, giving me besides some beautiful silver ornaments for the table. He likewise received from me an enamel portrait and was invested with the Grand Cross of the Indian Empire, which has been raised and increased from a mere Companion to three different grades, the one being a Grand Cross.

The Maharaja and Maharani of Kuch Behar came next, also beautifully dressed. She gave me a lovely pendant, a carved ruby set with fine large diamonds, and he an inlaid ivory writing and work-box in one. I gave her a miniature of myself.

Two views of the Royal Tent with Indian attendants at the Queen's Garden Party at Buckingham Palace in 1887.

Then followed the Thakores of Morvi, Limri and Gondal, the two last bringing their presents, and the two former were each knighted, and I placed the K.C. Cross of the Order of the Indian Empire round their necks, Arthur (The Duke of Connaught) helping me. The Deputations from the Nizam and from the Native Princes who could not come, entered last, each giving a present. After this I received Deputations from the Municipalties and Corporations of Calcutta and Bombay.

Sir Partab Singh then stopped forward, and, placing his sword at my feet, offered me a lovely pearl ornament, which he had taken off his own puggaree, as a mark of fealty, saying everything he possessed was at my service. After which Arthur, accompanied by his three gentlemen, presented four Addresses, in splendid silver cases, and Mr Fitzgerald presented, according to ancient custom, an Address on a shield from the District of Ajmere—Merwarra. Arthur presented his staff.

The richness and variety of gifts illustrate not only the degree of respect and loyalty accorded by native rulers, but also the immense wealth at their disposal, and thus ultimately at Britain's.

The address from the Madras Presidency of India is in a casket manufactured by Messrs. P. Orr & Sons, jewellers and silversmiths of Madras. Its chief feature is an elephant, of oxidised silver, ten inches high, richly caparisoned with a jewelled frontlet and breastplate, bearing a gilt embossed howdah, which supports the cylindrical casket; a keeper stands in front of the animal. The address on behalf of thirty-two million of the Queen's Indian subjects, was presented to Her Majesty at Windsor Castle, on Thursday week, by Sir Charles Lawson, who then received the honour of Knighthood. – *The Illustrated London News, 9th July 1887*

A gift fit for a Queen ... The Thakore of Morvi astride the richly bedecked charger which was his Golden Jubilee gift. Queen Victoria notes in her record of the Reception: 'We then went down to the entrance, where I stepped out and the Thakore of Morvi rode up on a young horse of his own Chettawa breed, splendidly caparisoned and completely covered with what looked like a sort of coat of mail, with heavy ornamented tassels hanging down and an amulet on one leg. Two natives led the horse, and the Thakore got off, begging me to accept it as a present from him. I expressed my sincere thanks for it.'

THE ILLUSTRATED LONDON NEWS: *10th July 1897*

The Indian Princes

EVERYONE IS AGREED that the Jubilee pageant would have lost one of its chief glories had not the Indian Princes been a part of it. For personal and political importance, no less than for picturesque appearance, they made a group which could hardly be anywhere surpassed. Here, there and everywhere in Windsor, they have been seen, and, happily, nearly always in their native dress. At the opera they and their precious stones have riveted attention; and they have been admired on their Arab steeds in the Row, with the light silk streamers of their turbans floating on the winds – sometimes the almost gales – of this summer. They gave colour to the Queen's Garden Party; and they have dined and lunched in the City. Among the seventeen native rulers of India who have been the nation's guests, a Prince has to be very distinguished to tower above the rest. Such a one is Maharaja Dhiraj Sir Partab Singh Bahadur of Jodhpur. He was Prime Minister to his brother, the late Maharaja, for fourteen years, and became Regent when the succession fell to his brother's son, still only a youth of eighteen. Sir Partab, during his sixteen years of virtual rule, has redeemed the State from bankruptcy, and has introduced the British system of finance, justice, education, and even to some extent, of marriage.

This engraving shows the procession of Royal Princes en route from Buckingham Palace to Westminster Abbey on the occasion of the Queen's Jubilee. Both in 1887 and 1897 the Indian Princes greatly added to the magnificence of the occasion, dressed as they were in splendid costumes and mounted on their superb horses.

(*left*) Indian cavalry, such as this splendid Sovereign's Escort, pictured on 22nd June 1897, the day of the Diamond Jubilee, are watched by the crowds as they pass by the Houses of Parliament.

(*bottom left*) An empire rejoices – Queen Victoria arrives at St. Paul's Cathedral to give thanks for her Diamond Jubilee preceded, as usual, by her Indian cavalry escort.

(*below*) A line of Indian cavalry on parade outside Buckingham Palace.

He has a crack cavalry regiment, of which he is Colonel; he is aide-de-camp to the Prince of Wales; he keeps open palace for English and other visitors, and he is the uncle of Prince Ranjitsinhji, the conqueror on English cricket-fields.

By reason of his additional and English title, Sir Jamsetjee Jejeebhoy – the third Baronet of his line – is another conspicuous figure. He is the head of the Parsee community and was born in 1851. The Raja Ajit Singh Bahadur of Khetri, Rajputana, is another conspicuous figure. He personally administers the State, and manages his six properties, one of which, yielding a rental of 150,000 rupees, was granted to him by the British Government as a reward for the military services of his ancestors. Two of the youngest Princes are Raj Kumar Umaid Singh, heir apparent to the Raja Dhiraj of Shahpura, who is twenty-one, and his younger brother, Raj Kumar Sardar Singh, both of whom begin their education under an English governess. The Rajputs of Maywar, from whom these young Princes descend, had brave fights to maintain their independence against the Delhi Emperors, with whose representatives they could meet in peace at last in London. The present chief has carried out large works of irrigation, and has made great reserves in safety against famine. Education, law and sanitation are all in a good condition in Shahpura, where, indeed, something like our county councils has been brought into being.

The Indian Princes who have done so much to decorate London crowds have themselves in many instances been further decorated by the Queen in honour of the Jubilee. Sir Partab Singh Bahadur has been given the Grand Cross of the Most Exalted Order of the Star of India; so have His Highness Maharaja Vyankatesh Raman Singh Bahadur, Chief of Rewa; His Excellency Sir Bir Shamsher Jang Rana Bahadur, KCSI, well known as the Prime Minister of Nepal; His Highness Raja Jagatjit Singh Bahadur of Kapurthala; and Sardar Bahadur Kashi Rao Sarve, Commander-in-Chief of the Maharaja Sindhia's army. The Grand Cross of the Most Eminent Order of the Indian Empire has been given to His Highness Sir Bhanwar Pal Deo Bahadur Yadukul Chandra Bhal, Maharaja of Karuli; His Highness Faiz Muhammad Khan, Talpur, Mir of Khairpur in Sind; Sir Lachhmeshwar Singh Bahadur, Maharaja of Darbhanga and His Highness Sir Bhagwut Singh, Thakore Saheb of Gondal. To be Knights Commanders of the same order of the Indian Empire the Queen has nominated Nawab Amir-un-din-Ahmed-Khan Bahadur, chief of Loharu; Mancherjee Bhownagree, Muhammed Munewar Ali Khan Bahadur, Prince of Arcot, and Nawab Bahadur Kwaja Ashan-Ulla of Decca.

Queen Victoria and the Empress Frederick entering St. George's Chapel, Windsor, for a service on Thanksgiving Day, 26th June 1897, the Queen on the arm of her Indian attendant.

CHAPTER TWO

Indian nobility:
the nineteenth century

'THE RESPONSIBILITY for governing India has been placed by the inscrutable design of providence upon the shoulders of the British race.' Kipling thus expressed the view of millions of his fellow-countrymen. Whole generations felt that the role of the British in India was to take up the white man's burden despite the discomfort and danger, and this they did. But who had governed before? India had, of course, been governed by the princes of India, hundreds of them, some ruling over states as large as a European nation, such as the Maharajah of Kashmir, many more ruling over states which were smaller in area than twenty square miles. These princes were absolute hereditary rulers and many of them offered a more just and sensitive régime than the prevailing British, although some others spent fabulous sums of money to realise their fantasies, leaving little in the state coffers for their subjects. But the British inexorably spread throughout India, and, where they could reach an agreement with the local Maharajah, they left him on his throne, always providing he recognised the 'paramountcy' of British rule.

Sometimes this forced accommodation developed into a relationship marked, on the one hand, by tremendous loyalty to the Queen-Empress, and then the King-Emperor, and, on the other, by admiration and respect. A less noble interpretation is that these rulers were given a free hand to behave as they wished, provided they maintained their loyalty to the British throne, and they connived with the British to stamp out any movement aimed at winning independence for India.

The truth is, as ever, more complex. Certain rulers, such as the Gaekwar of Baroda, were enlightened and liberal. In Baroda polygamy was outlawed, free education was made available to all before the end of Victoria's reign and the Gaekwar himself campaigned vigorously to improve the lot of the Untouchables. He was rewarded for his faithfulness and good government by being entitled to a twenty-one gun salute, the supreme honour, and one only extended to four other Indian princes.

When India finally regained self-determination the world changed for many millions of people, none more so than for the India princes. Their days of splendour were gone for ever. Gone the jewels, the brocades, the elephants; their palaces were left to crumble, or were turned into hotels or schools. Some went into business or took on roles in government, but the essence of what had been was dispersed, and their like will be seen no more.

THE ILLUSTRATED LONDON NEWS: *17th July 1852*

The Princess Gouramma

THE INTERESTING CEREMONY of the admission into the Christian Church of the Princess Gouramma, daughter of his Highness Prince Vere Rajunder, ex-Rajah of Coorg, was briefly described in the *Illustrated London News* of the 3rd instant. This, being one of the few instances on record of the abandonment of the Hindoo faith for the truths of the Christian religion, is an event more than commonly satisfactory to a country whose relations with the great continent of India are so vast and intimate as our own; and we cannot doubt that our readers will be pleased to possess the *vraisemblance* of the interesting Princess and her father, which we are this day enabled to give from a series of portraits recently taken by her Majesty's command.

The ex-Rajah of Coorg is one of the native Princes whose kingdoms have fallen, by their own internal dissensions and weakness, into the power of this country. The ex-Rajah, subsequently to the conquest of his dominions, has been residing at the city of Benares, a sort of state prisoner under the control of the East India Company, but possessing an establishment of ranees (wives) and servants, with an income of about £6,000 a year. The Princess Gouramma is the offspring of one of his Highness's favourite ranees, a native of the Coorg country. The Princess was born at Benares, on a Sunday in February 1841, and her mother died two days afterwards; a circumstance which seems to have led to an increased affection for the child on the part of the ex-Rajah, who, having forfeited his native caste, determined that his favourite daughter should be reared in the principles of the Christian religion, and hence his Highness's visit to England. The ex-Rajah has a family of eleven children, the eldest being a son nineteen years of age. In speaking of them, his Highness shows a marked preference for the Princess Gouramma, whom he describes familiarly as a 'pigeon among the crows', 'the fairest of the flock,' &c. The interest which her Majesty has shown for the Princess and her Royal condenscension in consenting to stand sponsor for the child cannot fail to have proved highly gratifying to the ex-Rajah. We have already stated that, in addition to her Majesty, the other sponsors were the Viscountess Hardinge, Mrs Drummond (wife of Major Drummond, 3rd Bengal Light Cavalry, who has been appointed by the directors of the East India Company to attend upon his Highness during his absence from India), and Sir James Weir Hogg. The ceremony was performed by the Archbishop of Canterbury, in the private chapel of Buckingham Palace, the Princess receiving from her Majesty the name of 'Victoria'. When the ex-Rajah, her father, gave up his child into her Majesty's charge, he addressed to her the following instruction and prayer: 'My dearest daughter – Endeavour to gain every day more and more the grace, and to merit the love and kindness of her most gracious Majesty the Queen; that thereby all Europe, India, and the rest of the world, may hear and be pleased with your good conduct and fame. May heaven bless you, and keep you always under its divine protection and special care! This is my advice to

This photograph, taken in 1852 by Roger Fenton shortly after her christening at the age of thirteen, shows the Princess Gouramma, goddaughter of the Queen, and named Victoria after her. The Princess was the daughter of the deposed Rajah of Coorg.

you, my dearest daughter, and my most earnest prayer to the Almighty on your behalf.'

The Princess is an interesting and intelligent child. Her complexion is but little darker than that of many Europeans, and her features are regular and pleasing. Her age is only eleven years, but she is far in advance of that period in intelligence. In addition to the Hauree and Hindostanee tongues, she is acquiring English.

The Princess is named after one of the Pagan divinities. A younger sister, the Princess Gungahmah was married, or rather betrothed to the Nepaulese Prince, Jung Bahadoor, a year ago.

By an agreement between the ex-Rajah on the one hand, and the board of directors of the East India Company and the Board of Control on the other, the Princess Gouramma has been placed under her Majesty's protection to be educated in the principles of the Church of England in this country; and her majesty, having fully considered the matter, has appointed Mrs Drummond to take charge of the child.

THE ILLUSTRATED LONDON NEWS: *11th April 1857*

The Guicowar of Goojerat

As EASTERN AFFAIRS at present occupy so prominent a position and seem likely to awaken a still-increasing interest, the Portrait of His Highness the Guicowar, who has lately ascended the throne of Goojerat, may prove acceptable to our readers. His Highness is seated with his daughter on his knee. His dress is of the richest silk, the borders embroidered with gold and pearls; while the brilliancy and value of his jewels almost realise the most gorgeous imaginings of the much exaggerated Eastern magnificence.

Kundey Ras has a pleasing intelligent expression of countenance. He appears to possess great muscular strength and is a capital shot. He also rides and hunts beautifully, using European saddle, and top boots and is a perfect Nimrod. As he has never hitherto been addicted to the miserable excesses which disgraced the reign of the late Guicowar, it is to be hoped his energy and intelligence will ensure to his dominions as much good government as we can hope to see developed in a native Court. At present his liberality of sentiment and apparently eager desire to be on the most friendly terms with the British promises much. He expresses the utmost interest in our success against Persia, and has even proposed to pay up and equip a regiment of infantry and a battery of artillery in our service; and when the news of the taking of Bushire arrived, he immediately ordered a Royal salute to be fired. Doubtless much of this good understanding may be attributed to the admirable management of the present Resident, and to his firm but kind and friendly treatment. Still, at the present crisis of our Indian affairs, the fidelity and good feeling of the native Prince ought to be more than ever valued. His Highness has as yet only reigned for two or three months and of course things are at their brightest. It remains to be proved whether his liberality extends so far as to permit the spread of European civilisation and Christian education, which have hitherto made lamentably little progress among the people of Goojerat.

Kundey Ras, the Guicowar of Goojerat, shown here with his young daughter.

This engraving shows the resplendent Maharajah of Mysore, a Hindu state which was administered by the British from 1832 onwards.

THE ILLUSTRATED LONDON NEWS: *22nd June 1867*

The Maharajah of Mysore

THE DEBATE in the House of Commons, on the 24th ult., upon the claims of the Maharajah of Mysore, or of his adopted son and heir, to be restored to the government of that State, which is now administered in his name by a British Commissioner, makes it opportune now to give an engraving of his portrait. The name of Mysore (Maisur or Maheshasur) is derived from 'Mahesh', a buffalo, and 'Azur', a demon; and this region of India is so called from the buffalo-headed fiend which was slain there by the goddess Kali, the consort of Seeva. The extent of the Mysore country is about 250 miles in length, and rather less in breadth: it is situated in the southern part of the peninsula of Hindostan, to the west of the Madras Presidency, having the Bombay Presidency and the independent native State of the Deccan on the north. Its population is nearly four millions, the peasantry and lower classes being chiefly Hindoos; but the aristocracy and military class belong to a Mussulman race, which conquered the country 300 years ago. The warlike reign of Hyder Ali and his son Tippoo, commonly spoken of as Tippoo Sahib, towards the end of the last century, was marked by continual hostilities with the British Government, till the final defeat and death of Tippoo in 1799, at the capture of Seringapatam, one of the most important victories we have ever gained in India. A portion of the territory of Mysore was then annexed to Madras, and another share bestowed on the Nizam of the Deccan, while the sovereignty of the remainder was restored to the legitimate Maharajah, the son of Cham Raj, born in 1793, and dispossessed by Tippoo. The question lately under the consideration of our Government turns upon the meaning of the treaty made by the Marquis of Wellesley in 1799 – whether it was intended to guarantee the sovereignty to the present Maharajah only during his own life, or to acknowledge his right of adopting a son to inherit the same. The State of Mysore, which had been ably and prudently governed, during his minority, by Purneah, the Brahmin Prime Minister, soon fell into great disorder when the Maharajah came to the throne. In consequence of a rebellion of his subjects, provoked by great misrule, in 1832, the British Government was obliged to take charge of the country. Under the just and wise administration of Sir Mark Cubborn, for more than thirty years, succeeded, in 1862, by Mr Lewin Bowring, one of the best members of the Indian Civil Service, at the present time, Mysore has become probably the most thriving and contented province of our India dominions.

An attempt was made in 1847 to persuade the British Government to intrust this fine country once more to the care of its titular Sovereign; but Lord Dalhousie refused to do so; and it would be a questionable benefit to the people of Mysore. The Maharajah, however, is a very respectable old gentleman, and rendered valuable assistance to the British Government during the sepoy mutiny and war of 1857.

THE ILLUSTRATED LONDON NEWS: *26th June 1886*

The Late Maharajah Holkar 1832–1886

THE INDEPENDENT MAHRATTA OF INDORE, in central India, is one of the Native Principalities most closely allied to the British Indian Empire. It has just lost, by death from a long illness, its able and successful ruler, the well-known 'Holkar', whose proper name was Tukaji Rao, and who was about fifty-four years of age. He was selected for the throne by the British Government as far back as 1843, being then eleven years of age. In 1852 he was declared of age, and ascended the seat of the Holkars of Indore, since which period he has ruled his people with much capacity, enriching himself by commercial, agricultural, and manufacturing speculations, and has observed towards the paramount Power a friendliness and loyalty unbroken. Under Jeswunt Rao the House of Holkar rose to great eminence, and even defied the British; but Lord Lake, by a series of marches and battles, completely broke his power in April, 1805. This Indore State has an area of 8,075 square miles, with a population approaching a million souls.

An engraving of the Maharajah of Holkar.

An early engraving of the Maharajah of Gwalior, wearing his distinctive hat.

THE ILLUSTRATED LONDON NEWS: *26th June 1886*

The Late Maharajah Scindia of Gwalior 1819–1886

WITHIN A FEW DAYS after the death of Holkar, the Maharajah of Indore, follows that of the other leading independent Prince of the Mahratta race, Baji Rao Scindia, the ruler of Gwalior. When the Rajah Daulat Rao died without an heir in 1827, the British Government recognised the adoption of a boy of the Scindia family, Bajirat Rao, then eight years old.

The late Maharajah was conspicuous for his loyalty to the English. In 1853 the fort of Gwalior, taken by the British ten years previously, was restored to the Maharajah on his coming of age. The following reflections in *The Times*, upon the deaths of Scindia and Holkar and upon the part they filled in India, seem worthy to be quoted:

> For years past the Maharajahs of Gwalior and Indore have been the solitary independent personalities among the native princes. None could accuse them of abandonment of vulgar and purposeless luxury. Whenever English thoughts dwelt on the number of the native Princes of India, Scindia and Holkar did duty for the rest. Theirs have been the only names which have called up a distinct impression. As Holkar had owed his accession to British favour, so Scindia owed to British power the retention of his throne. England has never had reason to question the sincerity of his recognition of this benefit. Gwalior and Indore sprang from a stock so sturdy that the temptations of oriental courts did not succeed in enervating them. They deserve admiration for not forgetting their duties as chiefs of their States.

(*right*) This is another Indian noble, His Highness Maharajah Dhiraj Mirza Maharao Shri Sir Khengari Savai Bahadur, the Rao of Cutch (1866–1942). This portrait by the fashionable painter Sidney Prior Hall shows him in 1887, when he was twenty-one and had already been on the throne for eleven years. He was a forward-looking noble, who took a keen interest in the education of women in his state, and helped many of his subjects to study in England.

(*left*) Sir Dolatsinhji, Thakore Saheb of Limdi. A Sidney Hall painting of 1887 now at Osborne House, Isle of Wight. Born in 1868, the Thakore went to the Jamnagar High School in Gujarat.

THE ILLUSTRATED LONDON NEWS: *1887*

'She is very pretty and attractive . . . such a dear, gentle woman.' That was Queen Victoria's verdict on the Maharanee of Kuch Behar, whom she met around the time of this portrait. A cultured, gentle woman, the Maharanee encouraged the emancipation of women in Bengal, with one exception – the removal of 'purdah' in Kuch Behar – though she herself moved freely all over India, including Bengal. She lived in the 'zenana' quarters in her own palace.

The Maharajah and Maharanee of Kuch Behar

THE MAHARAJAH and the Maharanee of Kuch Behar were amongst the distinguished Indian visitors to London during Her Majesty's Jubilee. Kuch Behar was an extensive territory during the Mogul reign, comprising almost the whole of Assam, the whole of Rungpore, Jalpaipore and Dinapore districts – an area almost half as large as England. The lavish but misguided charities of the earlier rulers, the result of which can even now be traced in the growth of the surrounding estates, and, later on, the double raids committed by the Moghuls on the South and the wild Bhootias on the North have reduced the State to a small fraction of its former self. Nevertheless, its importance as a staunch guard over Bhootan

(*right*) The Maharajah of Kuch Behar, who succeeded in 1863, is portrayed here by Sidney Prior Hall, a fashionable artist of the period.

cannot be overrated. Though the Kuch Behar family has always been orthodox Hindu, the Maharajah, who was wisely taken care of by our Indian Government during his minority, is devoid of all the blind prejudices of the Hindus, and is impressed with the many advantages of the Western civilisation. Both the Maharajah and the Maharanee – who, by the by, with her charming affability, has won the admiration of every lady who came in contact with her – have been heartily welcomed by English people, and the Queen has graciously invested the Maharanee with the Championship of the Indian Empire, and His Highness with the Order of the Grand Cross of the Indian Empire, so that we believe they carry back nothing but pleasant recollections of their English trip. In addition to numerous charitable institutions with which their Highnesses are connected. His Highness has established a club called the India Club for the more free and easy intercourse of the English and the natives, the beneficial effect of which has been manifest. He has also established, as a momento of the Jubilee year, a college in Kuch Behar, called Victoria College. The Maharanee Kuch Behar, Her Highness Suniti Devi, is the daughter of Baboo Kehsub Chandra Sen (1838–1884), the founder of the Brahmo Samaj who did much to reform the Bengali society in particular and the Hindoo society in general.

This contemporary engraving. taken from *The Illustrated London News* of 15th October 1887, shows the Nizam of Hyderabad, one of the wealthiest of all the Indian princes, who, in 1887, offered £600,000 to the Indian government to defend the North-West Frontier. The Nizam considered himself 'the oldest ally of the English in India' and promised that if India were invaded, 'England can count upon his sword'.

THE ILLUSTRATED LONDON NEWS: *28th October 1893*

Dhuleep Singh

THE MAHARAJA DHULEEP SINGH must have believed himself, to the day of his death, a very ill-used man. He was the son of old Ranjeet Singh, the 'Lion of the Punjaub'; but he had no experience as a ruler, for his dominions were annexed by the Indian Government when he was a child. The Government, no doubt, thought they behaved handsomely to Dhuleep by pensioning him with £40,000 a year, on which he endeavoured to maintain the state of a country gentleman in Suffolk. A few years ago the expenses of his establishment became insupportable, and he petitioned the Government for an increase of his allowance. It is said that he asked at the same time for the restoration of the great Kohinor diamond, which was part of the British loot in the Punjaub. Getting no satisfaction from the India Office, Dhuleep set off for India, but was stopped at Aden. In a fury, he betook himself to Russia, and offered his services to the Czar's military advisers. Probably he was convinced that his name and lineage would raise a revolt in the Punjaub against British rule, and he was prepared to impress the imagination of the

The benefits that British Rule brought to India during the later period of the Raj tend to obscure the ruthlessness with which they seized power. There were many victims of this policy, which began when the East India Company beat off the French and lasted until the time of the Mutiny, but none were more tragic than Maharajah Dhuleep Singh (1838–93). The pathetic story of his wasted life accompanies a photograph taken by the Prince of Wales in July 1856, and is recounted in his obituary in *The Graphic* of 28th October 1893.

Punjaubees by a mechanical trick by producing 'Pepper's Ghost'. At Aden he publicly abandoned Christianity, which he had professed during his career as a sportsman in England; and the Aden officials, with unspeakable gravity, authorised a number of Punjaub natives to travel from India for the express purpose of witnessing the ceremony of his return to the Hindoo faith. Discouraged by his reception in Russia, he took up his residence in Paris, and before his end he made his peace with the British Government, through the intercession of his son, who is an officer in the British Army.

THE GRAPHIC: *28th October 1893*

The Maharajah Dhuleep Singh

OBITUARY 1838–1893

AS THE SON of the famous Ranjeet Singh, who was one of the most remarkable men the soil of India ever produced, and the nominal head of that noble Sikh race which, first as our opponents, and then as our loyal friends and allies, has played so prominent a part in Indian history during the last fifty years, the late Maharajah Dhuleep Singh was a personage of considerable interest. Born in 1838, when his father the Lion of the Punjaub was dying, there were many to challenge his legitimacy, and the more than doubtful character of his mother, the Maharanee Zinda or Chinda, lent

While Queen Victoria looks down from a balcony at the wedding of her eldest son, the future Edward VII, the body of St George's Chapel, Windsor, is filled with a galaxy of nobility from every corner of the Empire. The Maharajah Dhuleep Singh, shown in the detail, cuts a splendid figure if, perhaps, a rather isolated one.

substance to allegation; but he was the second son, whose legitimacy the aged chief alone recognised, and the acts of the British Government subsequently ratified the fact. After Ranjeet's death, in 1843, Dhuleep Singh was proclaimed Maharajah, and duly placed under the charge of his mother as Regent. His first historical appearance was when, at the age of seven, after the defeats of the Sikhs at Sabraon, he proceeded to Sir Henry Hardinge's camp and tendered the submission. The treaty of Bhyrowal, which terminated the first Sikh war, provided that Punjaub should be placed under 'Dictatorship' of a British Resident and that Dhuleep Singh should become our ward. When the second Sikh War broke out, and the mutinous relics of the old Khalsa army perpetrated the outrages which rendered peace impossible, our measures were ostensibly taken in the name and for the authority of Dhuleep Singh. But the treaty of Lahore in 1849, to which are appended the signatures of both Lord Dalhousie [the Governor-General] and Dhuleep Singh, provided that 'The Maharajah Dhuleep Singh shall resign, for himself, his heirs, and his successors, all right, title and claim to the sovereignty of the Punjaub, or to any sovereign power wherever'. The property of the State and the famous jewel, the Koh-i-Noor, were also confiscated, and in return the young Maharajah was to receive for himself, his relations, and dependants a pension of four or five lakhs of rupees.

As a young man Dhuleep Singh gave no trouble and earned encomiums from everyone with whom he came in contact. As a boy he adopted Christianity and he made it appear as if his change of religion was due to absolute conviction. When he was presented at Court his manner and demeanour enlisted the sympathy of everyone on his behalf, and he was received with special consideration by the Queen and the Prince Consort. By the Prince of Wales and his brothers and sisters he was treated with frankness of a companion. On his side he made every effort, for a time, to show that he appreciated his consideration, and that he did not wish to take advantage of it. When the Koh-i-Noor was shown him he very gallantly said that it gave him great satisfaction to hand it in person to Her Majesty. But these harmonious relations were soon disturbed by more personal matters. In 1860 Dhuleep Singh was allowed to visit India, and he returned with a sense of his own political importance and of the loss he had incurred in the Punjaub. His mother, the ambitious and unscrupulous Zinda, who had lived in Nepaul for twelve years, came with him, and her advice was so pernicious that, at an early date after her arrival in England, she was separated from him; but not before she had inspired him with a belief that he had a valid claim to certain private estates of Ranjeet Singh which, owing to the discovery of salt, had risen to an extraordinary value. This claim which, well founded or not, proved impracticable, was destined to exercise an unfortunate influence over Dhuleep Singh's character. It became his one idea to recover these impossible, if not dubious, possessions; and from them he hoped to recoup himself for the heavy losses he had incurred in endeavouring to maintain a greater style than he was entitled to. His chief desire was to figure as a great county magnate; and at Elvedon Hall, in Suffolk – which was bought for him by capitalising a part of his pension – he kept up a state that alone absorbed the whole of the much-reduced income he received from the India Office.

Dhuleep Singh's financial difficulties soon made him an importunate and troublesome suitor at the India Office; whether rightly or wrongly, his demands were received with decreasing sympathy. At last Elvedon had to be given up; the shooting parties, which had been famous, could be held no more, and its too lavish master found himself in an embarrassed position that aggravated his sense of injury at official delays, and induced him to put forward untenable claims, among which the most senseless and ill-judged was a demand for the restitution of the Koh-i-Noor, which he had twice surrendered. When he found that it was impossible to obtain what he demanded he shook off the dust of his shoes against England and hastened to place his services as King of the Punjaub at the disposal of Russia. In this capacity he issued a high-flown, if not ridiculous, proclamation to his subjects in India, but it seems to have aroused little interest, and the Czar, who was just concluding an amicable arrangement with this country on the subject of the Afghan frontier, did not appreciate the offers of this Indian pretender. Dhuleep Singh left Russia disillusioned as to the advantages of being the Czar's protégé and took up his residence in Paris, where for a time he was reduced to great straits, having to sell the few jewels he still retained. During his absence, his wife, the Maharanee, an Egyptian lady with whom he had fallen in love when inspecting a school in the Delta, died, and he married an English lady in Paris, where he was chiefly resident since he quitted our shores. It was due to her influence that he conveyed an expression of contribution to the India Office in 1889, and that a portion of his pension was returned to him. It would be wrong to judge this unfortunate Prince too harshly, and great allowance should be made for his particular circumstances.

ILLUSTRATED LONDON NEWS: *24th June 1893*

Sir Takhtsinhji Jaswantsinhji, Thakore of Bhavnagar, 1856–1896

THE CHIEF FIGURE among the crowd of distinguished men upon whom the University of Cambridge conferred honorary degrees was that of His Highness the Maharajah of Bhavnagar, who received a very warm welcome as, in picturesque costume, he received the Degree of Doctor of Common Law. His Highness well deserved this high compliment, for the education benefits he has conferred certainly entitled him to the recognition of this ancient seat of learning. Besides establishing elementary and secondary schools, the Maharajah has also founded a High School and an Arts College. The latter is affiliated, with great advantage, to the University of Bombay. His Highness was created, in 1886, a Knight Grand Commander of the Most Exalted Order of the Star of India. His visit to this country, together with other illustrious Indians, has excited very much popular enthusiasm, which has been reciprocated on the part of the Maharajah by repeated expressions of delight. This was especially the case when he was recently entertained at the Crystal Palace. Another fact relating to His Highness is worth mentioning: he raised a troop of Imperial Hussars for

Thakore of Bhavnagar

Thakore Saheb of Gondal

service in the British Army. On every ground a better acquaintance on the part of the British public with those who fulfil such important duties in different portions of the Empire is to be desired, and we trust the visit of the Maharajah and other Indians will do much to strengthen the feeling of sympathy.

THE GRAPHIC: *May 1893*

Sir Shri Bhagvatsinhji, His Highness the Thakore Saheb of Gondal

GCIE, FRCP, FRS, DCL (OXFORD), MRCP, MRAS, MRI (GB), FCP&S *and* HPAC

THE THAKORE SAHEB OF GONDAL is known to our readers, he having been here more than once, and made a lengthened stay during his last visit. He is extremely fond of study, and has graduated in medicine in the University of Edinburgh. He is a social reformer, and has made his mark as one by tearing through the purdah system and bringing his consort out into Society. His efforts for social reform and his lengthened residence outside his own territory have not, however, precluded his taking a beneficial interest in the affairs of his own State. He has kept well abreast with the foremost of his brother-chiefs in giving his subjects the benefits of public works, railways, municipalities, courts of justice and police; and in these he has had a most competent practical assistant in the person of his Minister, or Dewan, Bezonjee Merwanjee.

His Highness Sir Rasulkhanji, managing, in this portrait, the difficult
feat of looking regal and relaxed at the same time, was the Nawab of
Junagad. He lived from 1859 to 1911.

India on display

To BRING INDIA home to Britain was the aim of the exhibitions that were held throughout Victoria's reign; the most enthusiastic of those promoting them was the Prince of Wales.

There was a threefold purpose in this desire to put on such exhibitions: a genuine appreciation of the magnificence that India could display in such abundance, but also a wish to make known that this exotic splendour was, ultimately, under British rule. The glory that was India's magnified the glory of a sovereign who counted kings amongst her subjects. The third and most vital issue at stake was what underpinned the entire Empire – trade.

Imperial splendour and the romance of distant possessions were hardly adjuncts to the process of making money, but in the last analysis they were dispensable and trade was not. It was the search for spices that first took Europeans to the East, and it was the production of one particular Oriental delicacy which kept the British in India just as much as any other factor – tea.

While *The Illustrated London News* describes with minute detail 'the richly coloured pottery . . . the very elaborately carved Bhaunagar screen . . . the alluring carpets' it is hardheaded enough to itemise precisely how valuable was our trade with India. 'The magnitude of the foreign trade of India enables it to rank as the fifth great commercial power in the world. The total value of the external sea-borne trade of India may be said, roughly, to be 155 millions of pounds sterling of which 70 million represents exports and 85 millions imports. Of this the commerce between India and the United Kingdom claims 86 millions – 36 millions exports and 50 millions imports.'

The Indian section of the South Kensington Museum, arousing much interest in the visiting families.

The Colonial and Indian Exhibition

ONE OF THE SECRETS of Queen Victoria's success as a monarch was that, for all her remoteness from the lives of her ordinary subjects, she shared many of their key perceptions.

So it was with India. The queen, who had brought that vast and diverse country under her sway, knew as much of it at first hand as most Britons, that is to say, very little.

Of course she met the Indian Princes, and the men and women who ran the Raj were there at her appointment. The man in the street, however, met the Indian beggars and hawkers who were hardly likely to grace a garden party, and it was the British working-class who made up the Army and the merchant fleet which tethered India to the Imperial apron strings. As for seeing the country with her own eyes, the nearest Victoria came was to visit the great Colonial and Indian Exhibition of 1886 – and, of course, that was the nearest most of her subjects got as well.

It was largely at the instigation of the Prince of Wales that the Exhibition was set up, and it was his idea to transform it into the Imperial Institute, as the national memorial of Queen Victoria's Jubilee. Later to become the Commonwealth Institute.

The archway into the courtyard of the Indian Palace.

The vestibule of the Durbar Hall.

The *Illustrated London News* brought forth a suitable introduction to the Exhibition on 8th May 1886, four days after the Queen had opened it:

> The Colonial and Indian Exhibition, projected by and carried out with the indefatigable assistance of the Prince of Wales, embraces examples of the products of the art and industry of many nations and in many races. But it is not a cosmopolitan show. It is intended to show to Britons at home of what stuff their brethren and fellow-subjects in distant climes are made. It is meant as a proclamation to all and sundry that Victoria rules an Empire as well as Three Kingdoms, that she is Empress as well as Queen, that from that dais at the Albert Hall, Kensington, she stretches forth the sceptre of a mild and beneficent, a just and equitable, but a firm and fearless rule.

Not content with that, however, the magazine produced a long, illustrated account of the exhibition two months later.

THE LONDON ILLUSTRATED NEWS: *17th July 1886*

Entering the chief entrance, we are at once transported to India – in a handsomely draped Indian Hall, furnished with beautiful models of P and O steamers, and lined with admirable figures of gallant Indian soldiers who have bravely fought shoulder to shoulder with British troops in Afghanistan, in Egypt and the Sudan and in Burmah.

The great Indian hunting trophy has been from the opening day one of the grand attractions of the Exhibition; a hunting elephant is seen beset by fierce tigers. Similarly there are other sections, such as the Natural History trophy, where a brace of gay peacocks as well as a colossal python may be seen. Alligators crawl from a pool, and buffaloes, hog-deer, sambur and bears are also to be seen in this signally vivid zoological masterpiece.

We pass on and pause to admire the fine carving on the handsome gateway presented by His Highness, the Maharajah of Jeypore. It is well worth strolling into this little court to inspect the coloured photographs which clearly illustrate life in an Indian city. In the Bombay and Baroda Courts, the richly coloured Bombay pottery and silk-work are worthy of the admiration they

The Durbar Hall of the Indian Palace.

The entrance to the central avenue in the Indian section.

Model of native fruit shop.

receive and the very elaborately carved Bhaunagar screen attracts general attention. Specimens of the famous Dacca muslin are shown in the Bengal Court. With respect to the alluring carpets with which the walls of the principal Indian avenue are made are of true Oriental designs.

The Indian Ethnological Court is small but wonderfully interesting. There are no less than three thousand specimens of useful timbers for building purposes in this noteworthy gateway. Immediately facing east, there is the remarkably fine seed and agricultural trophy and faithful models of native fruit and seed shops. The magnitude of the foreign trade of India enables it to rank as the fifth great commercial power in the world. The total value of the external sea-borne trade of India may be said, roughly, to be 155 millions of pounds sterling of which 70 millions represent exports and 85 millions imports. Of this the commerce between India and the United Kingdom claims 86 millions – 36 millions exports and 50 millions imports.

General interest is taken in the excellently executed models of villages and farms. In this broiling July, who will not revel in the cool vista of the handsome Durbar tent? The palatial Durbar Hall was entirely decorated by a couple of skilful native art-workmen. They took from midsummer of last year to April of this year for the carving and general decoration of this brilliant hall. The chased silver throne is a gift from the Maharajah Gunga Singh.

Many people prefer to enter the Courtyard of the Indian Palace through the famed stone gateway, presented by the late Maharajah Scindia. It should be added that in the Gallery of the Royal Albert Hall is a collection of oil paintings, water colour drawings and

photographs, executed by various artists and amateurs of art in India, presenting the scenery, the native figures and costumes and the architecture of different provinces.

On Thursday week, Her Majesty the Queen entertained at Windsor Castle about eighty Indians, Singalese and others employed at the Colonial and Indian Exhibition.

Gold brocade being woven by skilled weavers (*left*) and woodcarvers (*right*) working in the courtyard of the Indian palace.

Queen Victoria's letters

4th May 1886

A FINE BRIGHT MORNING. At eleven we left Windsor. At Paddington the Duchess of Bedford, the Great Officers of State, etc., met me. Immense and enthusiastic crowds. Got out at the entrance to the Exhibition amidst great acclamation. We first went into a tent at the entrance of which stood two Indian boys, and after a few minutes proceeded to a large vestibule.

Here all the Commissioners were presented to me in a body and a procession was formed, passing through the Indian Hall and the Indian Bazaar, where the sides were lined with Lascars, who looked most picturesque. Then we passed between rows, two or three deep, of Indians of all kinds, in the brightest costumes, all connected with the Exhibition and its exhibits, including the workmen. There were Parsees in white, with curious black glazed headgear, and numbers in turbans of every shade. We were warmly greeted with salaams, an old man of 100 held out a carpet for me to touch, and others held out their hands with pieces of money in them for me to touch. Then into the Albert Hall, through a sort of subterranean passage.

The Albert Hall was immensely full. We stood upon a large dais under the organ, where there was an Indian chair of state, standing on an Indian carpet. The national anthem was sung, the second verse in Sanskrit.

WINDSOR, *8th July 1886*

After lunch saw Sir H. Ponsonby about an interesting reception which is to take place viz of all Nations employed or connected with the Colonial and Indian Exhibition. The Indians came first, filing up one by one. They, one and all, 43 in number, knelt down and

An artist in metal meets an artist in oils . . . Mohammed Hussein was a coppersmith from Delhi, and was aged twenty-six when he came to the Colonial and Indian Exhibition in 1886. Whilst he was here the painter Rudolf Swoboda immortalised him.

3

kissed and stroked my feet and knees, some prostrating themselves more than others. They got up, they held out the palm of their hands for one to touch pieces of money they held in them. Their different coloured dresses had a very beautiful effect in the bright sunlit Hall. One of the Indians, a miniature painter, read out an address in Hindustani and presented it with two really wonderfully painted miniatures of me. Two of the Indians asked to sing, which they did sitting down and sang with most comical monotonous twang.

THE ILLUSTRATED LONDON NEWS: *3rd July 1886*

Our Colonial and Indian visitors

ON THURSDAY WEEK, a numerous company of the representatives of the British Colonies and India, connected with the Colonial and India Exhibition, visited this popular place of entertainment. After a grand concert, the visitors were entertained at dinner. Nearly four hundred ladies and gentlemen were present, those from India wearing their native costumes. In response to the toast, speeches were delivered by the Hon Graham Berry, Mr Bhownagree and Sir Charles Tupper.

The Lord Mayor of London and the Lady Mayoress on Friday week entertained the Colonial and Indian visitors at a grand ball at Guildhall. The scene was enlivened by the appearance of gorgeously-dressed native gentlemen (and a few ladies) from India and Ceylon.

Mr M.M. Bhownagree, Commissioner for His Highness the Thakur Saheb of Bhownagar, one of the Executive staff of the Colonial and Indian Exhibition.

(*below*) The reception of Colonial and Indian visitors in the Pompeian Court at the Crystal Palace.

Indian artificers at the Glasgow Exhibition.

THE OPPORTUNITY to view displays of Indian crafts and handiwork was not confined to the capital. An interesting exhibition was held in Glasgow in 1883, featuring workmen demonstrating their skills to the visitors.

THE ILLUSTRATED SPORTING AND DRAMATIC NEWS: *7th July 1888*

The Indian workman at the Glasgow Exhibition

ONE OF THE MOST INTERESTING FEATURES of the Indian contribution to the Glasgow Exhibition is the court devoted to the native artificers. The workmen, under their head man, a stately individual dressed in black, who occupies a compartment exactly in the centre of the row of shops, and who acts as interpreter, come from Bengal, the Punjab, &c., and are busily engaged all the day in wood-carving, making jewellery, manipulating the potter's wheel, &c. There is also one shop devoted entirely to Indian confectionery. The place is crowded with sightseers all day, who, however, are railed off by some Oriental palisading, but can at the same time enjoy a good view of the manufacturers and the products. The features which impress one most of all in viewing the thing are the quietness, deftness, and order with which the various crafts are pursued by the skilled and earnest workers.

The Imperial Institute – its origins

THE GREAT INTEREST excited throughout the British Empire by the Colonial and Indian Exhibition of 1886, which illustrated the vast wealth in natural products and the commercial, industrial, artistic and educational achievements of the various colonies and of India, led the Prince of Wales to suggest the setting-up of a permanent Institute. It would be designed to afford a thorough and living representation of the progress and the development of their resources, and set up on a scale commensurate with the importance of their relations to the prosperity of the Empire. The Institute would be a fitting national memorial to the fiftieth year of Queen Victoria's reign – 'an epoch within which some of our most important and thriving colonies passed from insignificance and even comparative barbarism to exalted positions in the commercial and civilised world'.

This suggestion became the germ of the proposal to establish an Imperial Institute. The next step taken by the Prince of Wales was to appoint a Committee of Organisation and before the end of the year 1887 promises of contributions amounting to nearly £350,000 had been secured. Private donations from India alone totalled £101,550.

The Queen laying the foundation stone of the Imperial Institute on the 4th July 1887.

The design by Mr T.E. Colcutt for the Imperial Institute, South Kensington.

The foundation stone of the Institute was laid by Her Majesty the Queen on the 4th of July 1887, in the presence of a brilliant assembly of more than ten thousand specially-invited spectators. The foundation stone was a huge block of granite from Cape Colony standing on a pedestal of Indian bricks. The main entrance to the temporary building where the ceremony took place, had served as the principal ingress to the Colonial and Indian Exhibition in Exhibition Road.

The Indian princes who attended the ceremony included the Rao of Cutch, Kumar Shri Kalooba (brother of Rao) the Maharajah and Maharani of Kuch Behar, the Thakore Sahib of Morvi, the Thakore Sahib of Limri, the Thakore Sahib of Gondal KCIE, the Maharajah Sir Pertab Singh KCSI, Kunwar Harman Singh, Ahluwalia CIE, of Kapurthalla, Prime Minister to the Nizam. The native officers of the Indian cavalry were on duty at the pavilion entrance.

Following the address by the Prince of Wales, Her Majesty read the reply:

> I believe and hope that the Imperial Institute will play a useful part in combining those resources for the common advantage of all my subjects, and in conducting towards the welding of the Colonies, India and the Mother Country into one harmonious and united community. In laying the foundation stone of the building devoted to your labours, I heartily wish you God speed in your undertaking.

In 1887 it was suggested that the School of Modern Oriental Studies should be organised as a branch of the Institute. This proposal led to negotiations with the authorities of University College and King's College, London, which resulted in their co-operation with the Institute in the establishment of the school. It was arranged that classes for Instruction in the oriental languages required by students qualifying for examinations for the Indian Civil Service should be held at University College, while Modern Oriental languages, other than the Indian languages, should be taught at King's College; the Imperial Institute should undertake the general administrative work. The school was officially opened in January 1890.

Royal activities got at least as much space in the Press of Queen Victoria's era as they do today, and the absence of the modern mass media – radio and television – meant that the descriptive powers of the journalists of the day were given full rein. Here, for example, is the description of the opening of the Imperial Institute from *Black & White* magazine of May 1893.

BLACK & WHITE MAGAZINE: *20th May 1893*

The opening of the Imperial Institute

IF FROM A FAIR BEGINNING fairest auguries of future prosperity may be drawn, the career of the Imperial Institute should be fortunate beyond parallel. No one, except apparently the responsible authorities, had formed an adequate idea of the magnitude of the popular demonstration; and surely nobody had clearly pictured in imagination anything like the beauty and majesty of the spectacle.

In the enclosure separating the Palace from the road were mounted guards drawn from volunteer corps, representing England, Ireland and Wales. Here also were drawn up the Royal escort – the Life Guards with their helmets, cuirasses and sabres flashing in the sunlight, the Colonial contingents and the Indian native cavalry, fierce-looking warriors in uniforms of the richest colours. The Queen thus paid to her Indian and Colonial troops the greatest compliment of making them the immediate guardians of her person.

The opening ceremony took place in a temporary building erected on the site of the great hall of the Institute. It was provided with seats for 2,000 spectators among whom were the Indian Princes, the leading members of the Ministry and Opposition, numerous representatives of the Diplomatic Body, the Judicial Bench, both Houses of Parliament, State dignitaries, the Lord Mayor and Sheriffs and other distinguished personages.

A fanfare of trumpets and a roll of drums heralded the approach of Her Majesty and the whole assembly rose to its feet. Her Majesty, who was dressed in black, trimmed with jet, and unrelieved by a single Order or jewel, walked with the aid of a stick, supported on either side by the Prince of Wales and the Duke of Edinburgh. With some assistance the Queen mounted the steps of the dais and took her seat in the chair of State, bowing right and left as she smilingly acknowledged the homage of those assembled.

The Prince of Wales, amidst perfect silence, read an address setting forth the objects of the Institute, and stating that all parts of the Empire had contributed to its erection.

With a profound bow the Home Secretary handed the Queen the reply which Her Majesty read. It is rarely that the Queen's voice is heard in public. After an Imperial March, specially composed by

'With soaring voice and solemn
  music sing!
High to Heaven's gate let pealing
  trumpets ring!
To-day our hands consolidate,
The Empire of a thousand years.'
— LEWIS MORRIS

Sir Arthur Sullivan, had been played, the Prince of Wales came forward and said, 'I have received the Queen's commands to declare this building open and inaugurated'. A grand flourish of trumpets in the porch of the great hall followed the declaration, and then the Prince of Wales, taking a jewelled key, opened a model of the Institute. Three strokes of a bell announced that the lock was turned, completing the circuit of an electric current to the bell-chamber of the 'Queen's Tower'. The Archbishop of Canterbury pronounced the benediction, after which Madame Albani sang 'God Save the Queen'.

The Queen, on rising to leave the building stopped before the Indian Princes, and cordially shook hands with them, a gracious departure from the official etiquette.

The distinguished Indians in the assembly within the hall were the Maharaja of Bhaunagar, the Raja of Kapurthala and the Thakore of Gondal. The rulers of Bhaunagar belong to one of the most ancient clans of Rajputs, and the present Maharaja, as an administrator, philanthropist and patron of arts ranks amongst the most enlightened princes of India. Of his loyalty to the Empress of India, he has given many proofs and he was the first chief in Western India to offer to contribute to Imperial defence.

The Raja of Kapurthala is also a man of culture, a warm advocate of progress and worthy representative on this Imperial occasion of the enlightened nobles of India, whose sympathies with their Empress are a source to her and her Ministers at once of pride and confidence. The Thakore of Gondal comes to us from his territories in Kattyawar, Western India, and, like the Maharaja of Bhaunagar, is a Rajput. He has travelled far and wide, having visited Europe and England more than once, besides America and Japan. As a social reformer he has proved himself most courageous, having gone as far as to emancipate the ladies of his household from the restriction of the purdah.

The British Empire Exhibition

In 1924, London was host to an exhibition designed to demonstrate to the world British power and achievement. All the nations of the Empire displayed their arts and their products in what was at once a colourful and an impressive show of imperial might.

THE British Empire Exhibition derives its absorbing interest from its intense realism. Stately and picturesque pavilions are constructed of materials brought from the countries they represent; trees and shrubs and flowers are growing around as they grow thousands of miles away.

Within these pavilions—just as one sees in the Palace of Engineering and the Palace of Industry the productive enterprise of the United Kingdom—are carried on the arts and crafts of all countries under the British flag.

But neither at Wembley nor in its home is the Empire always at work. When one has watched the making of Indian carpets by native experts, he may witness an Indian play performed by Indian actors in an Indian theatre, or, spellbound, gaze upon an Indian snake charmer compelling a huge cobra to do his bidding.

Not only are there displayed the products of the vast agricultural and mineral resources of the Empire; the visitor will see for himself how they are won and treated and brought to finished perfection for millions to use.

BRITISH EMPIRE EXHIBITION

Admission 1/6
Children 9d.

There are no extra charges for admission to Dominion, Colonial and Government buildings

Open
10 a.m. to 11 p.m.

CHAPTER FOUR

The Coronations

W HEN EDWARD VII was crowned in 1902, he became sovereign of a mighty Empire and, in accordance with the practice established by his mother, Queen Victoria, the new King wished to honour his loyal subjects. The congregation who gathered in Westminster Abbey comprised the most gallant and glittering display – dignitaries from all the ends of the earth, and the most colourful and magnificent of them were the Indian princes, their families and the officers and troops of the Indian regiments.

The coronation of George V in 1911 was attended by unalloyed celebration, with no hint that the world was moving towards war on a scale never known before. The crowned heads of Europe and the mightiest princes from Britain's Empire all converged on London as guests of the British monarch.

The accession of George VI was greeted with rejoicing, although the future King himself was shocked at being catapaulted on to the throne by so unlikely an event as his brother's abdication. As history was to reveal, he acquitted himself far better than could have been expected, this last of the King-Emperors, and it was he who saw India achieve her independence.

The Indian presence for this coronation was impressively large, with detachments from many regiments lining the route and certain cavalry members providing an escort to the royal carriage. The crowds who had come to see the procession greatly admired the dignity and splendour of these troops, while the maharajahs and their wives were seated among the guests of honour inside Westminster Abbey itself.

It is remarkable to note that Victoria, still only a girl, was crowned in 1837 and, precisely one hundred years later, the coronation of her great-grandson took place. During those hundred years a bond between Britain and India had been established and the lives of generations had been affected. Although British rule ended in 1947, the link between the two nations has remained.

The coronation of Edward VII

A FEW DAYS before the date fixed for the Coronation of King Edward VII, rumours began to circulate that the King was far from well.

Just two days before the proposed ceremony, on June 24th, an announcement was made, to the consternation of the public, that the King was suffering from perityphlitis. On the same day as the announcement, the King was operated upon with a completely successful result. Edward's recovery was such that a new date for the Coronation could be fixed for 9th August, but the ceremony was somewhat shortened in order not to tax the King too much.

The painting records the impressive sight of ranks of Indian troops in the grounds by Fulham Palace, silently praying for the recovery to health of the King.

THE ILLUSTRATED LONDON NEWS: *5th July 1902*

The King's illness: the sympathy of the Indian Troops

A STRIKING AND PICTURESQUE DEMONSTRATION of sympathy with the King was given by the representatives of the Indian Army attending the Bishop of London's reception at Fulham Palace on June 24. On hearing the news of His Majesty's severe illness, and the consequent postponement of the Coronation festivities, they lifted up their hands and said, 'We go to pray'. Then, with their carpets spread before them, they prayed for their Emperor for an hour and a half in the field opposite the Palace. The Christians in the Indian Army afterwards sent a message to the Bishop: 'The others have been praying in the camp for the King. May we come and join you, Bishop, at your evening worship?' The chapel was crowded with troops at the ten o'clock intercessionary service.

THE ILLUSTRATED LONDON NEWS: *9th August 1902*

Oriental and colonial guests at a historic English home

LORD AND LADY WARWICK'S Reception to Indian and Colonial Coronation visitors at Warwick Castle on August 2. A large and distinguished company travelled down to Warwick Castle from Paddington. Lord and Lady Warwick personally conducted the visitors over the castle, and pointed out its innumerable treasures.

Social life resumed its course upon the news of the King's recovery. Sir Baba Khem Singh, the splendidly robed figure on the left, was amongst the party which was invited down to Warwick Castle for a summer reception.

THE CORONATION SOUVENIR, *1902*

The coronation of Edward VII in Westminster Abbey

RANGED AGAINST THE SCREEN in the places of highest canonical honour, were a row of Indian feudatories, whose jewels rivalled in splendour those of the regalia which they had come to see assumed by their imperial suzerain. In the stall of the canon residentiary sat the Maharajah of Jaipur, the lord of the coral city where he presides over the solemn worship of the Hindu Sun-god. By him was another Rajput prince, the Maharajah of Bikaner, and then the Maharajah of Idar, better known as the gallant Sir Partab Singh, whose adopted son, Doulat Singh escorted the Prince of Wales in his procession. Near them were the young Maharajah of Gwalior from Central India, who served with the British forces in China: the Maharajah of Kolhapur, descendant of the founder of the ancient Maratha Empire; and the Maharajah of Cooch Behar, a brilliant officer of Bengal Cavalry, with his gentle Maharanee beside him. Then at the end of a row of divines of the Church of Scotland was seen the intelligent face of the Aga Khan.

Indian officers of the Imperial Service troops in magnificent military dress uniforms attending the Coronation of King Edward VII on the terrace of the House of Commons in 1902.

Less flamboyant than the soldiers and humbler than the princes, it was men like Gagan Chandra Rai who kept the wheels of the Raj turning. He was born in 1848 and began his working life as a civil servant in the famine department. He served the Government for almost forty years, and his services were so well thought of that he was granted the honorary title of 'Rai Bahadur' and was given a Certificate of Honour at the time of the Imperial Delhi Durbar in 1903.

He travelled widely and was present at the Coronation of Edward VII with his kinsman, Maharajah Tagore of Calcutta. In 1908 he retired from government service but carried on his work in various non-official capacities.

Colonel Yates and four of the King's Indian Orderlies at the House of Commons in 1902.

Indian army officers (*right, above*), models of military pomp and decorum, on the terrace of the House of Commons in 1902.

The Duke of Connaught on Wednesday inspected the Indian Coronation contingent (*right, below*) at their camp at Hampton Court. His Royal Highness, who was accompanied by Colonel Egerton, was received by Lieut-Colonel Dawson, who is in command of the troops, while the Indians themselves were smartly turned out to welcome their royal visitor.

(*left*) Riseldar Major Sir Partab Singh of the 12th Bengal Cavalry and two other officers present at the Coronation of King Edward VII in 1902.

(*below*) A group of Indian soldiers assembled for the Coronation in 1902.

Photo. Johnston and Hoffman.

COLONEL H.H. MAHARAJA SIR
MADHU RAO SINDHIA, G.C.S.I., A.D.C.,
Maharaja of Gwalior.

H.H. MAHARAJA SIR MADHO
SINGH, G.C.S.I., G.C.I.E.,
Maharaja of Jaipur.

H.H. SIR SHAHU CHHATRAPATI
MAHARAJ, G.C.S.I.,
Maharaja of Kolhapur.

Photo. Johnston and Hoffman.

MAHARAJ KUMAR PRODYOT
KUMAR TAGORE,
Representing Calcutta.

Photo. Johnston and Hoffman,

THE HON. ASIF KADR SAIYID WASIF
ALI MIRZA OF MURSHIDABAD,
Representing Bengal.

Photo. Johnston and Hoffman,

COLONEL H.H. MAHARAJA SIR PERTAB
SINGH, G.C.S.I., K.C.B., A.D.C., LL.D.
Maharaja of Idar, Commanding Indian
Contingent.

Photo. Wiele and Klein.

THE RAJA OF BOBBILI,
Representing Madras Province.

H.H. MUHAMMAD B. KHAN,
Nawab of Bahwalpur.

LIEUTENANT-COLONEL NAWAB
MAHOMED ASLAM KHAN, C.I.E.,
Representing the Frontier Province.

Under a majestic canopy representing the stars seen in the eastern sky, it was the Prince of Wales, due to the King's illness, who received the Indian princes who had come to Britain for the Coronation.

THE ILLUSTRATED LONDON NEWS: *12th July 1902*

A reception of Indian Princes at the India Office

Taken from the Coronation souvenir programme of 1902, portraits of a number of India's most illustrious princes.

THE COURT OF THE INDIA OFFICE was magnificently adorned for the most brilliant of all the receptions held in connection with the Coronation of King Edward VII. The Eastern Sky, studded with stars, was simulated by a huge painted velarium overhanging the hall, and under this gathered an assemblage rivalling that of the most magnificent Oriental Durbar. The chiefs and representatives were introduced to the Prince, acting as the King's deputy, by Lord George Hamilton, Secretary of State for India. Each bowed or touched his forehead, while the officers presented their sword-hilts for the Prince to touch.

The coronation of George V

THE CORONATION of the new King Emperor, George V, in 1911 was the signal for universal rejoicing throughout the Empire. The event was as glittering as any before it, and attended by thousands of loyal subjects of many races.

Inevitably, it was the Indians who made the biggest impact on the popular imagination, with their peacock uniforms and their fabulous wealth. The cream of the Indian nobility came to London, together with men from every unit of the Army.

Their every deed was eagerly chronicled in the popular press for an avid public who longed for a hint of the exotic and the romantic.

While the Indian troops camped in the Home Park at Hampton Court, to the west of London, the more illustrious guests lived in great style in the capital's grand hotels.

The most notable figures in the Royal Progress were the Maharajah Holkar of Indore and the Aga Khan (*above*) and (*below*) the Thakore Sahib of Gondal and the Thakore Sahiba of Gondal.

'Happy and contented' Indian officers of the Coronation contingent are presented informally to a smiling Lord Kitchener.

THE ILLUSTRATED LONDON NEWS: *24th June 1911*

The Indian Coronation contingent inspected by Lord Kitchener at Hampton Court

LORD KITCHENER, who is known to the native troops of India as their former 'Jung-i-lat Sahib' (Lord of Battles), the generic name given to the Commander-in-Chief, last week inspected the Indian Coronation contingent in its camp in the Home Park at Hampton Court. At the end of the inspection, with which Lord Kitchener expressed himself highly pleased, a few native officers were specially called up and presented to him, and after the parade was dismissed an informal levée was held, and many officers were introduced. Among those with whom he conversed were Lieutenant the Hon Malata Umar Hayat Khan Tirvana, a member of the Imperial Indian Council; Captain Shah Mirza Beg and Captain Mohammed Ali Mirza, of the Hyderabad Cavalry and Lieutenant Krishna Urs, Mysore Cavalry. Lord Kitchener asked one of the men how they were getting on. 'Raza bazy.' was the reply, meaning 'Happy and contented.'

Major-General His Highness Maharajah Sir Madhu Rao Scindhia Bahadur, of Gwalior

On the horse is the Hon Sir Cecil Edward Bingham at the Royal Mews, while, keeping his hand firmly on his sabre, is not his batman but one of the most distinguished guests for the Coronation of King George V. He is Maharajah Scindhia of Gwalior who came to the throne at the age of ten in 1886.

THE MAHARAJAH OF GWALIOR (1876–1925) succeeded to his State in 1886 and was given full powers in 1894 at the age of 18. He was made an Aide-de-Camp to His Majesty the King in 1901 and in 1902 received an honorary degree of LLD from the University of Cambridge. In 1903 he was invested with the insignia of Knight Grand Commander of the Victorian Order.

The Maharajah attended the Coronation of George V in 1911 and in 1917 was made Knight Grand Cross of the Order of the British Empire. In 1925, on his way to England the Maharajah died in Paris with a severe abscess on his neck and was cremated with Hindu rites at Père Lachaise cemetery near the tombs of Chopin and Oscar Wilde. His ashes were taken back to Gwalior.

When he came to London for the Coronation of George V in 1911 the following extract appeared in *The Times*:

> In 1889, the Darbars' offer of 1,200 cavalry and transport train of 200 carts of Imperial Services was accepted by the Government of India and the transport train has twice been utilised in active warfare. It was a matter of satisfaction to the Government of India to enable the Maharaja to gratify his intense desire for active service under the British flag by placing His Highness on the staff of General Sir Alfred Gaselee,

Commanding the Forces in China. The Gwalior Imperial Service Troops now consist of 1,892 cavalry and 1,794 infantry, including a transport corps of 446 men. Besides being a keen and able soldier, His Highness is a most enlightened administrator. His energy is indefatigable and he devotes close personal attention to all the details of the government of his vast estates. He is a great advocate of education in all its branches and is a patron of the Daly Chief's College at Indore. He is also a member of the Governing Body of the Mayo College of Ajmer, to which he has contributed handsomely. The Maharajah Scindhia is entitled to a salute of 19 guns with two additional guns in his own territory and to be received by the Viceroy.

The Begum of Bhopal, accompanied by Lieut-Colonel S.F. Bayley visiting the Coronation Exhibition at White City in 1911.

His son Jeewaji Rao Scindhia, born in 1916, succeeded his father in 1936. At the time he was the youngest of the princes, entitled to a salute of twenty-one guns. He named his son and daughter George and Mary after the King and Queen, who were their godparents.

The coronation of George VI

GEORGE VI WAS, like his father, a second son who was not expected to reign. In fact he regarded his brother's abdication as an unmitigated disaster, writing in his diary when the document was presented to him 'I broke down and sobbed like a child'.

His comments to Lord Mountbatten further demonstrates his very real reluctance to shoulder the burden of monarchy: 'Dickie, this is absolutely terrible . . . I'm quite unprepared for it . . . I've never seen a State paper; I'm only a naval officer. It's the only thing I know about.'

Nevertheless, he was one of the more successful British monarchs, bringing his country through its darkest hour and presiding over the peaceful passage of responsibility to the peoples of the Empire.

But in 1937 those peoples rejoiced wholeheartedly, as the last King-Emperor mounted his Imperial Throne. Two hundred and thirty representatives from India attended the occasion by special invitation.

This turbaned Indian visitor was determined to defy the British weather in order to have a good view of the Coronation procession in 1937, and joined many others at the Victoria Memorial in the heart of London.

With the exception of one man, the whole of the Indian Coronation contingent in camp at Hampton Court visited Brooklands and other places of amusements on 17th May 1937. The only remaining Indian was besieged for his autograph by visiting crowds. The picture shows the sole occupant of the Indian camp at Hampton Court signing autographs.

THE TIMES: *20th April 1937*

Troops for the Coronation

THE INDIAN CONTINGENT will be the largest of the overseas groups attending the Coronation. With followers, cooks, servants, and orderlies the total will approach 1,000, of which three parts will be serving soldiers. The mounted men in the procession will form an escort to the King Emperor, and part of the contingent will have a place on the line of route. The force will be made up of representatives and detachments from the many branches and regiments including Indian Lancers, Horse, Cavalry and Light Cavalry regiments; Six Punjab regiments; Two Frontier Force regiments; The Bombay Grenadiers; The Maratta Light Infantry; The Jat Regiment; The Baluch Regiment; The Sikh Regiment; The Royal Garhwal Rifles; The Hyderabad Regiment; The Burma Rifles; Officers, warrant officers, and seamen of the Royal Indian Navy; Superintendents, inspectors and constables of the Indian Police; and the Indian Air Force Squadron.

The King's Indian Orderly officers Rahim Ali and Sardar Khan (*left*) looking at a map of London. They liked to know the routes to their various entertainments.

Indian officers buying food in Cheals Stores, Cambridge Street, Pimlico, London. The proprietor, Mr Williams, obtains their curries and spices from London warehouses especially for them.

Most of the Indian Coronation contingent in camp at Hampton Court were farmers in civil life, and took the opportunity of learning something about English agriculture. They saw some of the finest model farms in Great Britain, including those belonging to the King at Windsor. They visited a farm near Bishops Stortford, Herts. The photograph shows one of the Indian contingent milking a cow on the farm on 7th May 1937.

The Indian Coronation contingent, composed of vastly different types of men from all over the huge country from which they came, were in camp at Hampton Court where this picture was taken on 4th May 1937. The picture shows a barber at work on one of the Burmese troops in the camp.

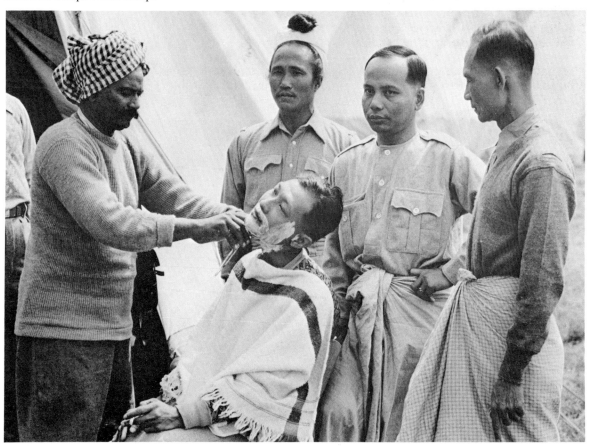

THE TIMES: *11th May 1937*

Indian guests at the Speaker's Reception for Overseas Guests

THE SPEAKER and the Hon. Mrs FitzRoy invited prominent members of the British aristocracy, together with some of the crowned heads of Europe, to meet the distinguished representatives of the Empire, who were the overseas guests of the King and Queen.

Those present included: the Maharajah of Jodhpur, the Maharajah of Ratlam, the Maharajah of Navanagar, the Maharajah of Palenpur, the Maharajah Gaekwar of Baroda, the Nawab of Bhopal, the Maharajah of Jaipur, the Maharajah of Bikaner, the Maharao of Cutch, the Nawab of Bhawalpur, the Maharajah of Kapurthala, the Rajah of Tehri Garhwal, the Rajah of Mandi, the Aga Khan and the Begum Aga Khan, the Yuvarajah of Mysore, the Rajah of Bhor, the Rajah of Jamkhandi, the Rajah of Koonjhar, the Rajah of Nilgiri, Sir Manekji Dadabhoy, Sir V.T. Krishnamachari and Lady Krishnamachari.

The correspondent from *The Times* reported enthusiastically,

The band of the Life Guards played in the red drawing-room, and Sydney Jerome's orchestra in the library. The main staircase was decorated with pink roses and the Speaker's library with red tulips, roses, and lilies. The House of Commons libraries were banked with pink tulips, rhododendrons, and hydrangeas, and there were white roses and lilac with salmon-pink roses and carnations in the blue drawing-room. The tables in the two main buffets were decorated with tulips, one room with pink and the other lemon-yellow.

Representatives of Indian regiments passing through Admiralty Arch in the Coronation procession of King George VI and Queen Elizabeth.

Some of the Indian Princes were the proud possessors of titles which were grandiose even by comparison with their peers. One such was His Highness Farzand-i-Duband Rasikh-ul-Ilikad Daulat -i- Inglisha Raja-i-Ragjan Maharaja Sir Jagjit Singh Bahadur GCSI, GCIE, GBE, the Maharaja of Kapurthala, (1872–1949). He attended the Silver Jubilee of King George V and the Coronation of King George VI, wearing in his turban his incomparable emeralds set in diamonds, which were amongst the legendary jewels of India. His travels were by no means confined to Britain and he saw more of the world than most of his fellow Princes, visiting both North and South America, Africa and most of Europe and Asia. This portrait from Osborne House is by the German artist Rudolf Swoboda and is dated 1898.

An Indian visitor is presented to King George VI, accompanied by Queen Elizabeth and Queen Mary.

CHAPTER FIVE

World War I

THE OUTBREAK of the First World War galvanised all parts of the Empire and Dominions into immediate action, and India's war effort was truly immense.

All opposition to the Government ceased at the beginning of the War and the feelings of Indians at large were well summed up by the Hon. Pandit Madan Mohan Malaviya, an ex-president of the Indian National Congress.

On 9th September, 1914 when the War was only five weeks old he assured the Viceroy and Governor-General that India would grudge 'no sacrifice of men and money in order that the British armies shall triumph'.

And there was indeed to be no holding back, with £100m. given outright to Britain, followed by an annual contribution of between £20m. and £30m. towards war expenses. India also undertook her

Poppies for the dead, spring flowers for the living . . . During a march past of Indian troops, ladies pin flowers on the Indian tunics.

Major-General H. H. Maharajah Sir Ganga Singh Bahadur of Bikaner, belonged to the great warrior clan of Rathore Rajputs. His long record of war service began with the expedition for the relief of the Legations at Peking, in which he commanded the famous Camel Corps. During the war he served both in France and Egypt. The Maharajah came to Britain in 1917 as the first Indian Prince to be delegated to the Imperial War Conference and Cabinet. He could not be spared from recruiting and other war work in India for the second War Conference and Cabinet, but in addition to providing a stream of recruits for the Indian Army between 1914 and 1918, His Highness gave many lakhs of rupees to the Imperial Treasury.

own defence, so that, for a time, there were less than 150,000 British troops in the sub-continent.

But it was in the field of manpower that she made her greatest effort. There was a total of 72,000,000 men between the ages of 18 and 50 in India who were eligible for active war service. As Nihal Singh pointed out in an article in the *Graphic* of April 1918, the Indian politicians who might have been expected to make recruiting difficult had, on the contrary, urged the authorities to make the greatest possible use of India's manpower.

The statistics show that the effort was truly prodigious for, according to the War Office figures of 1922, the strength of the Indian ranks was 239,561 at the outbreak, whilst by 1919 India had sent 1,096,013 men overseas. Most went to the theatre the troops called 'Messpot', with 675,391 Indian soldiers fighting the Turks in the Mesopotamia campaign. But the contribution to the main battle front in France was also significant, with 138,000 Indian soldiers serving there, and by the end of the war her soldiers had served in Belgium, Gallipoli, Salonika, Palestine, Egypt, Sudan, Mesopotamia, Aden, the Red Sea Coast, Somaliland and East Africa.

Impressive as all these figures are, the number that really lingers in the mind is the casualty roll, and here again India more than shouldered her burden, with a total of 121,598 casualties. This figure was made up of 53,486 dead, 64,350 wounded, 2,937 missing, 302 prisoners of war and 523 presumed prisoners at the end of 1919.

The intense savagery of the battles in which the Indian troops were involved is shown by the high proportion of dead as compared with wounded, although disease took a significant toll.

Hospitals in Britain took many of those sick and wounded, with a total of 368 officers and 14,182 other ranks receiving treatment in Britain for whom they were fighting.

Their sacrifices did not pass unnoticed by the British Government, and their suffering finally prodded the rulers into a recognition that things could not be the same after the War was over.

So in 1917 the Cabinet declared that its aim was the establishment of a responsible government in India, and the 1919 Government of India Act introduced a system of 'dyarchy' by which the government was divided between elected representatives and officials.

It was progress of a sort for the aspirations of the nationalists, but as the Americans say it was 'a day late and a dollar short'. That fact was almost tacitly recognised by another British concession, for India was accorded separate representation at the Versailles negotiations which concluded the War and at the fledgling League of Nations, just as if she were an independent state.

And that status was indeed the goal to which India now bent herself.

Sir Partab Singh, Maharajah of Idar, 1845–1922

JUST AS THE Maharajah of Bikaner's life summed up the latter part of British rule, the personal story of this man encompassed the first part. Sir Partab Singh, Maharajah of Idar, first made his mark by saving several Britons in the Mutiny, at great personal risk.

He fought in almost all of the incessant frontier wars, and at the age of 70 was amongst the first of the Indian Princes to appear at the front in France. He arrived there in the autumn of 1914, and summed up the purpose of his journey with admirable brevity: 'I wish to die leading my men, sword in hand.' Alas, France was not the place for a Bengal Lancer.

His long and outstanding military career should not make us forget his success as a ruler. Under his leadership the state of Idar was saved from bankruptcy and he introduced improvements in finance, justice and education.

Sir Partab was also on good terms with the British monarchy. He attended both of Queen Victoria's Jubilees and made a great

A portrait of His Highness
Maharajah Partab Singh by Spy,
reproduced in *Vanity Fair* in 1887.
Almost thirty years later, at the
age of 70, he was promoted by the
King to the rank of Hon. Lt-General.

impression on her. He was an ADC to her son Edward VII, and
attended the Coronation of his son, George V in 1911.

His military career was not harmed by the fact that as well as
knowing 'Bertie', he was an intimate friend of Field-Marshal Lord
Roberts, who was at the relief of Lucknow, led the retreat from
Kabul and commanded in the Boer War.

Aside from their shared gallantry and military interests, the
Field Marshal and the Maharajah shared one other distinction –
both were born in India.

Brighton Hospital 1914–18

IT WAS A BOLD STEP to attempt to convert buildings in the middle of an English town into an up-to-date hospital. To convert however, historic buildings such as the Pavilion and Dome, without making extensive structural changes or interfering with valuable mural decorations presented a problem: they lacked smaller rooms so necessary in a hospital for ward and kitchens. The ventilation of the buildings was most inadequate for a hospital. Places for operating theatres, convenient for all wards, had to be found. Space had to be found for many stores and offices, while room for the recreation of the patients had also to be thought out. The Pavilion could claim to be the first building in England in which this problem was solved.

There are three different kinds of kitchens attached to the hospital, one for Mohammedans, another for meat-eating Hindus and a third for vegetarians. All Indians are able to cook on the ground or on the plastered mud floor, using wood or charcoal for fuel. This, of course, was impossible in a hospital in England, so the cooks had to be taught to cook standing up. A fixed dresser made of slabs of stone was built round each kitchen and on this a series of gas rings was arranged for their pots. The Indians had never heard

(*opposite*) Cigarettes being presented to wounded Indian officers in the grounds of the Kitchener Hospital.

'There is some corner of a foreign field that is forever England'. That line from Rupert Brooke has come to serve as the epitaph for a lost generation of English youth, lost like Brooke himself, in the bloody turmoil of the First World War.

But for many of the 14,500 Indian soldiers admitted to hospitals in the United Kingdom, that corner was on the Downs above Brighton. For by a strange irony the Prince Regent's Indianesque conceit, the Royal Pavilion, was turned into the main hospital for the soldiers of the Raj serving in Europe.

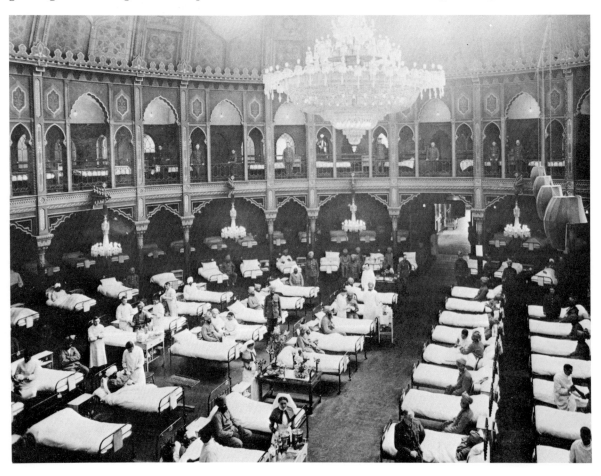

Convalescent sepoys working in the kitchen at the Royal Pavilion.

of gas, far less seen it, and the cooking hours were times of considerable excitement and anxiety till they learnt wisdom by alarming experience when lighting up. Many experiments were made before the right kind of flour could be obtained in this country for the making of chappatis. Eventually this was secured and passed by a Committee of Indian Officers representing all castes.

Dhal and ghee are imported and so are the various Indian spices. Sufficient caste cooks could not be got, so convalescent sepoys of different castes and men unfit for further fighting do much of the cooking. In every ward there are two water taps for drinking

Wounded Indian soldiers playing cards in the Royal Pavilion grounds.

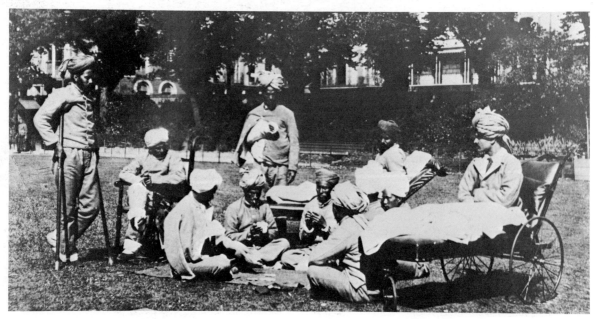

water, one for the Hindus and one for the Mohammedans. These are clearly labelled. All the notices throughout the hospital are in three languages, Urdu, Hindi and Gurmukhi.

The patients in each ward are grouped according to tribe or caste. Each patient has an English bed with spring and hair mattress.

Every effort has been made to make the wounded as comfortable and as happy as possible. Not only do they live in a Royal Palace, but the splendid grounds which surround it have been reserved for them. A 'Gift House' has also been opened. Many gifts for the wounded are sent by the public from all over England.

There are a number of Indian young doctors, studying in England when the war broke out, and now qualified. A staff of Indian medical students work as dressers whereas other students act as interpreters. They came forward to offer their services to the State and formed Indian Volunteer Ambulance Corps. The nursing is done by trained European orderlies.

The hospital has 724 beds and a British and an Indian doctor are on duty night and day.

By way of entertainment, organ recitals are given by local organists in the Pavilion and the music is much appreciated. In the Dome there is a powerful electric magic lantern with which frequent exhibitions of both English and Indian pictures are given. Cinema shows are also given there.

At the suggestion of Mr Chamberlain, the Secretary of State for India, parties of convalescent patients, one class at a time, are sent up once a week to London, where they are met by an officer conversant with Indian languages who takes them round in

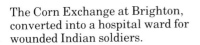

The Corn Exchange at Brighton, converted into a hospital ward for wounded Indian soldiers.

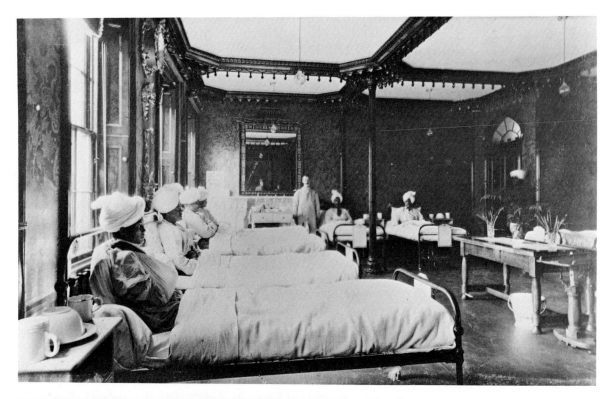

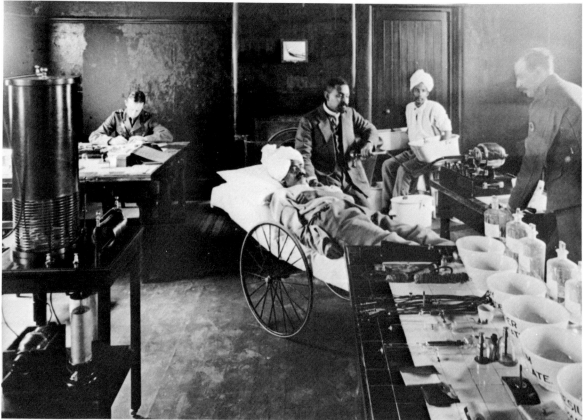

motors to see the principal sights of the capital. Small parties also go out regularly for short walks along the sea front in the charge of British NCOs of the nursing staff. Separate parts of the ground are specially reserved for the religious observances of both Mohammedans and Hindus and in a large marquee tent the Sikhs have improvised their temple.

The hospital was visited by HM King George and Queen Mary. Their Majesties, who spent a considerable time visiting each ward, were pleased to find the Royal Palace so much appreciated.

The Hospital was again visited by the King and Queen, accompanied by Princess Mary. The King had come specially to decorate with his own hands, for conspicuous gallantry in the field, ten of his wounded Indian officers and one Indian non-commissioned officer. It was royal weather, and the investiture took place on the lawn on the west of the Pavilion, where over 1,000 wounded Indians were gathered to greet their King Emperor. The recipients were:

> The VICTORIA CROSS – Jamadar Mir Dast, 55th Coke's Rifles who had already won the Indian Order of Merit in India. Though his wounds were healed, he was still suffering from effects of poison gas and had to be wheeled up in a chair, but he insisted on standing up in front of His Majesty. The King addressed him with these words: 'It is nearly sixty years since Queen Victoria instituted this cross for conspicuous bravery in battle. At the Delhi Durbar in 1911, I ordered that my Indian soldiers should be admitted to this high and coveted distinction. I have already bestowed with my own hand two VCs on Indian soldiers and I give this third cross with infinite pleasure. I earnestly hope that you will soon completely recover from your injuries and that you will live long to enjoy your honours.'

The official record of Jamadar Mir Dast's bravery is as follows:

> For most conspicuous bravery and great ability at Ypres on April 26th 1915, when he led his platoon with great gallantry during the attack and afterwards collected various parties of regiment (when no British officers were left) and kept them under his command until the retirement was ordered.
>
> Jamadar Mir Dast subsequently on this day displayed remarkable courage in helping to carry eight British and Indian officers into safety, whilst exposed to very heavy fire.

Then came the following:

> MILITARY CROSS: Jamadar Pancham Singh.
> ORDER OF BRITISH INDIA, *2nd Class*: Bahadur Subadar-Major Fateh Singh.
> INDIAN ORDER OF MERIT, *2nd Class*: Subadar Sasidhar Thapa, Jamadar Gunjbir Gurung and Jamadar Gunjar Singh.
> INDIAN DISTINGUISHED SERVICE MEDAL: Subadar Kedar Singh Rawat, Jamadar Ali Bahadur, Jamadar Bur Singh and Janadar Hawinda.

The last recipient was Havildar Ganga Singh, who was decorated with the Indian Order of Merit, 2nd Class. He arrived at the Pavilion with the first convoy in December 1914, severely wounded, and lay out on the battlefield for two days before he could be brought in. He killed eight Germans, using his bayonet till it broke, when he took the sword of a German officer he had already

The beautiful Red Drawing Room at the Royal Pavilion was also converted into a ward for the wounded.

Sepoys receiving electric and galvanic treatment at the Kitchener Hospital, Brighton.

As the 'war to end wars' dragged on through bitter winters and bloody summers, the first loyal flush of enthusiasm turned to the fatigue and resignation seen on the face of this wounded Indian soldier during his convalescence at Brighton.

killed to deal with the remainder. When the Investiture was over, their Majesties proceeded to the wards to see the Indians who were not well enough to come out on the lawn. After this Their Majesties inspected a typical group of hospital kitchen arrangements. On their way to the kitchens they heard the Sikhs chanting in their improvised temple. H.D. ROBERTS

When the Indian wounded soldiers had departed, Brighton felt that she had passed through an experience of extraordinary interest. It seemed that some visible monument should be raised in honour of India's faithful dead. Mr Austen Chamberlain, then Secretary of State for India and the Council of the Borough, decided that the form of the monument should be that a Chhatri be erected on the site of the burning ghat. Sir Swinton Jacob, the architect of many notable and beautiful buildings in India was consulted and under his supervision Mr E.C. Henriques, a brilliant young Indian architect (though bearing a European name) then completing his studies in London, prepared the design and plans. The Chhatri itself is of pure white Italian marble with a dome on eight pillars with an octagonal base. The steps are built of English stones. There are borders of delicate ornamental carving round the dome, about 25ft high. In construction and feeling, the memorial is purely Indian with the inscription:

'To the memory of all the Indian soldiers who gave their lives for their King-Emperor in the Great War, this monument, erected on the site of the funeral pyre where the Hindus and the Sikhs who died in hospital at Brighton passed through the fire, is in grateful admiration and brotherly affection dedicated.'

The memorial being of national character, HRH the Prince of Wales was pleased to consent to unveil and dedicate it on 1st February 1921. It was a notable event. As the Prince drove over the grass of the down, a salute to the dead of twenty-one guns was fired. The ceremony was short, simple and impressive. The Prince stood

More than fifty thousand Indian soldiers never returned home after World War I, and many of them died of their wounds in Brighton, Sussex. Those whose religion called for burial were interred at Woking, whilst cremations took place on this 'ghat' on the South Downs in Brighton. The spot where their souls ascended is now marked by a permanent memorial unveiled by the Prince of Wales in the presence of the Maharajah of Patiala.

behind the middle block of the three on which the pyres had been lit. The Mayor then invited him to unveil the Chhatri, which was swathed in Union Jacks and decorated with the Star of India. That done, the Prince delivered a speech:

> 'We are here met to dedicate a memorial to brave men, our fellow-subjects, who, after the fire and stress of Flanders, received the last sacred rites of their religion on this high eminence. It is befitting that we should remember, and that future generations should not forget, that our Indian comrades came when our need was highest, free men – voluntary soldiers – who were true to their salt – and gave their lives in a quarrel of which it was enough for them to know that the enemy were the foes of their Sahibs, their Empire and their King. It was a great adventure to them to leave home and a congenial climate, to pass over the Black Water, and to give all in a conflict of which the issues were to most of them strange and impersonal.
>
> This monument marks, too, another fact. When the wounded Indian soldiers were brought to England, there was no place ready for their reception. Your generous town came to the rescue, and, with a hospitality which will ever be remembered in India, gave not only her finest buildings, but gave also her friendship and respect to those gallant men. I can assure you, Mr Mayor, that India never forgets kindness and sympathy; and from this Chhatri a wave of goodwill will pass to India

Volleys were then fired and drums rolled. 'The Last Post' was sounded, followed by the 'Reveille', and the ceremony ended.

After the dedication in 1921, there were many visitors to the Chhatri, but within a few years the memorial became neglected. It also became the target for many stray bullets fired by Canadian soldiers carrying out exercises on the Down during the Second World War.

In 1951, the Patcham branch of the British Legion decided the renovate the Chhatri, and on the third Sunday in June the first Pilgrimage and Memorial Service took place. This Pilgrimage has been carried out every year, with the Service given by the Vicar of Patcham.

This is believed to be the only service of its kind in England.

THE ILLUSTRATED LONDON NEWS: *25th August 1917*

Indian patriotism throughout the Empire

The Rally to the Flag

INDIANS RESIDING in the remotest corners of the world came forward to serve the Empire in its hour of need. Take the case of Gurbuchan Singh, who is now fighting the Germans in the ranks of the Australian Imperial Force. At the time of the outbreak of the war, he owned a large general store in south-west Australia. The Sikh blood boiled in him, in spite of his being on the wrong side of forty.

In the middle of 1915, he managed to obtain his heart's desire: he was the first and the last Indian admitted into the Australian Field Force.

The outbreak of hostilities found Arjan Singh in the Argentine. He heard that the regiment in which he had formerly served had been ordered out to the Western Front from India, and more than anything else in the world, he wanted to be a member of the first Indian expeditionary force in France. He sailed for England on a steamer ferrying many Britons. Arjan Singh was the only man on board who had had military training, and his fellow-subjects got him to drill them on the voyage. That was the first time an Indian had drilled Europeans.

There were several Indians belonging to the Indian Military Service in England at the time war broke out. They at once went back to India. Among these men were Lieut. Colonel Bhola Nath and Lieut. Colonel Jivan Singh. Two Indian officers who had retired from the Indian Military Service and were living in London, Colonel Kanta Prasad and Colonel Warlekar, went out to India. Kanta Prasad's patriotism rose to such a high pitch that he did not mind serving, for a short time, as an orderly in a military hospital under an officer junior to him. He was recently given a first-class Kaisar-i-Hind medal as a reward for the valuable services rendered during the war.

The great march-past

No part of the Empire had fought harder or more gallantly than India, and, after the end of the First World War, the effect was officially recognised at a great march-past in August 1919. An official account chronicled:

In August 1914, the Indian Army entered upon a new phase of its history. It is hardly too much to say that in the days before the war Englishmen at home realized little more of that Army than that it existed. They read now and again of small campaigns on the North West Frontier, in Africa, or in China, in which bodies of Indian troops had taken part. They saw, perhaps, in Jubilee or Coronation processions a picturesque group of Oriental horsemen, clad, not in the native Indian khaki which the whole Empire was in time to make its own, but in the gorgeous uniforms that date from the days of the East India Company, in scarlet or yellow, blue or green, and gold; but here for the most part, and not unnaturally, their knowledge ended. The great Army from which these detachments were drawn, although maintained in a state of efficiency that might challenge comparison with any troops, was recruited primarily for service only within India or on her borders. Few could have foreseen that Indian troops were destined to stand one day in the cause of liberty, side by side with the soldiers of Britain, the Dominions, and the Allies in three continents, to fight the Hun and the Turk to a standstill, and to take their part in upholding the British Empire. It was therefore a fitting crown to their achievements that the forces serving or recruited in India, British troops, Indian Army, and the Imperial Service troops of the Native States alike should be invited to send a representative contingent to

march in the great peace celebration procession of 1919. Unfortunately an alteration of date, difficulties of shipping, and at the last moment an outbreak of influenza, prevented the contingent from arriving in time to join the procession, and it was not until the 26th July that the troops reached their quarters at Hampton Court. Their disappointment was, however, soon allayed by the King-Emperor's gracious decision that the Indian contingent should have a Victory March of its own through London, and that he would review the troops in person at Buckingham Palace.

This memorable event took place on August 2nd. The procession started at half-past two from Waterloo Station, where the contingent, consisting of a British detachment of 11 officers and 270 men, and an Indian Army detachment of 27 British officers, 465 Indian officers, 985 Indian other ranks, and 34 Imperial Service troops, had arrived by rail from Hampton Court.

The shadow of the Cenotaph fell long across the reign of George V, as it did over his second son and successor. Here some of the men who shared the joy of the 1911 Coronation share the grief that the next seven years brought. The four Indians are the Aga Khan, the Maharajah of Patiala, the Maharajah of Jodhpur and the Maharajah of Kashmir. The occasion is the tenth anniversary of the Great War's end, Armistice Day 1928.

CHAPTER SIX

Indian nobility: the early twentieth century

ALTHOUGH HE DIED YOUNG, His Highness Kishan Singh, the Maharajah of Rajputana, saw the ending of an era, with the death of Victoria, and lived through the early years of this century in a world which was changing enormously. Rapid technical advances, and a new economic and social climate combined with the devastating effects of the first World War to render life in the 1920s unrecognisable, when compared with that of Victorian times.

The circumstances of this young prince, who came to the throne in 1900 and died in 1929, represent those of all the maharajahs, who had to adjust to a new dispensation.

In 1902 the former Prince of Wales was crowned King, but only eight years later, in 1910, the young Kishan Singh attended his funeral. With the death of Edward VII, the last links with the nineteenth century disappeared, and Britain and the Empire looked to George V to guide them through uncharted seas.

The Maharajah of Bikaner was not only a gallant soldier but he showed courage and judgement in commissioning the most fashionable and talented painter of his day, Augustus John, to produce this picture. The Maharajah, dressed in his military uniform, sat for this portrait in 1919.

HIS HIGHNESS MAHARAJA KISHEN SINGH
OF BHARATPUR. RAJPUTANA INDIA
OCTOBER 1901

THE GRAPHIC: *27th August 1910*

H.H. Kishan Singh, Maharajah of Bharatpur

DURING THE LAST THIRTY YEARS many Indian Princes have visited this country, but if our memory does not play us false, the Maharajah of Bharatpur, who was one of the three representatives of India present in St. George's Chapel at King Edward's interment, enjoys the privilege of being the youngest member of his order to come to England. His Highness Kishan Singh is only eleven years of age and he is under a guardianship of the British Government. Bharatpur is the new official spelling for the place which the general reader would recognise more easily if spelt in the old fashion as Bhurtpore, a name recalling some remarkable achievements of failure and success in British military annals. The State of this name lies in Rajputana. Although it is only considered in the official sense to have existed since 1722, when the chief of that day 'committed suicide by swallowing a diamond' and earned the title of 'the Cincinnatus of the Jats' at the hands of the courtly Tod. The Jats whose name suggests affinity with the Getae and possibly Goths, fought on our side in 1803, when Lord Lake won the battle of Laswari and captured Delhi. In the following year, on Holkar's defection, Bharatpur went with him, and then occurred the first of the two memorable sieges of the fortress city of Bhurtpore. At the end of 1825 the second siege took place with a different result, with victory, and was restored to the ancestor of our present visitor. Kishan Singh succeeded his father in 1900. There can be no doubt that he and his people will benefit by the course of discipline through which he is passing and in years to come he will remember the vivid impressions formed during his visit to England, which happened to synchronise with so heart-stirring an historical event as the death and funeral of King Edward VII, the first British Emperor of India.

His Highness Maharajah Kishan Singh of Rajputana (1899–1929). This little boy looks exceedingly grave, as befits a Maharajah who is not yet three years old, claiming descent from the god Krishna. He came to the throne after his father's deposition in 1900. As the story from *The Graphic* of 1910 relates, he came to London for the funeral of King Edward VII. In the following year he was one of the pages for King George V and Queen Mary at the 1911 Coronation Durbar in Delhi. In 1918 he was invested with full powers by the Viceroy. He died very young.

The Maharajah and Maharani of Baroda

MAHARAJAH SAYAJI RAO, the Gaekwar of Baroda (1863–1939), personified the capricious tricks that only fate can play. He was born the son of a peasant farmer and grew up illiterate, but in 1875 at the age of 13 he was catapulted on to a throne he was to occupy longer than any British monarch ever reigned.

Sayaji Rao was the doyen of ruling princes. For the sixty-four years he was on the gadi, the State enjoyed progress and prosperity; he made education a fundamental feature of his policies and in 1893 introduced in Amreli Division an experimental measure making elementary education compulsory. He opposed early marriages, caste restrictions, untouchability and supported understanding and cooperation between different faiths. Dr Bhimrao Ramji Ambedkar, who was appointed chairman of the

The Maharajah and the Maharani at the House of Commons in 1905.

committee which drafted the Constitution to free India, was his protégé, educated and looked after by him when he was a young boy.

During the war, Baroda troops and resources were placed at the disposal of the British Government and the Gaekwar was a delegate to the Imperial Conference, as well as to the First and Second Round Table Conferences. He enjoyed travelling and toured most of Africa and Europe, even getting within a few hundred miles of the North Pole.

H.H. the Gaekwar of Baroda and the Maharani in a group at the House of Commons. On the extreme left is Sir M.M. Bhownagree. The photograph was taken on 5th July 1905.

All his three sons went to Oxford, the eldest to Balliol in 1901. Sadly they all died early in life, leaving his infant grandson Pratapsinhji to succeed him in 1939.

On his Diamond Jubilee, King George V sent a telegram, 'To few Princes is it granted to rule for so long a period of time and to look back with satisfaction upon sixty years of continued material and moral progress of their subjects'.

The Maharani of Baroda was the daughter of Sardar Bajirao Ghatge of Dewas and had beautiful manners. She was most simply, and with utmost assurance, a Queen. In 1926 she became honorary president of the National Council of Women and a year later presided over the first All-India Women's Conference. With her daughter Indira, the Maharani of Cooch Behar, she consistently opposed the purdah system and showed herself unveiled at the most formal religious festivals. Her ladies-in-waiting were all English. She often said, 'If only the right spirit could stir Indian women, what wonderful things could be done.' This concern for the status of Indian women led her write the book, *The Position of Women in Indian Life*.

This gold-encrusted figure is the Nawab Bahadur of Murshidabad (1875–1959), recognised by the Raj as 'Premier Hereditary Noble of Bengal, Orissa and Behar' and a direct descendent of Mir Jaffar. Prince Wasif Ali was born in 1875 and was the first of his house to receive western education – at Rugby and Oxford. He was renowned as one of the finest polo players in India and also excelled at shooting and billiards. But he was also famous for his more highbrow pursuits, notably for his fine poetry in both English and Urdu and was Founder President of the Hindu Muslim Association. Somehow he also found time to run his estates – as the original caption tactfully puts it, 'better than some of his predecessors had done'. He represented Bengal at Edward VII's Coronation.

Among the deeds preserved in his family for over two hundred years is Mir Jaffar's will recording the legacy to Clive.

(*right*) This splendidly flamboyant figure is the Maharajah Mádhav Rao of Gwalior (1876–1925), who could have acted as the progenitor of that grandiose American maxim 'If you've got it, flaunt it'. The original caption breathlessly describes the fabulous sum he spent on wishing his friends a Happy Christmas early this century: 'The Maharajah of Gwalior has paid £200 for 200 Christmas cards. They are described as being the last word in pictorial daintiness and costliness. Splendid views of the Durbar are included in the numerous pages which comprise the cards, together with hand-painted scenes illustrating incidents in the Maharajah's life.' The Maharajah received the Honorary degree of LL D from the University of Cambridge in 1903.

The Begum of Bhopal as a young child. This portrait was reproduced in *The Illustrated London News* in 1892.

Her Highness the Begum of Bhopal, who has taken Patteson Court, Nutfield, near Redhill, motored to town last week to be received by the King and Queen at Buckingham Palace, just before the first Court. On the following day she and her son, Sahibzada Hamidullah Khan, were received by Queen Alexandra. The Begum and her women observe the purdah strictly, wearing veils with holes for the eyes when out of doors.
– *The Illustrated London News*, 20th May 1911.

THE TIMES: *19th September 1911*

The Maharajah of Cooch Behar

OBITUARY

WE REGRET TO ANNOUNCE that the Maharajah of Cooch Behar died last evening at Bexhill. His Highness who came to England with a numerous suite for the Coronation, had been ill since the middle of July, suffering from heart trouble and kidney complications. Colonel His Highness Maharajah Sir Nripendra Narayan Bhup Bahadur of Cooch Behar GCIE, CB, and Hon. Aide-de-Camp to the king was born in 1862 and before he had completed his first year the death of his father, Narendra Narayan, brought him to the gadi of the important State of Cooch Behar in north Bengal. The young prince received a wholly European training. Soon after his accession he was made an hon. major in the British Army and received the insignia of the CB from Queen Victoria on coming to England in 1898. He had been made a GCIE ten years earlier.

The Maharajah stood first in reputation as a sportsman among the ruling Chiefs of India and he possessed the largest and the most varied collection of Indian sporting trophies ever brought together. He published the record of his long experience of jungle sport under the title of *Thirty-seven Years of Big Game Shooting* showing his record to be 365 tigers, 311 leopards, 438 buffaloes and 207 rhinoceroses.

He eagerly supported the cause of Indian social reform. By his

Two years after the death of his father, the young Maharajah of Cooch Behar married his bride Princess Indira, daughter of the Gaekwar of Baroda. They are photographed here in Indian dress following a ceremony to initiate the bride into the Brahmo religion.

genial hospitality and approachableness, and with the co-operation of his charming and accomplished consort, he did much to bring Europeans and Indians together. Their Highnesses were always welcomed by a wide circle of friends from the Sovereign downwards, on their frequent visits to this country. Their four sons and three daughters received education in this country and Princess Pretiva is specially noted for her charm and beauty. He will be deeply mourned not only by his subjects but a wide circle of friends here and in India.

The Maharajah was cremated at Golders Green Crematorium, London, as were his two heirs, Rajendra Narayan and Jitendra Narayan. There are commemorative plaques to this effect in the West Chapel of the Crematorium.

Maharajah and Maharani of Cooch Behar

AT THE CLOSE of the Edwardian era there took place in London one of those weddings which the world loves – a rich handsome young couple marrying in the teeth of parental opposition.

Both the families of the groom, the Maharajah Kumar of Cooch Behar (1886–1922), and the bride, Princess Indira, daughter of the Gaekwar of Baroda, were opposed to the match because she had

The Maharajah of Cooch Behar leaving Paddington Registry Office with his wife, who had formerly been engaged to the Rao of Gwalior.

previously been betrothed by her parents to the Maharajah of Gwalior.

Happily as in all the best romantic stories, both families were reconciled in the end but nobody knew that would happen on 26th August 1913, when *The Times* described the lengthy nuptials. The Maharajah was at Eton from 1899 to 1904 and later studied at Farnborough.

THE TIMES: *26th August 1913*

The wedding of Maharaj Kumar Jitendra Narayan of Cooch Behar and Princess Indira Gaekwad of Baroda took place privately in London yesterday, it being stated that circumstances in both families made it necessary to celebrate the marriage as quietly as possible.

Princess Indira had been staying at the Buckingham Palace Hotel and soon after 10 o'clock the Maharanee of Cooch Behar, wearing Indian robes of white silk and gold, arrived in a motor car from her London residence in Hyde Park Street. At 10.30 the first ceremony, the reception of the bride into Brahmo religion (which is the creed of the bridegroom), took place in the drawing-room of the hotel. During the ceremony incense was burned and conch shells were blown. An hour later the bridegroom, wearing a lounge suit and straw hat, drove to the hotel in a motor car, the interior of which was decorated with lilies. Just before noon the bride, wearing a gown of pink and rose du Barry silk, trimmed with white lace, and a hat to match, left the hotel, in a motor car accompanied by another lady and drove to the Paddington Registry Office in the Harrow Road where the Maharaj had arrived. Accompanying the Maharaj were his mother, the Maharanee, his brother-in-law Mr Sen, Sir Krishna Gupta and Mr Ali Baig. In the certificate the bridegroom was described as Jitendra Narayan of Cooch Behar, aged 26, bachelor of 59 Cambridge Terrace; the bride's name was given as Indira Gaekwad, 21, of Buckingham Palace Road.

After the ceremony the bride and bridegroom drove back to the hotel where the marriage service according to the rites of the Brahmo religion was held. Only two Europeans were present. Many of the ladies present were in native costume, as were both the bride and bridegroom, who changed from their European clothes on arrival at the hotel. The bridegroom wore a white costume and turban and the bride robes of yellow and gold. Subsequently a breakfast was given at the hotel, followed by a reception at the town house of the Maharanee, who presented the bride with dresses and ornaments.

It will be remembered that after considerable opposition on the part of the bride's parents the marriage was arranged to take place in India. Almost at the last moment, however, all the arrangements were cancelled and Princess Indira came to England.

As a curious footnote, the couple's daughter, the Maharani of Jaipur, Gayatri Devi, one of the most beautiful women in the world, is in the *Guiness Book of Records* for having achieved the largest ever personal majority in an election when she stood in the Indian General Election of February 1962 and won no less than 157,692 of the 192,909 votes cast.

The Maharajah of Patiala whose offer to accompany the British Expeditionary force was graciously accepted by His Majesty King George V.

The Maharajah of Patiala

ONE OF THE TITLES of Maharajah Sir Bhupendra Singh, the Maharajah of Patiala (1891–1938) was 'Favoured Son of the British Empire'.

Coming to the throne in 1900, he was renowned as a mighty sportsman – cricketer, shot and a fine polo player – and for his great generosity and hospitality. He also nurtured another passion dear to the English, breeding and training sporting dogs.

But it was in the field of politics that his greatest contribution was made. His state was known as 'the cradle of the Imperial Service troops' and on the outbreak of the First World War he placed all his resources at the disposal of the British Crown.

A tribute from India to the glorious dead. The Maharajah of Patiala saluting the Cenotaph in London.

He attended the Imperial War Conference in the UK in 1918 and represented India at the League of Nations Assembly in 1925, around the time he is pictured atop London's Savoy Hotel with Col. C.W. Bowles, his ADC, and was elected Chancellor of the Chamber of Indian Princes in the following year. In that capacity he led the delegation of Princes at the Round Table Conference in 1930, but later came under attack for his private life and the running of his State, accusations which were made in a publication called the 'Indictment of Patiala'.

He demonstrated his faith in British justice to the last, demanding an official inquiry which completely exonerated him.

The Maharajah of Patiala on the roof of the Savoy Hotel in London.

His Highness Thakore Saheb Sir Waghji, the Thakore of Morvi (1858–1942), pictured by Sidney Hall in 1887, the year of Queen Victoria's Golden Jubilee. He liked England, visiting it six times during the early part of his reign, even though in late Victorian and Edwardian times, the trip through the Suez Canal was an uncomfortable one. His last visit to England was in 1911.

THE TIMES: *23rd April 1928*

The Maharajah of Mayurbhanj

OBITUARY

OUR CALCUTTA CORRESPONDENT telegraphs that Maharajah Purna Chandra Bhanja Deo, of Mayurbhanj State, the most important feudatory Prince of Orissa, died on Saturday at Bombay of tetanus due to a cut on the cheek with a razor. The body has been conveyed to Mayurbhanj for the final rites.

The Maharajah's death while still in the twenties (he was born on 7th August 1899) follows about sixteen years after that of his father, who died at the age of 41 from injuries received from a spent bullet while shooting in his State. The Maharajah is survived by his mother, the Dowager Maharani, who is a daughter of the famous Brahmo leader, Keshub Chunder Sen, and the sister of the widow of Major General Maharajah Sri Nripendra Narayan of Kuch Behar. He was educated at Mayo College. He took great interest in the promotion of the Tata Steel Works, giving very extensive leases of iron ore. The Preference shares he received in return were turned to good account in the Great War, their sale at a high premium permitting of large investments, amounting to 35 lakhs, in Indian War Loan. The young Maharajah gave great assistance also in recruitment for labour corps, and was generous in contributions to various War Relief funds. The offer of his personal service for the field was duly accepted, and he was gazetted to the Royal Artillery; but before he reached France the Armistice was signed. The Maharajah took the opportunity to make an extensive tour of this country. He had been a page to the Queen-Empress on her visit to Calcutta in 1912, and he was received by their Majesties on this and subsequent visits to England.

It was not only the British who were happy to bestow titles on the Indian Princes. His Highness Sir Sajjan Singh of Rutlam (1880–1947), a polo player of international repute, was also a Chevalier of the Légion d'honneur, an honour bestowed after his World War I service in France. For their part the British gave him the honorary rank of Colonel in 1918, and he later became ADC to King George V. He ascended his throne in 1893 at the age of thirteen and married the daughter of the Rao of Kutch. Like so many other Indian nobles, he was a welcome guest at the Coronation of King George VI in 1937.

The Maharajah of Kolhapur

SIR SHAHU CHHATRAPATI, the Maharajah of Kolhapur (1874–1922) came to the throne as a ten-year-old child in 1884. His family went back to the Marathas and in 1811 his state was bound to Britain by Treaty, entitling him to a 19-gun salute on all his official appearances. He was much respected by the British, and he was a guest at the Coronations of both Edward VII in 1902 and George V in 1911. His loyalty was recognised in the New Year Honours List of 1931, when *The Times* announced that he had been made GCSI, Knight Grand Commander of the Star of India.

One feature of his life throws a bizarre light on the considerable difference which always existed between the Indian and British nobility, in spite of all the similarities. The Maharajah was awarded an Honorary Law Doctorate by Oxford, but could never return to his alma mater after ascending the throne, because his caste forbade it. It was for his sporting prowess, however, that he was best known, as a fine shot and a leading polo player. Like so many other Indian princes, he spent money freely on racehorses, and, despite his 28-stone bulk, he was a very active man. His great weight is not surprising in view of his habit of consuming three dinners in succession, whilst spending a quiet evening in his railway carriage.

CHAPTER SEVEN

Sporting encounters

(*left, above*) The first Indian team to tour the UK, the Parsees of Bombay, whose Club was founded in 1848. *The Times* commented, 'Their cricket proved to be of the most elementary description.'

(*left, below*) The second tour of 1888 saw the Parsees in much better form, their star performer, Dr M. E. Pavri, taking 170 wickets at under 12 runs each.

(*below*) 'In 1911 the first India side came to England, and . . . English people realised India was not lacking in cricketing talent' – *The Times*. The team was captained by the Maharajah of Patiala. Gaekwar of Baroda, extreme right, standing.

OF ALL THE BONDS linking India and Britain, none has been tighter than the shared passion for cricket. It was first played in India by English sailors, the first recorded match being at Cambay in 1721.

The Calcutta Cricket Club was founded, just after the MCC, in 1792. The first Indian cricket team to come to Britain was the Parsee Cricket Club of Bombay in 1886. Both that tour and a subsequent one in 1888 were financed by Indian philanthropists. It was not until 1911 that the next touring side arrived in the United Kingdom, captained by the Maharaja of Patiala and including the Gaekwar of Baroda.

But the most famous Indian cricketer of the age had already been playing in Britain since 1895 – His Highness Prince Ranjitsinhji, later to be the Jam Saheb of Nawanagar, Gujarat. Known simply as 'Ranji' wherever the game was played, he was a Cambridge Blue, captain of Sussex for five years and an England Test player. He scored 1,000 runs in each of the twelve full seasons he played, including a Test tour of Australia, and a record seventy-two first-class centuries.

It was not until the late 1920s that India was granted full Test match status, and the first Test match between England and India was played at Lord's, London, in 1932. England won, as they did again in 1936 and in 1946, in the last tour before India's Independence.

If England at first proved masters in the game they took to India, they had a harder time of it when it came to hockey and polo, and the Indian love of horses ensured that many of the English classic races were won by Indian owners.

Nothing could better illustrate the relationship between India and Britain than the history of sporting contact between the two nations.

Playing for England against Australia at Old Trafford in 1896, the great 'Ranji' rescued his side after two shaky starts by scoring 62 and 154 not out.

The contribution that sportsmen made in other spheres was

Ranjitsinhji edited the *Jubilee Book of Cricket* and was acclaimed by G.L. Jessop as 'the most brilliant figure during cricket's most brilliant period.' W.G. Grace went further, 'I assure you', he said soberly at an after-dinner speech in 1908, 'that you will never see a batsman to beat him if you live for a hundred years.' *Punch* gave him the nick-name 'Run-Getsinhji'. 'By becoming the first Indian to play cricket for England, at the height of Victorian prejudice, he demonstrated that a coloured man could not only be the equal of any Englishman in the field of endeavour but, in his case, indisputably superior' wrote one sports journalist of the time.

(*left*) Ranji's incomparable leg glance – part of a remarkable range of skills from a man who suffered all his life from hay fever. He was nick-named 'Smith' at his university in England.

exemplified by the same man, who in later life served on the League of Nations with his former Sussex colleague, C.B. Fry.

In 1929 Lord Hailsham, then president of the MCC and Lord Chief Justice commented: 'At least in the sphere of cricket, India has been granted Dominion Status if nothing else.' Eighteen years later, the politicians followed where the cricketers had led.

Prince of cricketers

LIKE MANY OF sport's immortals, the great Prince Ranjitsinhji (1872-1933) was as renowned for his modesty as for his incomparable leg glance. In a letter to the *Strand* magazine in 1896 he wrote:

'I take this opportunity also of thanking the British public for the very kind way in which they have always received me on all grounds, and that has in no small way conduced to my success in cricket.

Trusting that I have not encroached too much on your valuable space, I remain,

Yours truly,

RANJITSINHJI

The *Strand* magazine's correspondent wrote: 'When the time arrives for cricket history to be written, the name of Prince Ranjitsinhji, the young Indian player, will be inscribed upon the roll of fame.

'Several things will conduce to such an event occurring. In the first place, the Prince has rapidly played himself into the hearts and favour of the British public. At the present time it would be difficult to discover a more popular player throughout the length and breadth of the Empire. The roar of welcome that goes up from the throats of the assembled thousands as 'KS' steps upon the field is equal even to the outburst of enthusiasm that greets the champion, the immortal 'WG'. It may be explained that 'KS' stands for 'Kumar Shri', meaning 'Prince'.

Another thing is that, although known to first-class county cricket for barely two reasons, Prince Ranjitsinhji, after having been most unaccountably passed over by the executive sitting at Lords in the first of the test matches against Australia this year, attained the summit of a cricketer's ambition by being requested to play for the mother country at Manchester, when the second of the international fixtures was decided.

His performance on that occasion is now a matter of history, but I must be pardoned for referring to it. After the failures of such men as Mr W.G. Grace, Mr A.E. Stoddart, and others, with the bat, an easy victory for the Colonials appeared within measurable distance. But the Prince came to the rescue of his side. He treated the Antipodean bowlers with indifference. Jones sent down his express deliveries; Giffen, the wily, sent up full tosses for catches; Trott tempted him to hit, but every ball was met and dispatched, clean and hard, far out of the reach of the fieldsmen.

At the end of the second day's play, Prince Ranjitsinhji was not out, and it appeared as though he might even then retrieve the fortunes of his side. Unfortunately, however, he was unable to secure a partner who could stay with him, and when the last of the English wickets fell he was not out for a grand contribution of 154, made at a time when even the bravest heart might have been pardoned had it quailed at the stupendous task before it.'

SKETCH: *4th September 1901*

Two cricket stars of the season: Prince Ranjitsinhji and Mr C.B. Fry

MR C. B. FRY, K. S. RANJITSINHJI AND KILLICK: the first two named have proved themselves the brightest 'stars' of the season in which other 'stars' have burned brilliantly. Each has scored over two hundred in an innings. Ranjitsinhji has, indeed, done it twice consecutively, and of this wonderful cricket it may, with truth, be said that he has never played with greater variety of hit, or stroke, than in the

Two stars of the 1901 cricket season: Prince Ranjitsinhji and C.B. Fry.

present year. Mr Fry's 105 against Surrey at the Oval last week was another source of rejoicing for Sussex.

Over the Indian Prince's batting one is never likely to be found nodding. He has not scored nearly so many runs as Mr Fry, Tyldesley, or Abel, yet, with the old Oxford Blue, he stands apart from the rest of the batsmen in the matter of average and, in individual innings, is second to none, for his 285 (not out) tops all others of the year, during which eleven other batsmen have scored 200 or over in a single innings.

THE ILLUSTRATED LONDON NEWS: *17th June 1893*

Ranjitsinhji

AN INDIAN PRINCE on the cricket-field earning the applause of the most critical crowds by his brilliant batting is a spectacle sufficiently novel to awaken the sympathy of all who have a spark of interest in either the vast Empire from which the player comes or in the great national game which is so characteristic of England. Kumar Shri Ranjitsinhji, whose excellent achievements in the Cambridge University Eleven have led to his obtaining the coveted honour of a place in the annual inter-University match is a Rajput Prince of Jadeja descent and a relative of Jamnagar. After study at Rajkumar College, in Rajkot, he came to England in 1888, and two years later he entered Trinity College, Cambridge. In 1891 he had, by his cricketing prowess, won his college colours, and at the end of the season his average was fifty-four runs. In addition, he is an excellent player at tennis and racquets and a good shot. Mr Ranjitsinhji has this season had remarkable success with the bat, scoring 58 and 37 (not out) in the match against the Australians on June 10. Many years ago the Prince of Wales occasionally took part in a game of cricket at the Oval, while the sons of Prince Christian have constantly gained honours in the game. It is particularly appropriate that in these days when the 'crimson thread of kinship' is, happily, a popular idea an Indian prince should play for an ancient English University in the year when the Imperial Institute was opened.

Among those watching the England–Australia Test match at Old Trafford in 1930 was His Highness the Jam Sahib of Nawangaris (*third from left*) who is better known as the immortal Ranji. Also present were (*from left to right*) Arthur Gilligan, Sir Edwin Stockton and Lord Belper.

THE TIMES: *November 1921*

Ranji

RANJI was a generous man, except to opposing bowlers, as this story from *The Times* of November 1921 shows.

'The Maharajah Sahib of Nawangar, still better known in this country as Prince Ranjitsinhji, has presented two pairs of lions to the London Zoo. The lions are African by origin, the native Indian animal being now excessively rare. Both were born at Nawangar. They were sent to Bombay, where the Natural History Society took them over until they could be shipped to London.

They came by the British India SS *Chanda,* which berthed at Tilbury yesterday. The lions were packed each in a separate case, but the lionesses travelled together. Owing to the size and weight of the animals, which are full grown, and their cases, three lorries had to be arranged to bring them to Regent's Park. They arrived soon after 8p.m. last night, but will not be put on exhibition until today. They are reported to be in good condition and to have fed well throughout the journey.'

Jahangir Khan played in both the 1932 and 1936 Test sides, and also for Cambridge University. Said *The Times*: 'The 1932 Tour really placed Indian cricket on the map, for such men as Amar Singh, C.K. Nayudu, Jahangir Khan, Wazir Ali and Mahommed Nissar were worthy to rank with the best players England could produce at the time.'

K.S. Duleepsinhji (*right*), nicknamed 'Tulip', off to bat with Prickett in the Freshers' match.

THE ILLUSTRATED SPORTING AND DRAMATIC NEWS: *16th May 1925*

Cricket at Cambridge: the 'Varsity's good start

MR C.T. BENNETT, who is captain of the Cambridge University cricket season, cannot have felt unhappy at the result of his team's first matches, though, in common with all cricketers, he may reasonably have expected something better in the shape of weather. However, the Freshmen's and Seniors' matches were both satisfactorily played out and in the initial first-class encounter the 'Varsity brilliantly defeated Sussex. K.S. Duleepsinhji, a nephew of the H.H. the Maharajah of Nawanagar ('Ranji'), has started well with the bat, and this Freshman, who had such a remarkable record at Cheltenham, is a very strong candidate for the eleven which will ultimately come to Lord's.

THE ILLUSTRATED SPORTING AND DRAMATIC NEWS: *24th June 1916*

Wartime cricket at Lord's: five of 'Ranji's' nephews

A FEATURE of a match which took place at Lord's the other day between a team of Indian students and Lt-Col Bailey's XI was the presence with the former team of no less than five nephews of the Jamsaheb of Nawanagar. Although one of the nephews was reserve man and another acted as umpire, the remaining three scored 131 out of a total of 182, the captain K.S. Pratapsinhji, making the highest score of the afternoon with 75. Lt-Col Bailey's team responded with 154.

(*left*) Another of cricket's greats came from Nawangar: Ranji's nephew Kumar Shri Duleepsinhji. Educated at Cheltenham, he played in four of the five Tests against Australia in 1930. Tragically, ill health forced him to retire from the game in 1933.

Ranji's five nephews. From left to right: K.S. Digvijaysinhji (*umpire*), K.S. Himatsinhji, K.S. Pratapsinhji (*captain*), K.S. Raisinhji (*reserve man*) and K.S. Rajendrasinhji.

The first Test match between England and India: 1932

IN APRIL 1932 the first Indian Test team arrived in Britain. The only Test match of the tour was played at Lord's on 25th, 27th and 28th June, and England won by a comfortable 158 runs against an Indian side hamstrung by injuries. Even so, India dismissed the home side's first three batsmen, Holmes, Sutcliffe and Woolley for 19 runs in a sensational opening. This match marked the debut of

W.E. 'Bill' Bowes, and he took 4 for 49 in the first innings as India slumped to 189 all out in reply to England's total of 259.

The Indian captain, the Maharajah Rana of Porbander, was absent and so was vice-captain K.S. Ghanshyamsinhji, and India was led by C.K. Nayadu. He badly damaged his hand attempting a catch in England's first innings, and the team was further weakened by leg injuries to Nazir Ali and P.E. Palia. England declared their second innings at 275 for 8, and India were all out for 187 in the second innings, in spite of Amar Singh scoring India's first Test Match fifty, and adding 74 in 40 minutes with Lall Singh. When the team left Victoria in September, they were better accustomed both to English cricket and the English weather.

The All-India team meets the King-Emperor at Lord's.

(*left, above*) The All-India cricket team arriving at Victoria Station in April 1932. They were obviously prepared for the British weather.

(*left, below*) The teams for the opening match of the Indians' 1932 tour against Mr T. Gilbert Scott's XI at Pelsham. The Maharajah of Porbandar is seated third from the right and among those at the rear are three England captains, Percy Chapman, Douglas Jardine and Freddie Brown.

England v. India 1932 (Only Test)

Played at Lord's, London, on 25, 27, 28 June.
Toss: England.   Result: ENGLAND won by 158 runs.
Debuts: England – W.E. Bowes; India – All.

ENGLAND

P. Holmes	b Nissar	6	b Jahangir Khan	11
H. Sutcliffe	b Nissar	3	c Nayudu b Amar Singh	19
F.E. Woolley	run out	9	c Colah b Jahangir Khan	21
W.R. Hammond	b Amar Singh	35	b Jahangir Khan	12
D.R. Jardine*	c Navle b Nayudu	79	not out	85
E. Paynter	lbw b Nayudu	14	b Jahangir Khan	54
L.E.G. Ames†	b Nissar	65	b Amar Singh	6
R.W.V. Robins	c Lall Singh b Nissar	21	c Jahangir Khan b Nissar	30
F.R. Brown	c Amar Singh b Nissar	1	c Colah b Naoomal	29
W. Voce	not out	4	not out	0
W.E. Bowes	c Nissar b Amar Singh	7		
Extras	(B 3, LB 9, NB 3)	15	(B 2, LB 6)	8
Total		**259**	(8 wickets declared)	**275**

INDIA

J.G. Navle†	b Bowes	12	lbw b Robins	13
Naoomal Jeoomal	lbw b Robins	33	b Brown	25
S. Wazir Ali	lbw b Brown	31	c Hammond b Voce	39
C.K. Nayudu*	c Robins b Voce	40	b Bowes	10
S.H.M. Colah	c Robins b Bowes	22	b Brown	4
S. Nazir Ali	b Bowes	13	c Jardine b Bowes	6
P.E. Palia	b Voce	1	(11) not out	1
Lall Singh	c Jardine b Bowes	15	(7) b Hammond	29
M. Jahangir Khan	b Robins	1	(8) b Voce	0
L. Amar Singh	c Robins b Voce	5	(9) c and b Hammond	51
Mahomed Nissar	not out	1	(10) b Hammond	0
Extras	(B 5, LB 7, W 1, NB 2)	15	(B 5, LB 2, NB 2)	9
Total		**189**		**187**

INDIA	O	M	R	W	O	M	R	W
Nissar	26	3	93	5	18	5	42	1
Amar Singh	31	10	75	2	41	13	84	2
Jahangir Khan	17	7	26	0	30	12	60	4
Nayudu	24	8	40	2	9	0	21	0
Palia	4	3	2	0	3	0	11	0
Naoomal	3	0	8	0	8	0	40	1
Wazir Ali					1	0	9	0
ENGLAND								
Bowes	30	13	49	4	14	5	30	2
Voce	17	6	23	3	12	3	28	2
Brown	25	7	48	1	14	1	54	2
Robins	17	4	39	2	14	5	57	1
Hammond	4	0	15	0	5.3	3	9	3

FALL OF WICKETS

Wkt	E 1st	I 1st	E 2nd	I 2nd
1st	8	39	30	41
2nd	11	63	34	41
3rd	19	110	54	52
4th	101	139	67	65
5th	149	160	156	83
6th	166	165	169	108
7th	229	181	222	108
8th	231	182	271	182
9th	252	188	–	182
10th	259	189	–	187

Umpires: F. Chester and J. Hardstaff, sr.

The man who captained the first all-India touring side in 1911, His Highness Sir Bhupendra Singh Mahinder Bahadur of Patiala. In memory of Ranjitsinhji, he donated the Ranji Trophy, which is presented each year to the winner of the Indian National Championship. This is a 1935 caricature from Marylebone Cricket Club.

(*right, above*) Members of the Indian cricket team are pictured on the deck of the liner *Viceroy of India* which brought them to England for a series of Test Matches in the 1936 season.

(*right, below*) Sir Vijaya Vizianagram, captain of India against Freeman's 6th at Gravesend, was bowled for eight in this opening match of the Tour on 4th April 1936.

The second tour in 1936

THE SECOND INDIAN TEST TOUR of England took place in 1936 and the team arrived at Tilbury on the P & O liner *Viceroy of India* in April of that year.

In 1937 *The Times* commented: 'During the visit of India to England last summer only four first-class matches were won, but the Indians showed their best form in the representative games.

England had a big fright before winning the First Test by nine wickets – India actually led on the first innings – the tourists worthily drew the second and in the third were by no means disgraced.'

The Times also wrote poignantly: 'In India team selection has always been complicated by the many races, creeds and politics. It is to be hoped that by the time England and India meet in the winter of 1939 some of these differences will have been forgotten so that the inherent skill of the Indians can find full expression.' That tour never took place because of a political difference *The Times* had not anticipated – the Second World War.

England *v.* India 1936 (2nd Test)

Played at Old Trafford, Manchester, on 25, 27, 28 July.
Toss: India.　Result: MATCH DRAWN.
Debuts: England – A.E. Fagg, L.B. Fishlock, A.R. Gover; India – K.R. Meherhomji, C. Ramaswami.

England scored 571 for 8 in only 375 minutes and India's opening partnership of 203 (still their record against England) took just 150 minutes; on the second day 588 runs were scored for the loss of six wickets – this is still the most runs scored in a day of Test cricket.

INDIA

Player	Dismissal	Runs	Dismissal 2	Runs 2
V.M. Merchant	c Hammond b Verity	33	lbw b Hammond	114
Mushtaq Ali	run out	13	c and b Robins	112
L. Amar Singh	c Duckworth b Worthington	27	(6) not out	48
C.K. Nayudu	lbw b Allen	16	st Duckworth b Verity	34
S. Wazir Ali	c Worthington b Verity	42	b Robins	4
C. Ramaswami	b Verity	40	(3) b Robins	60
M. Jahangir Khan	c Duckworth b Allen	2		
C.S. Nayudu	b Verity	10		
Maharaj Vizianagram*	b Robins	6	(7) not out	0
K.R. Meherhomji†	not out	0		
Mahomed Nissar	c Hardstaff b Robins	13		
Extras	(B 1)	1	(B 9, LB 7, NB 2)	18
Total		**203**	(5 wickets)	**390**

ENGLAND

Player	Dismissal	Runs
H. Gimblett	b Nissar	9
A.E. Fagg	lbw b Mushtaq Ali	39
W.R. Hammond	b C.K. Nayudu	167
T.S. Worthington	b C.K. Nayudu b C.S. Nayudu	87
L.B. Fishlock	b C.K. Nayudu	6
J. Hardstaff, jr	c and b Amar Singh	94
G.O.B. Allen*	c Meherhomji b Amar Singh	1
R.W.V. Robins	c Merchant b Nissar	76
H. Verity	not out	66
G. Duckworth†	not out	10
A.R. Gover	did not bat	
Extras	(B 5, LB 9, W 1, NB 1)	16
Total	(8 wickets declared)	**571**

ENGLAND	O	M	R	W	O	M	R	W
Allen	14	3	39	2	19	2	96	0
Gover	15	2	39	0	20	2	61	0
Hammond	9	1	34	0	12	2	19	1
Robins	9.1	1	34	2	29	2	103	3
Verity	17	5	51	4	22	8	66	1
Worthington	4	0	15	1	13	4	27	0
INDIA								
Nissar	28	5	125	2				
Amar Singh	41	8	121	2				
C.S. Nayudu	17	1	87	1				
C.K. Nayudu	22	1	84	2				
Jahangir Khan	18	5	57	0				
Mushtaq Ali	13	1	64	1				
Merchant	3	0	17	0				

FALL OF WICKETS

	I	E	I
Wkt	1st	1st	2nd
1st	18	12	203
2nd	67	146	279
3rd	73	273	313
4th	100	289	317
5th	161	375	390
6th	164	376	–
7th	181	409	–
8th	188	547	–
9th	190	–	–
10th	203	–	–

Umpires: F. Chester and F. Walden.

1946 Test Tour

THE 1946 TOUR was the last before Independence, and was the first test series India had played against England for ten years. But they were still unable to master an English side under their own conditions, and were not to win a series until the winter of 1961/2 in India, where they won two tests with three drawn.

In 1946, however, India lost the first test at Lord's by ten wickets, and drew the other two, in spite of the inspiring presence of the Nawab of Pataudi. He held two rare distinctions in this series, first by playing for India after three test appearances for their opponents before the war, and second by making his debut as India's captain.

V.M. Merchant, India's vice-captain who is famous for his McCartneyesque style. He had a dazzling late cut and held the record score in India of 359 not out.

India's skipper, the Nawab of Pataudi at net practice

IFTIQUAR ALI KHAN, NAWAB OF PATAUDI, was another in the line of great cricketing noblemen produced by India. He captained the 1946 Tour, having made his Test debut fourteen years earlier, scoring a century for England against Australia in Sydney.

The Nawab came to England at the age of sixteen, and was coached by the legendary Frank Woolley. His was a natural talent, but his batting technique was formidable and he always relished a challenge. In the Oxford vs Cambridge game at Lord's in 1931 the gauntlet was tossed down by Alan Ratcliffe, who scored a double hundred for Cambridge. Pataudi responded in typical fashion with 238 not out, the record innings in the contests.

After representing England against Australia at Trent Bridge,

The Nawab of Pataudi at net practice during the 1946 Tour.

The Nawab of Pataudi played for Oxford against Cambridge at Lord's in 1929 and 1930, and in the former year made the top score in each innings for his side – 106 and 84 runs. He is pictured here taking a turn with the roller.

however, he was forced to return to India because of the ill health that was to trouble him for the rest of his life.

In spite of the twelve-year gap in his Test career, the Nawab again took up the challenge when leading the 1946 Tour. Although his Test performances were not all he might have hoped, he still scored 981 runs on the Tour, including four centuries, and averaged over 46 runs an innings.

England *v.* India 1946 (1st Test)

Played at Lord's, London, on 22, 24, 25 June.
Toss: India.   Result: ENGLAND won by ten wickets.
Debuts: England – A.V. Bedser, J.T. Ikin, T.F. Smailes; India – Gul Mahomed, V.S. Hazare, A.H. Kardar (*Abdul Hafeez Kardar, who played for India as 'Abdul Hafeez' but later took the name of 'Kardar' and appeared for Pakistan as 'A.H. Kardar'. For consistency he is listed throughout this book under the latter name*), V.M.H. Mankad (*real names Mulvantrai Himmatlal Mankad but was known as 'Vinoo'; his son, Ashok, has taken 'Vinoo' as his second name*), R.S. Modi, S.G. Shinde. *Nawab Iftikhar Ali of Pataudi made his deput for India after appearing in three Tests for England.*

INDIA

V.M. Merchant	c Gibb b Bedser	12	lbw b Ikin	27
V.M.H. Mankad	b Wright	14	c Hammond b Smailes	63
L. Amarnath	lbw b Bedser	0	(8) b Smailes	50
V.S. Hazare	b Bedser	31	c Hammond b Bedser	34
R.S. Modi	not out	57	(3) lbw b Smailes	21
Nawab of Pataudi, sr*	c Ikin b Bedser	9	b Wright	22
Gul Mahomed	b Wright	1	lbw b Wright	9
A.H. Kardar	b Bowes	43	(5) b Bedser	0
D.D. Hindlekar†	lbw b Bedser	3	c Ikin b Bedser	17
C.S. Nayudu	st Gibb b Bedser	4	b Bedser	13
S.G. Shinde	b Bedser	10	not out	4
Extras	(B 10, LB 6)	16	(B 10, LB 2, NB 3)	15
Total		**200**		**275**

ENGLAND

L. Hutton	c Nayudu b Amarnath	7	not out	22
C. Washbrook	c Mankad b Amarnath	27	not out	24
D.C.S. Compton	b Amarnath	0		
W.R. Hammond*	b Amarnath	33		
J. Hardstaff, jr	not out	205		
P.A. Gibb†	c Hazare b Mankad	60		
J.T. Ikin	c Hindlekar b Shinde	16		
T.F. Smailes	c Mankad b Amarnath	25		
A.V. Bedser	b Hazare	30		
D.V.P. Wright	b Mankad	3		
W.E. Bowes	lbw b Hazare	2		
Extras	(B 11, LB 8, NB 1)	20	(LB 1, W1)	2
Total		**428**	(0 wickets)	**48**

ENGLAND	O	M	R	W	O	M	R	W
Bowes	25	7	64	1	4	1	9	0
Bedser	29.1	11	49	7	32.1	3	96	4
Smailes	5	1	18	0	15	2	44	3
Wright	17	4	53	2	20	3	68	2
Ikin					10	1	43	1
INDIA								
Hazare	34.4	4	100	2	4	2	7	0
Amarnath	57	18	118	5	4	0	15	0
Mahomed	2	0	2	0				
Mankad	48	11	107	2	4.5	1	11	0
Shinde	23	2	66	1				
Nayudu	5	1	15	0	4	0	13	0

FALL OF WICKETS

	I	E	I	E
Wkt	1st	1st	2nd	2nd
1st	15	16	67	–
2nd	15	16	117	–
3rd	44	61	126	–
4th	74	70	129	–
5th	86	252	174	–
6th	87	284	185	–
7th	144	344	190	–
8th	147	416	249	–
9th	157	421	263	–
10th	200	428	275	–

Umpires: H.G. Baldwin and J. Smart.

This picture shows bowler Sarwate during batting practice. With Banerjee, he broke the record with a last wicket stand of 249 in June 1946.

England *v*. India 1946 (2nd Test)

Played at Old Trafford, Manchester, on 20, 22, 23 July.
Toss: India.   Result: MATCH DRAWN.
Debuts: England – R. Pollard; India – C.T. Sarwate, S.W. Sohoni.

Rain prevented play until after lunch on the opening day. India's last pair survived for 13 minutes to earn a draw.

ENGLAND

L. Hutton	c Mushtaq Ali b Mankad	67	c Hindlekar b Amarnath	2
C. Washbrook	c Hindlekar b Mankad	52	lbw b Mankad	26
D.C.S. Compton	lbw b Armanath	51	not out	71
W.R. Hammond*	b Amarnath	69	c Kardar b Mankad	8
J. Hardstaff, jr	c Merchant b Amarnath	5	b Amarnath	0
P.A. Gibb†	b Mankad	24	c Modi b Amarnath	0
J.T. Ikin	c Mankad b Amarnath	2	not out	29
W. Voce	b Mankad	0		
R. Pollard	not out	10		
A.V. Bedser	lbw b Amarnath	8		
D.V.P. Wright	lbw b Mankad	0		
Extras	(B 2, LB 4)	6	(B 6, LB 10, W 1)	17
Total		**294**	(5 wickets declared)	**153**

INDIA

V.M. Merchant	c Bedser b Pollard	78	c Ikin b Pollard	0
Mushtaq Ali	b Pollard	46	b Pollard	1
A.H. Kardar	c and b Pollard	1	(7) c and b Bedser	35
V.M.H. Mankad	b Pollard	0	(8) c Pollard b Bedser	5
V.S. Hazare	b Voce	3	b Bedser	44
R.S. Modi	c Ikin b Bedser	2	(4) b Bedser	30
Nawab of Pataudi, sr*	b Pollard	11	(3) b Bedser	4
L. Amarnath	b Bedser	8	(6) b Bedser	3
S.W. Sohoni	c and b Bedser	3	not out	11
C.T. Sarwate	c Ikin b Bedser	0	c Gibb b Bedser	2
D.D. Hindlekar†	not out	1	not out	4
Extras	(B 10, LB 5, NB 2)	17	(B 5, LB 8)	13
Total		**170**	(9 wickets)	**152**

The Indian Touring Cricket Team, who had just completed a tour of this country, were the guests of the Raymond Electric Company at the Berners Hotel, London, when they were presented with the latest Raymond 1947 Indian Model Radio sets as a gift from the manufacturers. The presentation was made by Deborah Kerr, the famous British actress. She is shown here presenting a set to V.M. Merchant, vice-captain of the Cricket Team.

INDIA	O	M	R	W	O	M	R	W
Sohoni	11	1	31	0				
Amarnath	51	17	96	5	30	9	71	3
Hazare	14	2	48	0	10	3	20	0
Mankad	46	15	101	5	21	6	45	2
Sarwate	7	0	12	0				
ENGLAND								
Voce	20	3	44	1	6	5	2	0
Bedser	26	9	41	4	25	4	52	7
Pollard	27	16	24	5	25	10	63	2
Wright	2	0	12	0	2	0	17	0
Compton	4	0	18	0	3	1	5	0
Ikin	2	0	11	0				
Hammond	1	0	3	0				

FALL OF WICKETS

Wkt	E 1st	I 1st	E 2nd	I 2nd
1st	81	124	7	0
2nd	156	130	48	3
3rd	186	130	68	5
4th	193	141	68	79
5th	250	141	84	84
6th	265	146	–	87
7th	270	156	–	113
8th	274	168	–	132
9th	287	169	–	138
10th	294	170	–	–

Umpires: F. Chester and G. Beet.

THE ILLUSTRATED SPORTING AND DRAMATIC NEWS: *2nd July 1902*

Gymkhana at Ranelagh

A VERY INTERESTING ENTERTAINMENT was that given the Indian Princes at Ranelagh by the Committee of this popular West End club. The Gymkhana was certainly the most magnificent yet attempted in England, and as several of the visitors took part in the most important events, the competitions quite partook of an international character. Some of the horses ridden by the princes were wonderfully good-looking, but both in the bending races and the tent-pegging, they were not under such good control as those handy ponies ridden by menbers of the club. They also seemed over 14.2, the regulation height but, as no polo was played, this rule was not rigidly enforced. Emerald and Spinster, the ponies competing in the final of the bending race, are very smart, the first named, owned by Mr J.B. Dale, a Yorkshire member of the club, having previously won the event three years in succession. She was beaten last week, however, by half a length by Mr Guy Gilbey's mount, bloodlike in appearance, and possessed of a rare turn of speed, outpacing her opponent in the run in.

At the gymkhana which took place at Ranelagh, Maharajah Sir Partab Singh of Idar, Kunwar Girdhari Singh, Thakur Baktawar Singh and Thakur Kishore Singh took three pegs at their first attempt.

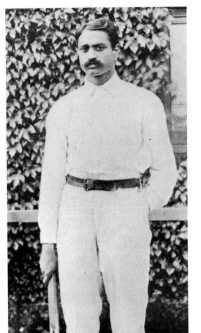

Sirdar Nihal Singh, one of the competitors in the All-England Lawn Tennis Championships at Wimbledon in 1909.

THE TIMES: *12th May 1921*

Indian Gymkhana Club: purchase of new ground

THE INDIAN GYMKHANA CLUB, of which Lord Hawke is president, has acquired 16 acres of land at Thornbury-avenue, Osterley, near the Osterley Park station on the Hounslow Branch of the District Railway.

The club, formed in 1916 to provide athletic facilities for Indian students, has had as home ground that of the Mill Hill Park Cricket Club at Acton, which has had such great additions to membership since demobilisation that it notified last summer its wishes to resume exclusive use of the ground. The Indian Gymkhana Club thereupon issued an appeal for £15,000 for the purchase and equipment of a ground. To this appeal there was a good, though not widespread, response from a few Indian princes and men of wealth.

The purchase price is £6,560, of which a deposit of £1,000 has been paid, and the balance must be forthcoming by September 20. The Maharajah of Patiala has generously signed a guarantee, and in the event of his not being called upon to pay any part of the balance he has promised a further donation of £1,000. W. Adcock, the club's old groundsman, has undertaken to provide a cricket pitch and nine tennis courts for play by Saturday, 28th May. The problem of finance for a pavilion causes some anxiety to the committee, and they appeal for prompt support both in this country and from India.

THE TIMES: *26th August 1921*

LORD LYTTON, the Under-Secretary for India has written to Lord Hawke expressing the hope that the committee of the Indian Gymkhana Club will be successful in raising the whole of the £15,000 required for the purchase and lay out of the ground at Osterley Park. Lord Lytton writes: Indian students in this country soon realise how large a part athletics and games play in our universities, which I had visited lately (as chairman of the Indian Student Committee). I find that they are anxious to avail themselves of every opportunity of joining in these games. Apart from the aid to health of athletic recreation, it affords opportunities for social intercourse which are not otherwise available. This Gymkhana Club in London is the very thing which is needed, and all who wish to benefit the Indian student should help to make it a success.

THE TIMES: *10th April 1923*

Polo

AN INDIAN NATIVE POLO TEAM will arrive in England on May 1. Two matches have been arranged for them at Hurlingham. The first of them will be played on Saturday May 26 and the second on

Saturday June 16. The team will include three Patiala State players, Jaswant Singh, Jogindra Singh and Chunda Singh. Captain E.G. Atkinson, of the Indian cavalry, will be the fourth player. The public will be admitted to watch the matches, which will be begun at 3.30 each afternoon.

THE ILLUSTRATED SPORTING AND DRAMATIC NEWS: *9th May 1925*

The Maharajah of Jodhpur in London for the polo season

WITH THE APPROACH of the London polo tournament season, interest in the visiting Jodhpur team increases and their form on the English grounds will be followed as closely as that of the American Army team now here. Last year in India, Jodhpur were the strongest combination in the game, winning the Calcutta Championship and the Prince of Wales's Tournament at Delhi. The young Maharajah of Jodhpur is himself in England and will probably take part in some of the games. The actual team, however, is composed of Thakur Prithi Singh, Captain A.H. Williams, Captain Rajah Hanut Singh and Thakore Ram Singh. Captain Williams, who is Military Adviser to the Maharajah of Jodhpur, is a brilliant player and is one of the five members of the Indian Polo Association.

By the middle of August the Maharajah had enjoyed a most successful season, his polo side having won, among other trophies, the Hurlingham Champion Cup. He then travelled north to Scotland to indulge in some salmon fishing on the River Spean in Inverness-shire.

The Maharajah of Jodhpur

The Maharajah salmon fishing on the River Spean.

After cricket, the Nawab of Pataudi's other great sporting love is polo. But his love-affair with the game had a tragic ending in 1952, when he had a fatal heart attack on the polo field. In spite of his premature death at the age of only 42, the name Nawab of Pataudi continued to grace the cricket record books, for his son also captained the Indian Test team.

The winners of the Champion Cup Final at Hurlingham: the famous Jodhpur polo team, with the Maharajah of Jodhpur holding the cup. The Duke of Westminster's Eaton team was beaten by eight goals to six.

Back to the ship. The Maharajah of Jaipur's polo ponies crossing Barnes Bridge from Ranelagh Club on their way to the docks for shipment to India. The Maharajah's team was the outstanding success of the London season, being too good for its opponents throughout the summer.

The polo ponies being shipped from the Royal Albert Docks. This 1933 picture shows the little pony 'Snowdrop' which is for the Maharajah's two-year-old son and heir.

Major His Highness Maharajah Vijayasinhji Chhatrasinhji (1890–1951), came to the throne in 1915 at the age of 25 and was educated at Rajkumar College, Rajkot in Gujarat. The ruler of Rajpipla, a keen sportsman, was a frequent visitor to this country, having endeared himself to the sporting public as a patron of the turf and achieved his ambition with his 1934 Derby winner, Windsor Lad.

The Gaekwar of Baroda and his daughter the Maharanee of Cooch Behar at a cubbing meet of the Cottesmore at Stapleford Park.

THE ILLUSTRATED SPORTING AND DRAMATIC NEWS: *1st March 1924*

A victory of the Dark (Half) Blues: Inter-'Varsity hockey

DEFEATING CAMBRIDGE three to nil at Beckenham in the Inter-'Varsity hockey match, Oxford maintained their unbeaten record. This was the thirtieth of these encounters and the victory was the nineteenth recorded by the Dark Blues since this season opened. The occasion again called attention to the fact that a full blue is awarded at Cambridge for hockey, whereas a half-blue is still only granted at Oxford. The Oxonian Jaipal Singh's name is already mentioned in connection with international honours.

THE ILLUSTRATED SPORTING AND DRAMATIC NEWS: *26th December 1925*

An All-India hockey tour

UNDER THE CAPTAINCY of the famous Jaipal Singh, who is a tower of strength to Oxford University hockey, an 'All-India' hockey team is touring during the Christmas vacation in Belgium and Spain; this is the first team of this kind to visit the latter country. The tourists, who are selected from London, Cambridge, Manchester,

During the Christmas vacation of 1925 an 'All-Indian' hockey team made up of students from British Universities, captained by Jaipal Singh of Oxford University, toured Belgium and Spain.

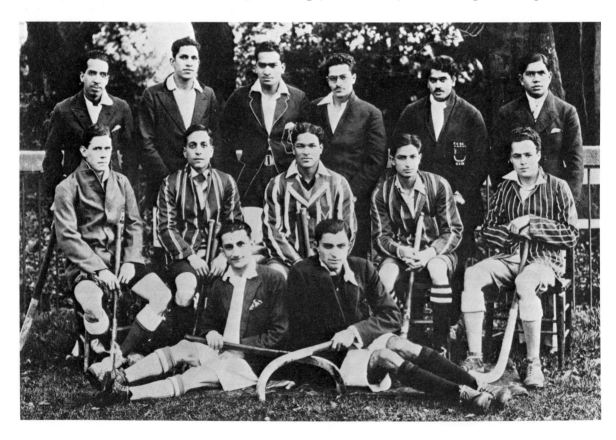

Oxford's brilliant
Hindu back, Jaipal
Singh.

Edinburgh, and Oxford Universities, will play at Brussels, Antwerp, Barcelona, Valencia, Madrid, and Bilbao. Our group shows, from left to right: (*back row*) W. Mahmood (Aligarth), R.M. Khan (Indore), J.A. Fernandez (Poona), J.S. Davar (Bombay), T. Murari (Mysore), and F.A. Ahmed (Lahore); (*centre*) C.W. Little (Madras), S.M. Yasut (Punjab), I. Jaipal Singh (Ranchi), N.A. Ahmed (Delhi), and R.Afzal (Calcutta); (*front row*) A.A. Baig (Lucknow), and M.A. Beg (Allahabad).

THE TIMES: *3rd April 1928*

Hockey: London v. All-India

THE ALL-INDIA TEAM played their second match yesterday at Merton Abbey, against a moderately strong side representing London, and gained a comfortable victory by five goals to two.

With the conditions quite good, the All-India side proved themselves to be a very fast and clever team, and made certain of victory by scoring five times in the first half without reply from the London side. Allen made many fine saves and is a really high-class goalkeeper. The half-backs made a good, hard-working line, and are better in defence than attack. Chand again made a very good impression at centre forward, and he, with the two inside men, worked very well together and showed good combination.

From the start All-India set a strong pace and were not long opening their score, through Khan. A second goal followed a little later from Marthins. London played hard but found Allen in great form and were unable to score. On the other hand, All-India missed very few chances and added three more goals before the interval, through Khan, Chand and Gateley. London did better in the second half and had rather the better of the play.

The teams were: LONDON– A.H. Boys, goal; R. Scott Freeman and G.F. Summer, backs; A.W. Sharpe, Lieutenant J.D. Fisher and T.H. Ely, half-backs; W.A. Brown, C. Morley Brown, A.W. Sharpley, L.H. Shelly and A.D. Ogilvy, forwards. ALL-INDIA – R. Allen, goal; M.E. Rocque and L. Hammond, backs; Keshar Singh, E. Penniger and J. Goodise Cullen, half-backs; M. Gateley, Feroze Khan, Dhyan Chand, G. Marthin and F.S. Seaman, forwards.

THE TIMES: *16th April 1928*

Hockey: Indian team wins again

THE INDIAN OLYMPIC ELEVEN gave another fine display of hockey at Merton Abbey on Saturday, when they beat a combined London University and Hospitals side by seven goals to three.

The combined side gave the Indians a good match, the first half being fairly evenly contested. The Indians found the cold weather a disadvantage, and they experienced some difficulty in holding their sticks. After the tourists had led by four goals to two at half time, their opponents brought their deficit down to one, but afterwards the Indians outplayed the home team and scored three more goals. With five goals in this match, Dhian Chand brought his total of goals scored during the tour to 26 out of a total of 49, although in one of the six previous matches he did not play. The other goals for the winners on Saturday were scored by Shaukat Ali and the Nawab of Pataudi, the combined side's points being scored by Hatton (London University), Clayton (Hospitals), and Gillam (Hospitals).

Y. Kumar, right-back in the 1938 London University hockey team.

Y. Kumar: an outstanding all-round athlete

NOT ALL of the Indian sportsmen who made their mark in Britain were cricketers, and this man, Y. Kumar, was an outstanding all-round athlete. Says a 1938 Press report: 'London University have this season almost reconstructed their hockey team, as eight of last year's players are not available. An outstanding newcomer is Y. Kumar (London School of Economics), a right-back who may develop into a front rank player. Kumar, an Indian, became known in London University sporting circles last season as an unbeatable boxer, and he won the University Middleweight Championship.'

CHAPTER EIGHT

Indians in Westminster

THE FACT that three Indian MPs have sat in the House of Commons, representing three different English constituencies must be the best-kept secret in the annals of British political history.

Few outside of Parliament or its students have ever heard of them, and whilst their achievements might have been limited, the precedent that they set may be of immense significance for the future relations between the British and Indian peoples.

All the parties now acknowledge that it is only a matter of time before another Indian is elected to take his or her seat in the Parliament. The examples of these three men show that this eventuality, far from being a threat to the established political order, represents rather a broadening of it, a new dimension but not a new experience.

The first Indian Member of Parliament, Mr Dadabhai Naoroji.

In fact their politics say as much about Indian society as about British society. Their convictions could not have been more different – a Liberal centrist, a Conservative lawyer, and a radical Labour firebrand, who became one of the handful of Communist MPs ever to be elected. They may have made little impact on political history then or since, but their enduring achievement lies in their having been elected at all.

The first of them was Dadabhai Naoroji, who won Finsbury Central for the Liberals in 1892 with a wafer-thin majority of five over his Conservative opponent. This figure emerged after a recount, and though it may seem slim, it was a 66 per cent increase over the first count, which gave him the seat by three votes.

He was renowned as the founding father of Indian nationalism, taking part in the formation of the Indian National Congress, the East India Association and the London Indian Society. He was also the first of his countrymen to be appointed to the Royal Commission on Indian Expenditure.

As he made clear in his maiden speech in the House, in August 1892, neither his election nor his age of sixty-seven had in the slightest dimmed his progressive instincts.

Maiden speech by Mr Dadabhai Naoroji

MR D. NAOROJI (*Finsbury, Central*): It may be considered rather rash and unwise on my part to stand before this House so immediately after my admission here; and my only excuse is that I am under a certain necessity to do so. My election for an English constituency is a unique event. For the first time during more than a century of settled British rule an Indian is admitted into this House as a Member for an English constituency. That, as I have said, is a unique event in the history of India, and, I may also venture to say, in the history of the British Empire. I desire to say a few words in analysis of this great and wonderful phenomenon. The spirit of the British rule, the instinct of British justice and generosity, from the very commencement, when Parliament seriously took the matter of Indian policy into its hands, about the beginning of this century, decided that India was to be governed on the lines of British freedom and justice. Steps were taken without any hesitation to introduce Western education, civilisation, and political institutions in that country; and the result was that, aided by a noble and grand language, in which the youth of that country began to be educated, a great movement of political life – I may say new life – was infused into a land which had been decaying for centuries. The British rulers of the country endowed it with all their own most important privileges. A few days ago, Sir, you demanded from the Throne the privileges which belong to the people, including freedom of speech, for which they have fought and shed their blood. That freedom of speech you have given to us, and it enables Indians to stand before you and represent in clear and open language any desire they have felt. By conferring those privileges you have prepared for this final result of an Indian standing before you in this House, becoming a Member of the great

Dadabhai Naoroji was born in Bombay in 1825, and was one of the first batch of students to attend Elphinstone College. While there he became assistant to the mathematics professor, the first Indian to hold such a post in a government college. He came to London in 1855 at the age of thirty as a partner in the first purely Indian firm to be established in the City of London, that of the mercantile Cama family. In his later years he was venerated as a sage, both in India and in Britain.

Imperial Parliament of the British Empire, and being able to express his views openly and fearlessly before you. The glory and credit of this great event – by which India is thrilled from one end to the other – of the new life, the joy, the ecstasy of India at the present moment, is all your own; it is the spirit of British institutions and the love of justice and freedom in British instincts which has produced this extraordinary result, and I stand here in the name of India to thank the British people that they have made it at all possible for an Indian to occupy this position, and to speak freely in the English language of any grievance which India may be suffering under, with the conviction that, though he stand alone, with only one vote, whenever he is able to bring forward any aspiration, and is supported by just and proper reasons, he will find a large number of other Members from both sides of the House ready to support him and give him the justice he asks. This is the conviction which permeates the whole thinking and educated classes of India. It is that conviction that enables us to work on day after day, without dismay, for the removal of a grievance. The questions now being discussed before the House will come up from time to time in practical shape, and I shall then be able to express my humble views upon them as a Representative of the English constituency of Central Finsbury. I do not intend to enter into them now. Central Finsbury has earned the everlasting gratitude of the millions of India, and has made itself famous in the history of the British Empire, by electing an Indian to represent it. Its name will never be forgotten by India. This event has strengthened the British power, and the loyalty and attachment of India to it, ten times more than the sending out of one hundred thousand or two hundred thousand European soldiers would have done. The moral force to which the right hon. Gentleman the Member for Midlothian (Mr W.E. Gladstone) referred is the golden link by which India is held to the British Power. So long as India is satisfied with the justice and honour of Britain so long will her Indian Empire last, and I have not the least doubt that, though our progress may be slow and we may at times meet with disappointments, if we persevere, whatever justice we ask in reason we shall get. I thank you, Sir, for allowing me to say these few words, and the House for so indulgently listening to me, and I hope that the connection between England and India – which forms five-sixths of the British Empire – may continue long with benefit to both countries.

SPECIAL REPORT

Important conference at Westminster Town Hall

THE ANNUAL CONFERENCE of Indians resident in the United Kingdom was held on the afternoon of Wednesday, December 28, 1898, in the Westminster Town Hall, under the presidency of Mr Dadabhai Naoroji. There was a large attendance of members of the London Indian Society and their friends.

THE CHAIRMAN said the Committee of the Indian Society had asked him to propose the first resolution in the following terms:

'That in accordance with the oft-declared and pledged policy of the British people, through Acts and Resolutions of Parliament and Proclamations of her Majesty the Queen, to treat Indians exactly as British subjects in this country; and considering that Indians have distinguished themselves by their loyalty, heroism, and all soldierly qualities in the recent war beyond the frontiers and in all preceeding wars, this Conference is of the opinion, and urges upon the Government in the name of British justice and honour, that Indians should be allowed commissions and command in the Indian army in the same manner and through the same methods as are open to Englishmen by competition and training and by promotion for distinguished ability and gallantry in the field.'

The motion, he said, divided itself into two parts. The first dealt with the policy of the British people in India. It had been clearly and emphatically laid down that there should be equality between Indian and all other British subjects. (Cheers) Such a policy was laid down not only by Act of Parliament but also by the Proclamation of the Queen, and it was a very sad thing that the policy had been perverted by what Lord Salisbury called 'political hypocrisy'. (Hear, hear) He now came to the second part of the resolution as to the manner in which the Indian soldiers had behaved. It would be sufficient for him to say that it would be an act of suicide on the part of their British rulers if they did not recognise their services and if they still looked upon the natives of India as mere slaves and helots. (Hear, hear) The people of India claimed not only justice; they also claimed gratitude, for upon Indian blood had the British Empire been built up and maintained, while thousands upon thousands of millions sterling had been contributed to the British Treasury. In 1896 he had some correspondence with the War Office as to the conditions and qualifications of Indian candidates for army commissions. He received a very courteous reply to the effect that Indians were entirely excluded.

MR A.A. KHAN supported the motion and insisted that it was absurd to suggest that while the Indians were good warriors they could not make good captains.

The resolution was then put to the meeting and carried unanimously.

THE TIMES: *19th March 1911*

The future of India: 'Orderly and just government'

Mr Churchill on the Prime Need

A MASS MEETING organised by the Indian Empire Society, 'to insist on orderly and just government for the Indian peoples' was held in the Albert Hall last night. The Duke of Marlborough presided and the speakers were Mr Churchill, Lord Burnham, Colonel John Gretton, MP, Mr Esmond Harmsworth, Major-General Sir Alfred Knox, MP, Rear-Admiral Sueter, MP, and Mr Warris Ameer Ali.

Mr Churchill said that it was rather hard that the burden of organizing that great meeting should be thrown on the Indian Empire Society, composed as it was mainly of retired administrators of deep experience in the East. What spectacle could be more sorrowful than that of this powerful country casting away with both hands, and almost up to now by general acquiescence, the great inheritance, which centuries had gathered? A hideous act of self-mutilation was being performed, to the astonishment of every other civilized nation in the world. (Cheers). 'I am against all this surrender to Gandhi. I am against these conversations and agreements between Lord Irwin and Gandhi. Gandhi stands for the expulsion of the British from India, for the permanent exclusion of British trade from India. Gandhi stands for the substitution of Brahmin domination for British rule in India. You will never be able to come to terms with Gandhi. (Cheers). Already Nehru, his young rival in the Indian Congress, is preparing to supersede him the moment that the last drop has been squeezed from the British lemon. In running after Gandhi and imagining that Mr Ramsay MacDonald and Mr Gandhi and Lord Irwin are going to bestow peace and progress upon India, we should be committing ourselves to a crazy dream, from which there would be a terrible awakening.' (Cheers).

THE GRAPHIC: *17th January 1914*

The Grand Old Man of India: Mr Dadabhai Naoroji

BY ABDICATING HIS RULE at the age of sixty-one to devote himself to religious meditation, the Raja of Cochin is about to become a 'sanyasi'; the 'Grand Old Man of India', Mr Dadabhai Naoroji, is one by right of age, for he is in his eighty-ninth year and at eighty-four the Hindus regard a man as a saint, quite irrespective of his character or career. But Mr Dadabhai Naoroji has every claim to canonisation apart from that of longevity. His descent from an uninterrupted line of the Zoroastrian priesthood in Persia is marked by a Grecian classicness of feature and fairness of skin which gave peculiar inappropriateness to the late Lord Salisbury's 'blazing indiscretion' in describing him as a 'black man'. The great simplicity and purity of his life have been recognised and admired by all who have come into contact with him. Mr Dadabhai Naoroji has spent no inconsiderable portion of his active life in this country, being a member of the first Indian firm established in London, now nearly sixty years ago and working incessantly by speech and pen and organisation for the political causes associated with the Indian National Congress movement, of which he was a founder. He was the first Indian to enter the House of Commons, being elected to the 1892–5 Parliament for Central Finsbury, but was unsuccessful in subsequent endeavours to secure a seat. He continued his active public career until he was an octogenarian, presiding at the Indian National Congress at Calcutta in 1906. But during the last seven years he has lived in quiet retirement at a seaside suburb some fifteen miles from Bombay, enjoying the warm affection of his countrymen without distinction of party, and the esteem of the heads of the Indian Administration. When the King and Queen went out to India for the Durbar they exchanged greetings with the distinguished veteran and recently he was visited by the new Governor of Bombay, Lord Willington, at the retreat where the evening light falls so gently upon him.

THE TIMES: *1st August 1917*

The saint of modern India

SIR WILLIAM WEDDERBURN, who presided yesterday at Caxton Hall, Westminster, over a meeting of Indian residents and British sympathisers called to express India's loss in the death of Mr Dadabhai Naoroji, said that India had long been the home of saints and sages, and Mr Dadabhai Naoroji might be called saint of modern India. He was the author of India's new aspirations and spiritual father of worthy disciples.

Sir Mancherjee Bhownagree

THE SECOND of the three Indian MPs to sit in the House of Commons was Sir Mancherjee Merwanjee Bhownagree, the only one of the trio to walk the corridors of Westminster for more than ten years. He was elected twice for the East London seat of Bethnal Green North-East on the Conservative ticket, having majorities of 160 in

Sir M.M. Bhownagree at the House of Commons.

1895 and 379 in 1900. In fact these figures are not as small as they may seem nowadays, since his electorate was a mere 7,431. He stood again in 1906, but the tide had turned against him and he was not re-elected.

SON OF A PARSEE MERCHANT in Bombay, Sir Mancherjee Bhownagree (1851–1933) came to Britain at the age of thirty and was called to the Bar by Lincoln's Inn in 1885.

For more than forty years he was the most prominent figure amongst the Indians who had settled in Britain and was the only Indian to sit in the House of Commons continuously for ten years. A most versatile and practical man, he impressed the House by the vigour and eloquence of his speeches on Indian subjects. He also fought for the rights of Indians in South Africa. During the war he wrote a booklet *The Verdict of India* to crush the German propaganda detrimental to the British connexion in India.

Sir Mancherjee was one of the first Indians to press forward the need for technical and vocational education in India as well as the need to raise the educational standard of women to the same level as that of men. He was also deeply interested in the education and welfare of students in London. As the chairman of the Northbrook Society he was in helpful contact with the Indian student element. He was also the chairman of the Indian Social Club in London and vice-chairman of the council of the East India Association. For a very long time he dominated the Parsee Association of Europe. To the Imperial Institute, he contributed a corridor in memory of his only sister, named the Bhownagree Corridor.

Lady Mancherjee could not stay in London as a permanent resident – the British weather was not suitable for her health – but she visited her husband frequently. Their only son died young, on the threshold of a promising career, and his only daughter married Dr Bahadurji. She was widowed quite young leaving a daughter who later became a barrister.

Shapurji Saklatvala: the third Indian Member of Parliament

THE THIRD INDIAN MEMBER of the British Parliament, Shapurji Saklatvala was twice elected for Battersea North. In 1922 he had a majority of 2,021 on the Labour ticket, but he lost his seat in the following year. In 1924 he stood again, this time as a Communist and won by 542 votes.

SHAPURJI SAKLATVALA was born in Bombay in 1874, the son of Dorabji and Jerbai Saklatvala, who later moved to Manchester. His mother was a sister of J.N. Tata, who, with his brother, had founded the Tata Steel Works in India.

After an early education in Bombay, Shapurji went on to study law and became a member of Lincoln's Inn in London. He joined the British Socialist Party and was actively engaged in forming the People's Russian Information Bureau, as well as the Communist Party of Great Britain, following the revolution in that country.

Shapurji Saklatvala addresses the crowds in Trafalgar Square, London.

He first entered the British Parliament in 1922 as Labour member for North Battersea. He is also the last Indian to enter the Parliament at Westminster.

Saklatvala was a founder member of the Worker's Welfare League of India which aimed at equalising European and Indian labour standards. In 1923, he stood again as a Labour candidate but lost his seat. In the 1924 election he stood as a Communist and won with a majority of 554 votes. In the following year he was appointed a member of an inter-parliamentary delegation to visit America but his visa was revoked on the grounds that the United States did not admit revolutionaries.

In 1926 Saklatvala was imprisoned for two months on a charge arising out of a May Day speech he made in Hyde Park. He was a strong critic of the Indian National Congress and of Gandhi's methods in the freedom fight.

In 1927 he returned to India and when he arrived back in England, his permit to re-enter India was cancelled at the request of the Indian Government. He lost his seat in the House in the 1926 general election.

Saklatvala was known as a revolutionary and a fiery figure. He was also extremely critical of the continuance of British rule in India. He was married to Sheri, daughter of Henry Marsh of Derbyshire, in 1907 and had three sons and two daughters, who were initiated to the Parsee religion – for which he was censured by the Communist Party.

THE TIMES: *23rd January 1919*

Sir Satyendra Prassano Sinha, KC

SIR SATYENDRA PRASSANO SINHA, KC, will go down in history as representing in his own person more fully than any contemporary Indian the progress of his country towards the ultimate goal of self-government within the Empire.

The romance of his advancement from the obscurity of an Indian village home is scarcely less remarkable than that of our own Prime Minister [Lloyd George]. He came to England to study for the Bar at Lincoln's Inn thirty-eight years ago after secret preparation, owing to the strong prejudice then prevailing in Bengal against foreign travel.

He was the first Indian to be appointed permanent Advocate-General of Bengal and to become just under ten years ago, a member of the Viceroy's Executive Council.

He is the first Indian to 'take silk' (an honour hitherto jealously confined to the Bar practising in this country), to be a member (in association with the Maharajah of Bikaner) of the Imperial War Conference and Imperial War Cabinet in 1917, and now to participate in the Peace Conference, to be made a member of the Ministry in Whitehall, and finally, to be raised to the peerage, for he is to represent the India Office as Under-Secretary in the House of Lords.

He is the second Indian, (Mr Ameer Ali being the first) to be named of the Privy Council. These signal honours, so gratifying to his countrymen, have been earned by high capacity, earnest labour, and gifts of statesmanship.

Lord Sinha: maiden speech

THE INDIAN CONTRIBUTION to British politics was not limited to the three Members of Parliament. An equally influential figure was the first Indian peer, Lord Sinha, whose life spanned the high-water mark of the Raj. From his birth in Bengal in 1864, just seven years after the Mutiny, to his death in 1928, twenty years before Independence, Satyendra Prassano First Baron Sinha personified all that was good in the co-operation between Indians and Britons.

He took his seat in the Upper House in February 1919, under the gaze of a group of Indian officers in the Strangers' Gallery.

LORD ISLINGTON: My Lords, before the noble Lord answers for the Government I would like to say a word in addition to what has already been said by Lord Sydenham. Perhaps I may be permitted to seize this opportunity of offering a very warm expression of congratulation to my noble friend the Under-Secretary on his first assumption of active work as the representative of the India Office. I have had the privilege of close and intimate association with Lord Sinha in public work both in India and in this country during recent years, and therefore I, along with other noble Lords present, can readily understand how it has come about that Lord Sinha has occupied posts of the very highest distinction and responsibility

Lord Sinha, who was raised to the peerage in 1919.

6

both in connection with India and the Empire during the past ten years. The post he now fills is one that, to every Englishman, is perfectly easy and simple, as your Lordships are well aware. But the post occupied, and occupied for the first time under the new movement of Imperial evolution, by an Indian like my noble friend will present difficulties, in many instances serious difficulties, and I feel sure that those who know India best will realise what I mean when I say that. Nobody will realise it better than my noble friend himself, and I feel that it is an act of characteristic public spirit on his part in assuming the position. I feel sure his high qualities will enable him to overcome those difficulties in the same way as he had successfully overcome difficulties in other posts, but he will find it difficult to attain complete success unless he can be assured – as I confidently hope he may be – during the whole term of his office, of the whole-hearted and sincere support and co-operation of his fellow-subjects in India, whether they be European or Indian. That he will receive the sympathy and support of your Lordships during the time he is in office he can, I am certain, be assured.

THE UNDER-SECRETARY OF STATE FOR INDIA (*Lord Sinha*): My lords, it is with considerable diffidence that I rise this evening to address your Lordships, and I hope I may be not altogether out of order if I begin by thanking my noble friend Lord Islington, from whom I have in the past had a great deal of courtesy and consideration, for the more than generous terms with which he has been pleased to refer to me; and I thank your Lordships also for the very kind reception you gave to the remarks.

THE TIMES: *27th October 1922*

India's claim

Mr Sastri on Peaceful Revolutions

THE RIGHT HON. SRINIVASA SASTRI was entertained at luncheon yesterday by the Royal Colonial Institute, Sir Godfrey Lagden presiding.

Replying to the toast 'Our Guest', proposed by the Chairman, Mr Sastri said that he had arrived at a most interesting time in English public affairs. He found the country engaged upon one of its periodical pastimes of pulling down a Government and setting up another.

He wished that other nations knew the secret of accomplishing a revolution in so unsanguinary and peaceful manner. They in India had taken very good care not to be linked with any political party, and expected from any Government the entire fulfilment of pledges and promises that had been made. He had been surprised during the last few days to hear so many people of influence ask what was the best thing to do with regard to India. It was not always possible to take the ideal course, and it was sometimes better to take the second best course in good time rather than to take the best course at some distant time.

Great Britain was committed in 1919 irrevocably to the grant of responsible government to India, and it was a matter of grave concern to read speeches delivered by statesmen of Cabinet rank who treated the subject as though it had not been settled, as if

Parliament had not over and over again pledged its solemn word to the accomplishment of that high aim. Nothing remained now but to go forward.

Those present included: Mr W. Turnbull, Mrs M. Chrimes, Mr F.C. Wade (Agent-General for British Columbia), the Hon W. Ormsby-Gore, MP, Admiral the Hon Sir Edmund Fremantle, the Hon Sir Arthur and Lady Lawley, Sir Charles McLeod, Sir William Duke (Permanent Under-Secretary of State for India) and Lady Duke, H.H. the Jam Sahib of Nawanagar, GBE, KCSI, Colonel the Hon Sir James Allen (High Commissioner for New Zealand), Mr N.C. Sen, Khan Bahadur M. Prestonji, Mr G.S. Bajpai, Mr N.W. Smith-Carrington and Mr Edward Salmon.

THE TIMES: *13th May 1927*

Parliaments of Empire

Mr McCormack on Loans – Tariff Policy

MR W. McCORMACK, Premier of Queensland, Mr V.J. Patel, President of the Indian Legislative Assembly and other visiting members of Empire Parliaments, were the guests at a luncheon of the United Kingdom branch of the Empire Parliamentary Association at the House of Commons yesterday. Mr Amery presided. In Mr Patel they had the first Speaker of the Indian Parliament.

Mr Patel said the branch of the association had affiliated with the British branch in the spirit of comradeship and honourable cooperation. The Central Legislature in India was not yet the sovereign body as Parliament was in the United Kingdom. Their franchise would have to be generously extended and their powers considerably widened to bring the Indian Parliament, if he might so call it, in line with the various self-governing countries within the vast combination of races and creeds, but he hoped that the advent of that devoutly wished-for consummation would be largely accelerated by the fraternal and friendly intercourse between the members of the various constituent units of the Empire Parliamentary Association. The association furnished in the very heart of the Empire a central place where the representatives of its branches could meet and freely discuss not merely the technique of parliamentary procedure, but the larger question of broadening and widening the basis of freedom. Since the Indian branch was inaugurated last year, a number of Indian members had visited this country and had testified to the usefulness of the association, and they were also glad to welcome in India some of the British members during this last cold weather.

He hoped that before long the Legislature in India, with its powers and status largely extended, would have the pleasure of welcoming to Delhi the representatives of all the parliamentary bodies within the British Commonwealth to a joint discussion of problems common to all. He believed that brief visits of a month or two would do more to bring to the minds of all the realization of needs and difficulties than years spent on reading books written about each other by authors who, with all their learning and labour, might be ill-equipped for the task, owing to the absence of a sympathetic insight into their affairs. For that reason he was consulting the Speaker, as joint president of the United Kingdom branch, and also with Sir Howard D'Egville, as to the prospect of a visit from some members of the British Parliament. He was convinced that the association had a great mission before it – no less than that of uniting together the different units of the world-wide organization. It would have failed of its purpose if its activities did not tend in the direction of increasing – however indirectly – the bounds of freedom in all parts of the Empire.

THE TIMES: *18th April 1928*

Indian reforms: Swarajists and Simon Commission

Letters to the Editor

Sir, – The return of the Simon Commission lends interest to the recent manoeurvres of the Swaraj party that is unsuccessfully attempting to boycott it. The Lahore cable in *The Times* of April 14 summarizes the views placed before the Congress meeting at Amritsar by Mr Jawahir Lal, son of the extremist leader, Pandit Moti Lal. After rebuking the Punjab, the 'Indian Ulster', for its lack of 'great speakers or thinkers' and its consequent failure to join in the boycott, he outlined the Swaraj programme as follows: Dominion status would be useless to India, as she would still remain under British economic subjection. Hence complete independence, with the severance of the British connexion is the only sound political deal. India could defend herself; if not, better foreign invasion than British protection. Then follows the bait that has so often deluded our British Socialists into supporting a Brahman oligarchy striving under the catchwords of democracy to recapture its lost Dominion:

> India should be made an independent democratic State, aiming at Swaraj for the masses, based on Socialism, and not on a transfer of power from a British oligarchy to an Indian oligarchy.

It was anti-British incitements of this nature that stirred up the revolutionary outbreaks of 1919; and, however futile they may be in Madras or Bengal, they may be a real danger in the 'virile province' of the Punjab.

Mr Jawahir Lal's rhetoric cannot conceal his misgivings; he urges that the boycott should continue 'in spite of the defections of the weak and the well-meant attempts to bridge a gulf which is not easily bridged.' He and his kind are looking out for that bridge.

The Commission is now master of the situation; it has realized that the Swarajists do not speak for the diverse Indian peoples, but only for a small minority, whose real aim is to restore a Brahman-controlled autocracy of the higher Hindu castes, under a camouflage of democratic form with which they hope to delude the British people.

I am, &c.,

M.F. O'DWYER

The Athenaeum, 15th April 1928

Pandit Moti Lal Nehru with the young Jawharlal.

THE TIMES: *18th February 1930*

Special India number

EDITORIAL

THE PROJECT of a Special Number of *The Times* to be devoted entirely to India was set in hand more than a year ago. It was believed at that time – with what accuracy recent events have shown – that the year 1930 would find public opinion in England more deeply concerned with Indian problems than at any time for half a century; that the Report of the Statutory Commission, which is due within the next month or two, would be the better understood by English readers for a general account beforehand of various phases of life in India; and that there was occasion also, at a time when it is the fashion in some quarters to disparage the British connexion, to recall some of the great achievements in the moral and material development of the country for which it is responsible. With these objects in view the present Number has gradually taken shape. It does not profess to be either uniform or exhaustive. The whole character of the Number, as its readers will find, is historical and descriptive rather than controversial.

The project has the blessing of the VICEROY, and includes among its contributors a large body of distinguished administrators, past and present, British and Indian. In some cases their contributions are signed; in other cases they prefer, for various reasons, to remain anonymous. The reader will find abundant and recent information about the structure of the Government, the compliated and important land revenue system, the public services, the great cities, the railways and shipping, the agriculture and manufacturers, and the antiquities, the literature, the daily life and sports and pastimes of India.

THE TIMES: *7th March 1931*

The position in India

Mr Chamberlain on the Agreement

MR CHAMBERLAIN, speaking at Birmingham last night, said that the conversations between the Viceroy and Mr Gandhi, which had given rise to a great deal of anxiety here and India, had at last resulted in an agreement which, so far as he could judge, gave us reason for genuine if sober satisfaction.

There were two special causes of anxiety to those who were watching Indian affairs. The first concerned the preservation of law and order. It was well known that the Congress Party, the most extreme party in India, had been demanding that there should be an inquiry into the conduct of the police. Yet all who knew India felt that to set up an inquiry of that kind into the conduct of the police, who had acted throughout with great forbearance and courage in face of the most tremendous provocation, would be to undermine and destroy their own confidence that they would be backed up in doing their duty. It was a relief to find that, as a result of this agreement, that demand had been abandoned.

Another subject of natural concern to us, in this country in particular, was the boycott of British trade, which for 12 months had done immense injury to one of our greatest industries – the Lancashire cotton trade. The boycott was now to be raised on British goods. It is true that the Congress Party had stated that they still intended to advocate the purchase of Indian cloth in preference to foreign cloth. And a great deal depended on how they interpreted that advocacy. If it meant that the cry would be 'Buy Indian Goods' as we said British, that need not be intepreted as a hostile act to Great Britain.

THE TIMES: *7th March 1931*

Sir W. Jowitt's Plea for Free Hand

SIR WILLIAM JOWITT, Attorney-General, speaking at Sunderland last night, said the days had gone by when we could treat the Indians as a kind of inferior race.

'Our justification for being in India', he said, 'is simply that we may contribute to the peace and order and good government of India for Indians. We have played a great role. But the time has come when the Indian, politically, is growing up, and, notwithstanding all the difficulties, we have got to help him to grow up. We have got to help him in his first tottering steps towards self-government: but we have got to realise that that is a perfectly laudable goal and an ambition which has got to be realised.

'There is a movement growing up in the Tory Party which has found expression from the mouth of Mr Winston Churchill. He has used insulting phrases about Indian leaders, and has done a great deal of harm to the cause of peace in India.

'It is common knowledge that, only last week, the members of the Tory party expressed their desire to Mr Baldwin that he should protest about these very meetings between Gandhi and Lord Irwin which have led to this settlement. Therefore it is essential for the peace of India that this government should have the chance in the autumn of continuing the Round Table Conference.'

THE TIMES: *25th March 1931*

Killing no murder

EDITORIAL

NOTHING COULD ILLUSTRATE more completely the deplorable confusion of thought prevailing in large bodies of Indian politicians than their attitude towards the execution of three Indian terrorists at Lahore. Yesterday Mr RANGACHARIAR, the Brahmin squire from Madras who leads the Nationalists in the Legislative Assembly, read a statement in the House expressing angry resentment of his party at the execution of these three men, criticising their trial and condemnation by a special tribunal set up by a Viceregal Ordinance, and alleging that the public believed that BHAGAT SINGH was not connected with the murders of which he was convicted and had expected the Government to respond to their desire for clemency. In spite of the HOME MEMBER'S defence of the action of the Government the Nationalists soon left the House in demonstrative protest. At Karachi, where the Congress delegates hold their first meeting to-day, there are signs that Mr GANDHI and his supporters will have difficulties with the extremists, who will use the executions as an argument for refusing to endorse his agreement with LORD IRWIN. Their leader, PANDIT JAWAHARLAL NEHRU, clearly hopes to increase their excitement by theatrically proclaiming that the corpse of BHAGAT SINGH is an obstacle to a settlement; there have been HARTALS and protestatory processions at Lahore and elsewhere, and the three murderers are, for the moment, regarded as martyrs. The craze no doubt will pass; but its prevalence even among normally moderate politicians is of evil omen.

On what grounds do the Nationalists and other Indian constitutionalists object to the executions? It can hardly be on the ground that these murderers were unfairly condemned by the very competent special tribunal, set up under a Viceregal Ordinance, which tried them after they and their accomplices had adopted every form of obstruction before a magistrate's court. Their Judges, British and Indian, after hearing over 600 witnesses found that BHAGAT SINGH, who had already been sentenced to transportation for his part in the bomb outrage in the Legislative Assembly, and the men who were hanged with him were guilty of the murder of Mr SAUNDERS, a promising young police officer, and of an Indian head constable at Lahore in December 1928; of conspiracy to murder other Europeans, and to wage war on the Government; and, among other revolutionary activities, of the establishment of bomb factories in various towns. The judgment and its confirmation by the Privy Council left no doubt of their guilt. Nor is the agitation due to any repugnance to the infliction of capital punishment as such. These protests are purely emotional and sentimental. Conciliation is in the air; therefore, it is argued, the Government must not execute criminals who have murdered its servants and conspired to wage war by assassination and outrage. No self-respecting Government could accept such an argument for the exercise of clemency, and if the present Government of India had yielded to the confused emotionalism of a group of politicians, or to the threats and demonstrations at Lahore, it would have abdicated its trust by a dishonourable surrender. The Nationalist members of the Assembly forgot that the consequences of such an abdication would simply recoil upon the self-governing India which is their ideal.

CHAPTER NINE

World War II

BETWEEN 1939 and 1945 over two and a half million Indians came to the colours without conscription, making up the largest voluntary army ever formed anywhere.

Some of the Indian Army's most famous regiments made their final appearance during the Second World War, before Independence swept away two hundred years of Anglo-Indian military tradition. Throughout the war a relationship of mutual trust and respect existed between the British and Indian officers.

(*left*) In October 1944, Major Sarbjit Singh of the 1st Punjabs was decorated with the DSO by His Majesty King George VI. He is shown here, after the investiture, outside Buckingham Palace.

'We shall fight them on the beaches . . .' This Indian Army officer and British sentry are pictured during a tour of coastal defences, and symbolise the close cooperation between the two countries during World War II.

(left, above) A number of Indian Officers seen inspecting coastal defences in Southern Command.

(left, below) The Princess Royal visiting the Royal Indian Army Service Corps (Mule Transport) of the 7th/9th Battalion, The Royal Scots.

Of the 2,393,891 Indian soldiers who enlisted, 36,092 were killed or missing; 64,354 wounded; 79,489 taken prisoner. As these figures show, Indian troops fought with distinction and often with incredible valour in every theatre in which they were committed.

During the War, a total of 30 VCs were awarded to Indian soldiers, the largest number, fourteen, in 1944. The first recipient was Second Lieutenant Premindra Singh Bhagat of the Corps of Indian Empire.

Trained in Britain

Captain B. E. Rodrigues leaving Brompton Oratory with his bride Monica Das Gupta.

Many of those who fought in the Second World War were to continue their military careers as lynch-pins of the Independent Armed Forces, and the excellence of the training offered in Britain was never lost. One such officer was Captain B. E. Rodrigues, pictured here in uniform on the day of his wedding to his radiant bride, Monica Das Gupta, at Brompton Oratory, London, in 1947. He had been sent to England by the Indian Government for training as an Air Force Officer.

(*left, above*) The Maharajah of Kashmir with the Mayor of Bermondsey inspecting Civil Defence Units.

(*left, below*) The Maharajah with Sir Firoz Khan Noon, former High Commissioner for India, and Mr Leo Amery, Secretary of State for India, on the steps of the Burma Office in April 1944.

(*right*) The Duchess of Gloucester with two Indian volunteers at India House, London, who are engaged in packing parcels for Indian POWs.

'Some chicken – some neck . . .' Thus Winston Churchill responded to Hitler's threat '. . . to wring Britain's neck like a chicken.' This group photograph of the warriors of the Empire and its allies shows just what he meant.

(*above*) Their Majesties King George VI and Queen Elizabeth inspecting Royal Indian Army troops at Shirley, near Derby, in August 1940.

(*right*) Sergeant-Major Sher Singh was a much-decorated soldier. This photograph of him was taken while he was in London for the 1946 Victory celebrations and shows him wearing the Indian DSM and the Military Medal and Bar.

Three Indian VCs, Lance Naik
Dhanbhakta Gurung, Naik Gian
Singh and Havaldar Umrao Singh,
received their decorations at
Buckingham Palace on 16th
October 1945. Outside the Palace
they were mobbed by the crowd
who surrounded them as they posed
for the photographers.

The Indian influence

WE MAY ALL READ THE HISTORY of a country, study its political structures and its geography and analyse the agricultural and industrial bases of its wealth, but what we learn can never have as much impact as what we feel. Our reactions and impressions are based on the way in which a society organizes itself, the disposition of the people and the external expression of the national character in its arts, crafts, and architecture. Knowledge of the society of ancient Greece may be approached by many paths, but the most attractive must be by reading Homer, by looking at a statue by Praxiteles and by climbing the Acropolis to gaze at the Parthenon.

While many Britons have had first-hand experience of the glories of India, the majority have to get something of her flavour

A once-familiar sight, an Indian salesman with his scarves and ties, trying to interest the lady of the house. If a purchase was made, he might give away a lucky bean.

by way of the seaports. Since the earliest days, when the Company were spreading across the subcontinent, until today, Indian crafts have been acclaimed. Every Victorian woman of substance had a shawl made of the finest cashmere worked in the classic Paisley pattern and hand-woven rugs and rich fabrics were, and still are, prized items. The openwork rattan furniture, so suitable for hot climates, was admired, and Osborne House on the Isle of Wight was chosen by Queen Victoria as the site for the construction of a wing to be 'decorated according to ancient Hindu and Sikh pattern of ornament'.

Indian entertainers were greatly appreciated for their exotic charm: conjurers, snake charmers and illusionists had tremendous appeal, and a reporter in 1886 claimed 'the Hindustanee Nautch Girls will attract you with their graceful movements and the Tanjore Nautch Girls will teach you more than ever you will learn in any English theatre of graceful movements and poise.' Indian music, too, with its rhythms and cadences so foreign to Western ears had its admirers.

In 1913 the attention of the world was focused on Indian literature when the poet Rabindranath Tagore was awarded the Nobel Prize for Literature and the interest of the 'Orientalists' ensured that new translations were made of the classic Indian religious texts, the *Rig Veda* and the *Upanishads*.

A less spiritual aspect of Indian culture has had perhaps the most pervasive influence of all – its rich and varied cuisine which ranks alongside the world's greatest. The British may have stuck solidly to their roasts and school puddings in even the remotest parts of the subcontinent but native dishes began to find their way into the kitchens of the British in India and then into the repertoire of the cooks back home. Kedgeree was a popular breakfast meal and curry, in particular, although a peculiarly British interpretation of it, became an established dish in the nation's homes.

Since the Second World War the trends which were evident in these earlier years have grown with speed and vigour and the Indian culture has made a much greater impact since independence than it ever did during the days of the Raj.

THE TIMES: *20th July 1852*

Indian beggars

Letter to the Editor

Sir, – I was not a little surprised on my arrival from India in this glorious part of the world to see in this metropolis several Indian beggars, who are of great annoyance to the public, but more so to the Indian gentlemen who visit England. Now, I frequently entered into conversation with them, and inquired the cause of their begging in London; the only reply that I could obtain was that their masters died and they were left unprovided for; no other resort is left to them but to beg. England is overstocked by various people already, and the following rule should be strictly adhered to and acted upon by the authorities in India, which would in a great measure put a stop to the coming of Indian beggars to this free land

and it would be highly beneficial to the public as well as to the Indian delinquents, who often perish for want of care and the effect of climate.

GENERAL DEPARTMENT

The Hon. the Governor in Council is pleased to intimate for general information, that under instruction from the Hon. the Court of Directors, the customary deposit of five hundred rupees (500) will in future be required on account of all servants leaving Bombay by any route for Europe, whether such servants be Asiatic, or African or other persons of colour, born within the limits of the East India Company's charter.

By order of the Hon. the Governor in Council

W. ESCOMBE,

Secretary to Government

Bombay Castle, 11th February 1846

At present there are upwards of 200 Indian beggars in London itself, and many of them are certainly left through the treachery of the parties who brought them, and are anxious to return to India, but for want of means they are unable to do so, actually starving and suffering, and if all the Indian beggars be called upon, many of them will volunteer to return home, and it would be an act of infinite charity to send them to India, and to call upon the authorities of the port from which they were allowed to embark for England, for infringing the above order, and to adopt such measures as to totally put an end to the suffering of Indian foreigners in this country. I sincerely hope that this may attract the attention of those in this country who have got the power of interfering and taking up the matter, and to obtain passage for their poor Indian subjects, whom circumstances have thrown in their land.

Yours obediently,

AN INDIAN GENTLEMAN

London, 18th July

THE ILLUSTRATED LONDON NEWS: *14th October 1865*

The Social Science Congress at Sheffield

THE INAUGURAL ADDRESS of Lord Brougham at the opening meeting of the ninth annual Congress of the National Association for the Promotion of Social Science, on the evening of Wednesday week, appeared in our last number. An illustration of the scene at this meeting, which was held in the Alexandra Music Hall, is presented to our readers. We have selected for the subject of another illustration the meeting, on Friday, of the Eductional Department, Mr Thomas Chambers MP presiding, when Sir Manockjee Cursetjee, a Parsee gentleman of Bombay, not less distinguished by his liberality and enlightenment than by his wealth and commercial position, made an interesting statement with regard to the improvement of female education in India, of which he has long been a zealous and influential promoter. He described the means by which, two years ago, an institution was opened at Bombay for the education of a limited number of daughters of respectable native families. He had previously tried the experiment in his own family, and it had proved successful. A strong prejudice, however, still subsisted in the country against female education; and, without the co-operation of their European brethren, it was impossible for enlightened natives to accomplish all those changes which they were desirous of seeing carried out. The speech of Sir Manockjee Cursetjee, which was fluently delivered, was listened to with attention, and appeared to excite general interest.

THE ILLUSTRATED LONDON NEWS: *19th January 1884*

The Late Keshub Chunder Sen

THE DEATH of this eminent Hindoo religious reformer, who was personally well known in England, took place at Calcutta last week. Baboo (a title of social rank) Keshub Chunder Sen was born in

A portrait by an unknown artist of Keshub Chunder Sen.

1838, and received English education. He became, about 1860, the leader of an active and zealous section of the Native Unitarian Christians in Bengal, a community founded about fifty years ago by Rajah Rammohun Roy, who died in 1833. The younger and most progressive part of this community, led by Chunder Sen, further tried to carry their religious theories into practice by excluding all idolatrous rites from social and domestic ceremonies, and rejecting the distinction of caste. This society of Hindoo Unitarians, or, as they call their church, the 'Brahmo Samaj of India', have made considerable progress. They built a chapel in Calcutta, and they encourage the establishment of branch societies in different parts of the country. The greater part of the educated natives of Bengal sympathise more or less with the movement. In 1870, Keshub Chunder Sen visited this country, preached or spoke in several Nonconformist chapels in London, and received a good deal of attention from many religious leaders in this country, including some who did not endorse his theological views. Lord Lawrence, for instance, presided at one of the meetings addressed by the Indian Reformer, and spoke highly of the value of his work in India. The late Dean Stanley was also one of his English friends.

THE ILLUSTRATED SPORTING AND DRAMATIC NEWS: *9th January 1886*

India in London – Langham Hall

CONSTANT and varied entertainments, too short and fitting in duration to become monotonous, leaving behind them a sense of something akin to lively satisfaction, form the chief attraction of the new Indian venture, as distant, both in character and variety, from its earlier rival as well could be. From the opening of the doors to the last moment of closing, Banoo Khan's nimble fingers, much less his tongue, are never still. 'Have you one s'illin'? Veri Well! One han'kchef? All right. One ring? Oh, yes! T'ank you' Or he shows a little ball in the palm of his hand, and proceeds, in his broken way, to rack his brains for its English equivalent identifying its substance. This is his formula: 'Dis soap – soot, suit no! shoot, shoot-no? no! sop? zot? sot! shot? shot! dis shot! ah, yes, t'ank you, shot all right;' and immediately, with noisy incantations, he works divers ingenious wonders with his own and the borrowed property. He is a dabster at card trickery, and the hundred and one sleight-of-hand feints, so popular with his own countrymen, will scarcely prove less attractive to English visitors. Unfortunately, by the loss of sixteen out of his twenty-two snakes, his performances with them lose some of their charm; and till they can be replaced one must be content to handle the harmless creatures remaining. Banco will even allow anyone who has nerve enough to twine them round their necks, &c., for they are, to use his own words, 'Vera goot, no no bad!' With his pets I must leave him, and if you will follow me I can show and point out to you many a charming little scene. Look at that youngster, she is but three years of age, little Knuka they call her; she is the daughter of Vanzacksi and Virluxumi, of Mysore, Madras; watch her dainty little feet, you see, with all the chic imaginable, she dances to the strains of the Austro-Hungarian band. That's an admiring companion kneeling by her side, a merry, happy girl of some twenty summers, swathed in sumptuous gold-striped drapery; she eggs the youngster on to fresh efforts; look, she is unable to contain herself, with a rush she hugs the child in her arms, smothers her with kisses, and bolts as hard as she can to the Nautch girl's house. With your permission we will follow them. Here again the little mite is the centre of attraction. Do you speak Hindustanee? If so the whole bevy of girls will favour you with their attentions, and go into raptures over their faraway home. You would possibly like to see them in a change of costume? Very well, wait till seven o'clock, you will then see them in far prettier headdresses and drapery. There is the ivory-worker, the four-handed man – he uses both hands and feet indiscriminately – watch him, and when you tire visit the adjacent shops (there is plenty that is of interest along here in the gallery), and, when you are satisfied, meet me over in the corner there – by the luncheon stall, the home of the guitar player. The musical quartet are tuning up, and you will have an opportunity of studying the peculiar weird rhythmic measure of the native music if you are so inclined. Downstairs there are shops galore, and should you not yet have ferreted out the goat, pay your respect to him, and don't forget your cup of Indian tea in the bungalows. But wait! Before you empty your pockets at the many native stalls – you have a choice of purely native work – you had better take your seats in the body of the hall, the curtain is up, and behind the footlights – we must not miss this, the *tour de force* of the village – the Parsee Victoria Dramatic Company present themselves in a Burmese pantomimic sketch. Could anything be more comical? They change the programme every week. You enjoy the Parsee gymnasts, the juggling, the wrestling entertainments, and the Hindustanee sketch. Yes; but now, if you will sit out the entertainment, the Hindustanee Nautch Girls will attract you with their graceful movements, and the Tanjore Nautch Girls will teach you more than ever you will learn in any English theatre of graceful movements and pose. Come again? Of course you will. The dance has many movements as varied as the hills, and always beautiful. L.W.

THE ILLUSTRATED LONDON NEWS: *12th August 1893*

The Indian Durbar Hall at Osborne . . .

HER MAJESTY THE QUEEN, as Empress of India, takes great interest, especially of late years, in studying the affairs of her vast Asiatic dominion, the condition of its different populations, their habits and manners, and the rank of its native princes, some of whom have been her visitors in England, with whom she has learnt to converse, sufficiently for ceremonial intercourse, in the current Hindostani language. The portrait of her native Indian private secretary, who is a Mohammedan, recently appeared in this Journal. Another instance of her Majesty's disposition to show all her possible friendly regard to those who come from India as representatives of her loyal subjects and faithful allies is equally

A selection of the exotic entertainments available to the Victorian visitor who went to the Indian 'village' is seen through the eyes of a contemporary engraver.

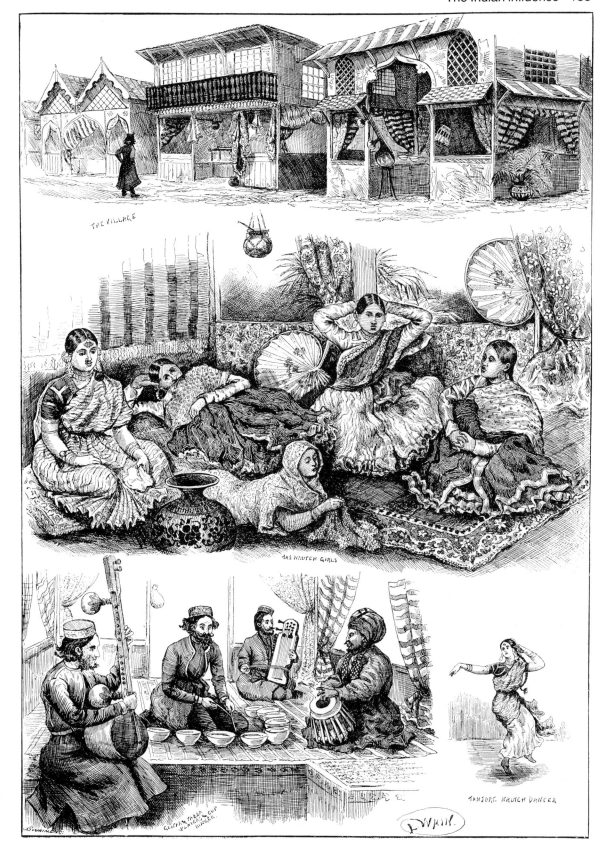

THE VILLAGE

THE NAUTCH GIRLS

GUITAR, TABLA & CUP PLAYER, RINGER.

TANJORE NAUTCH DANCER

deserving of public notice. This is the construction, in the new wing of Osborne House, East Cowes, the Queen's favourite residence in the Isle of Wight, of a beautiful apartment, decorated according to ancient Hindu and Sikh pattern of ornament, to be used as a 'Durbar' or hall of State and Court receptions, upon occasions particularly concerning Asiatic guests of her Majesty. The work, at the Queen's private expense, was performed during the years 1891 and 1892, under the personal superintendence of the designer, Ram Singh, a native of the Punjab, formerly a pupil of Mr Kipling CIE – father of the popular novelist, Rudyard Kipling – in the Mayo School of Art at Lahore. It was the Duke of Connaught, when his

Not all Victorians' rooms were stuffed with mahogany and aspidistras. In 1893 Bhai Ram Singh designed a Durbar Room in Indian style for one of Queen Victoria's palaces, Osborne House on the Isle of Wight. This portrait was painted in 1892 by Rudolf Swoboda of the German School of painters.

Royal Highness was in India, who appreciated the merits of Ram Singh, and recommended him to the Queen for this employment, before which that ingenious and tasteful native artist – a master of architectural decoration, wood-carving and cabinet-work – had achieved high success with his designs for the Chiefs' College at Lahore, the Lahore Jubilee Museum, and the Municipal Halls of Ferozepur and Allahabad, winning the prizes and the preference in open competitions. He also designed caskets, of ebony and silver, for presentation to the Queen and to the Duke of Connaught and furnished the decorations of the billiard-room and carridor in the mansion of his Royal Highness at Bagshot Park. We therefore willingly, in the belief that much is to be learned from India, as, indeed, has been already confessed, in these branches of ornamental art, give the portrait of Ram Singh.

The city of Amritsar, where Ram Singh got his early training as a workman, is a great centre of trade, as well as the original headquarters of the Sikh national and religious community in the Punjab. Many of its houses are ornamented internally with the finest wood-carving, an art which has there been practiced by Indian workmen almost to an equal degree of manual skill with those of China and Japan, and with far better notions of richness and magnificence of effect, gracefulness of design, and the artistic treatment of surface reliefs. The ancient Hindu temples were probably unequalled in the beauty of the elaborate sandalwood carvings on their ceilings and doors, of which the existing gates of the Somnauth temple are only a copy; these were carried off to Ghuzni, in 1024, by the Moslem conqueror, Sultan Mahmoud, and were recovered and brought to Agra by Lord Ellenborough in 1842, after the first Afghan war.

THE GRAPHIC: *17th October 1893*

Mr Cowassee Jehangir

MR JAHANGIER COWASSEE JEHANGIR, a well known and wealthy gentleman of Bombay has just presented the Imperial Institute, South Kensington, with the magnificent donation of two lakhs of rupees, a sum amounting to between £13,000 and £15,000, on the condition that the sum shall be applied for the benefit of the Indian section. The Governing body of the Institute have decided to devote the money to completion of the Indian Conference Room and in building the Eastern Hall, in which lectures will be delivered and discussions raised on commercial subjects relating to Greater Britain.

Mr Jehangir, who, with Mrs Jehangir, has recently been on a visit to England, and was present at the opening of the Imperial Institute, is the nephew and adopted heir of the late Sir Cowassee Jehangir who was famous in Western India for his public charities and for his independent character. He represents one of the oldest and wealthiest of the Parsee families in India, which identified their interests with those of the East India Company. Another of his ancestors was the first native of India who established direct trade between Bombay and England.

Infamy and investiture. Buck Ruxton (*left*), born Buckhtyar Rustomji Ratanji Hakim, and Khan Saheb Aspindiar Coverjee Jassawalla (*above*) were contemporaries but could not better illustrate the extremes of action which bring men into prominence. Ruxton, who was a doctor, killed his common-law wife, Isabelle, in a fit of jealousy, and then the nursemaid who witnessed the murder. After surgically removing all distinguishing marks from their bodies, he drove to Scotland and hid them in a gully, but they were discovered and Ruxton, shown here hiding his face, was executed in 1936. One year later, his fellow-countryman was appointed to be a Companion of the Imperial Service Order for services rendered at Army headquarters and he is seen here leaving Buckingham Palace after the investiture by King George VI.

SPHERE: *23rd March 1907*

Mr Bomanjee Dinshaw Petit

PARSEE AND PHILANTHROPY are almost convertible terms, in Bombay at least. The late Sir Dinshaw Maneckjee Petit, who received the second and last baronetcy conferred on any native of India, was the greatest benefactor of his race and city in his generation, and his only surviving son, Mr Bomanjee Dinshaw Petit, has carried on the family tradition with great credit. The surname is derived from the French: over a century ago, Mr Bomanjee's ancestor was agent to a French firm and being of short stature received the nickname of 'le petit', which has been handed down ever since as the surname of this family. Born in 1859 and educated at St Xavier's College, he is not merely the principal mill owner in Bombay but a leading authority on finance and banking.

Mr Petit has also shown special interest in institutions connected with the sick poor and in all questions relating to public health and matters of hygiene. His principal endowment has been the founding of a Parsee hospital in Bombay and another great benefaction was his gift of a lakh (£6,666) to the London School of Tropical Medicine. During a visit to England last year Mr Bomanjee was entertained at a banquet given by the authorities of

The family pictured here is that of Sir Jamsetjee Jejeebhoy, head of the Parsee community of Bombay. He was the 4th Baronet Cowasjee Cursetjee (1852–1908), to hold the title since it was created in 1857 for his great-grandfather, a wealthy and generous merchant born in 1783. An act passed in 1860 stipulated that each holder of the title must relinquish his own name to take that of the first Baronet, Sir Jamsetjee Jejeebhoy.

Seen here in 1902 with his son and daughter, he visited the House of Commons to be entertained by the Rt. Hon. Jesse Collings.

the Seamen's Hospital Society and the gift referred to was described as the real foundation of the long-neglected institution of a school of tropical medicine, in connection with that hospital and its work among the seafaring population of the London docks.

THE ILLUSTRATED LONDON NEWS: *29th November 1913*

The Indian poet who has brought East to the West

THE NOBEL PRIZE FOR LITERATURE for 1913 has been awarded to Mr Rabindranath Tagore, the Indian poet and teacher, who has been called 'the Prophet of Indian Nationalism'. Mr Tagore who is fifty-two years old, is a son of Maharshi (Great Sage) Debendranath Tagore, a member of the most ancient Bengali families, and his grandfather was Prince Dwarkanath Tagore, who was received at Queen Victoria's Court. Mr Tagore, not liking school, practically educated himself, and wrote his first poem when he was very young. In early manhood, he came to England to study law, but feeling out of his element, returned to his native land, to become poet, philosopher and playwright. He has a large school at Bolepur where his pupils are instructed in the open air.

As we have said, he is a Nationalist but he is a great admirer of England, and is certain that this country and his own are held together by unbreakable ties and have a great destiny to fulfil together. His poems have been sung for a long while by the people. He himself has translated them into rhythmical prose.

Rabindranath Tagore, to whom the Swedish Academy has awarded the 1913 Nobel Prize for Literature (worth about £8,000).

In January 1931 Tagore stopped over in London on his way from America to India and had a long talk with Bernard Shaw at a luncheon which *The Spectator* gave for him at the Hyde Park Hotel.

Rabindranath Tagore, 1861 to 1941

RABINDRANATH, the fourteenth child of Dabendranath and Sarda Devi Tagore, went to school early and wrote his first verse at the age of eight. At the age of seventeen, in 1878, he arrived in London, on his way to Brighton, to join his brother's family and attend school there. London made a poor impression on him. He described it as a dismal city, smoky, foggy, and wet, with everyone jostling and in a hurry.

Though he was happy at Brighton, a friend of the family persuaded his brother to send him to London in order to benefit from his education in the West. He was put in a lodging-house facing Regent's Park but later moved to the house of a professional coach, a Mr Barker, as a paying guest.

Young Tagore joined London University, where he attended Henry Morley's lectures in English literature and read *Religio Medici* and Shakespeare with him. He often visited the Houses of Parliament and listened to Gladstone and John Bright's debates on Irish Home Rule.

Away from the home of his brother's family, he was lucky to find a friendly English family with whom he spent some time, but not without some initial opposition from the two daughters in the family, who were rather taken aback with the presence of a 'blackie' in the house and went away to stay with relatives. They returned only after being reassured that the stranger was harmless. Dr and Mrs Scott, the girls' parents, in fact treated him like a son.

In 1880, Rabindranath was called back to India. His letters, full of admiration for English society made his family think again about the wisdom of letting him loose in England alone. He returned home without any qualifications of distinction.

THE GRAPHIC: *23rd June 1923*

An Indian composer

A NOVEL EVENT in the history of musical production in London will take place in the evening of July 3 at the Steinway Hall, when Miss Comolata Banerji, the daughter of Mr Albion R. Banerji CSI, CIE, the Dewan of Mysore State will give a recital of her compositions. She has been under the training of Signor di Veroli, after a special course of study at the Conservatoire at Paris.

Her compositions include pieces which are quite English in style, yet conform to her ideal of showing the adaptability of the East to the West. Her ambition is to carry yet further the happy development in recent years of mutual appreciation and understanding of British and Indian art and culture. That this should be

Rabindranath Tagore with his son, on a visit to London in 1912, left the briefcase containing the manuscript of the English translation of his *Gitanjali* in an underground train while travelling between Charing Cross and Russell Square. Luckily it was recovered from the lost property office the next morning.

Anna Pavlova dancing the role of *Radha* to Uday Shankar's *Krishna.*

done in the realm of Indian music is the more desirable, since it is one in which misconception and misunderstanding are rife from lack of the knowledge indispensable to adequate appreciation.

Anna Pavlova asked one of her aides to go to Miss Banerji's recital. His favourable report made her invite Miss Banerji to Ivy House, her Hampstead home in London, where she asked her to write the score of the dance 'Hindu Wedding'.

Later Miss Banerji introduced Pavlova to dancer Uday Shankar who was studying painting at the Royal College of Arts in London. Anna, who was deeply interested in Indian art and dance and who had already performed in the ballet, 'Ajanta Frescoes' had the opportunity of learning from Uday Shankar the Indian-style movements.

Later he himself danced Krishna to Pavlova's Radha for which Miss Banerji also wrote the music. The dance was popular with the Indian community in London but was a greater success in the United States and together they travelled to Canada, Mexico and India.

THE TIMES: *23rd September 1924*

Religions of the Empire

LONDON CONFERENCE OPENED

The Indian community in Britain was by no means confined to London. These smiling nannies from Madras are brightening up a section of the Great Western Road in Glasgow on a damp Clydeside afternoon in 1925. They are evidently rather better accustomed to the camera than their charges, Ian Davidson and his cousin, Mary.

THE CONFERENCE on some Living Religions within the Empire, which will continue until the end of next week, began yesterday afternoon in the Upper West Gallery of the Imperial Institute. It is under the auspices of the School of Oriental Studies and the Sociological Society, but the organization has devolved on an executive committee under the chairmanship of Sir Denison Ross, director of the school of Oriental Studies. The gallery was decorated with Oriental tapestries, carpets, and paintings and at the close of the proceedings a reception was held by Lady Ross.

The chairman said that every effort had been made to secure

papers by representative speakers on all the important religions of the Empire not widely known in this country.

Colonel Sir Francis Younghusband, in his inaugural address, said that included in the Empire there were more Mahomedans than Christians, and at least twice as many Hindus as Mahomedans. The British Government aimed at being strictly impartial in its dealing with all these forms of faith; but this necessary neutrality of the State did not mean indifference to religion as such.

Sir Francis went on to declare that the ultimate basis upon which the British Empire should stand must be religion, not political constitutions nor economic agreements. Even patriotism was not enough. Above and at the base of patriotism and suffusing it through and through must be religion – love of the whole great world in which every nation and all creations were included.

Professor E.J. Rapson, of Cambridge, subsequently took the chair and introduced the exponent of orthodox Hinduism, Pandit Shyam Shankar, formerly a Professor at the Central Hindu College, now the Hindu University of Benaras.

Pandit Shyam Shankar drew a hearty cheer from the audience when he said that such a conference was a token of the religious toleration of the British Government, which deserved the appreciation of the world and a tribute from that conference.

THE TIMES: *2nd February 1931*

Asiatic art

Letter to the Editor

Sir – Indians of all shades of opinion will welcome the proposal made at a meeting of the India Society last week (a report of which appeared in *The Times* on Thursday) for the establishment in London of a museum in which objects representative of the arts of all parts of Asia will be effectively grouped and displayed. Art in the East and in the rest of the world, is the living expression of the soul of the people – only perhaps more so. A true appreciation of Eastern art is therefore the surest means of understanding the spirit and the general outlook on life of the Eastern races. And in so far as there never was a time when such an understanding was more necessary for the happiness of the world than it is now, the suggested museum, it appears to me, will fulfil a great purpose. I might add that the art of India cannot be fully appreciated except in its relation to that of Asia as a whole, and today it seems almost as necessary to understand India as to understand the whole of Asia.

In the period of the world's development that lies before us mutual appreciation of East and West, based on sympathetic understanding, will be a material factor in the preservation of peace. Misunderstanding may entail much heavier cost than it would take to make London into the foremost centre of the Western world for the study and appreciation of the fundamental ideas of the East. The movement to achieve this high aim should receive support not only in Britian and India, but throughout the Empire and in many other countries of the world.

Your obedient servant,

Savoy Hotel, W.C.2   K.N. HAKSAR

CHAPTER ELEVEN

Indians and their British alma maters

THE BENEFITS OF the British public school education were extended to many sons and daughters of the better-off citizens of the Empire, and India was no exception.

Though, by the time most of them arrived, the schools had moved from Nicholas Nickleby to Tom Brown's School Days, the experience could still be depressing, if instructive, for children unaccustomed to the customs, climate and food.

The first impressions of Rabindranath Tagore, who won the Nobel Prize for Literature, in spite of, rather than because of, his English education, are fairly typical.

Those who survived the system intact often went on to the Bar or the universities and these institutions shaped the thinking of many of the most influential figures in the British-Indian dialogue. It was his legal work defending his fellow countrymen in South Africa which first made Gandhi's name. Nehru, too, was influenced by his British higher education at Cambridge and the Bar, and recalls in his autobiography how many of his contemporaries followed the same path.

Queen Victoria's grandson, the eleven-year-old Duke of Albany, is seated in the front row, second from the left, with three Indian classmates. This 1896 photograph shows that, for the British upper classes at least, multi-racial education was accepted as completely unremarkable. It would take another sixty years before they would accept girls for co-education.

After Queen Victoria's Diamond Jubilee celebration in London in 1897, she visited Eton, to be greeted, amongst others, by four Indian student princes, stationed by the Triumphal Arch, and dressed in their national costumes. They were (*shown in the detail*) Nawab Wali Ud Deen, Nawab Mir Ekram Hussain, Kumar Shri Jareja and Raj Rajendra Narayan.

Raj Rajendra Narayan, later to become the Maharajah of Cooch Behar drank himself to death in 1913 after failing to get family approval to marry an English actress. He vowed to drink himself to death and did so by living exclusively on champagne. He died three weeks after the marriage of his younger brother, and successor, to Princess Indira of Baroda.

An unusual portrait of Mahatma Gandhi wearing European clothes.

Mohandas Karamchand Gandhi

TEN YEARS AFTER Queen Victoria was proclaimed the Empress of India and in the year of her Golden Jubilee, in 1887, eighteen-year-old Mohandas Karamchand Gandhi arrived in England to study law. It was not a happy time for him, as he explains in this passage from his autobiography.

'Everything was strange – the people, their ways and even their dwellings. Even the dishes that I could eat were tasteless and insipid. England I could not bear, but to return to India was not to be thought of.' The rest of his stay in England, until he was called to the Bar on 10th June 1891 and returned home three days later, was spent trying to understand the English as well as learning more about Indian history. 'During my wonderings in the city at last I hit on a vegetarian restaurant in Farringdon Street. Before I entered, I noticed books for sale behind a glass window near the door and among them Salt's Plea for Vegetarianism. This I purchased for a shilling and went straight to the dining room. There I had my first hearty meal since my arrival.

'The clothes which I had brought from Bombay now seemed to me to be unsuitable for English society and I got new ones made at the Army and Navy Stores. As if all this was not enough, I began to direct my attention to other details that were supposed to go towards the making of an English gentleman. I was informed that it was necessary for me to take lessons in dancing, French and elocution. I thought I should learn to play the violin in order to cultivate an ear for Western music. All this infatuation must have lasted about three months. The punctiliousness in dress persisted for years.

'My living with a family meant the payment of a regular weekly bill so I decided to take rooms on my own account. Soon after this I came across books on simple living, and after reading them abandoned the suite of rooms and rented one instead, invested in a stove and began cooking my own breakfast at home.

Towards the end of my second year in England, I came across two Theosophists. They talked to me about the Gita. I felt ashamed, as I had neither read the Divine Song in Sanskrit nor in Gujarati. I was constrained to tell them I had not read the Gita. They also took me on one occasion to the Blavatsky Lodge and introduced me to Mrs Besant.

'It was easy enough to be called to the Bar in England but it was difficult to practise. Whilst I was studying law at Inner Temple I was torn with doubts and confided my difficulties to some of my friends. One of them suggested that I should seek Dadabhai Naoroji's advice. Though I had brought an introduction to him from India, it seemed to me that I had no right to trouble such a great man. Whenever an address by him was announced, I would attend it. In order to come in close touch with the students, he had founded an association. In course of time at last I mustered up courage to present to him the letter of introduction. 'You can come,' he said, 'and have my advice whenever you like.' But I never availed myself of his offer.'

THE TIMES: *4th October 1911*

Lieutenant-Colonel Jayakar

OBITUARY

THE DEATH TOOK place at Bandra, a suburb of Bombay, last month, of Lieutenant-Colonel Atmaram Sadasiva Grovindin Jayakar, late of the Indian Medical Service, who made important contributions to scientific knowledge of the fauna of South-Eastern Arabia and the shores of the Persian Gulf.

Born in Bombay in 1845, Colonel Jayakar was educated at the mission institution of which Dr John Wilson had charge. As the first holder of a scholarship founded to encourage Hindu graduates to complete their training in this country, he came to London in 1867, and after obtaining the MRCS and LRCP degrees, passed into the Indian Medical Service, being one of the first Indians to do so.

During the greater part of his official career, namely for nearly 30 years, he was residency surgeon at Muscat. Here he got together a large number of zoological specimens for the museum authorities in this country.

The most important discovery was that of a new goat, which Mr Oldfield Thomas named after him, *Hemitragus Jayakari*. Two new species of lizards and two of snakes are named after him. In the great collection of fishes he made on the Arabian coast and presented to the Natural History Museum here, no less than twenty-two new species have been identified and seven of them bear his name.

CROYDON HIGH SCHOOL MAGAZINE: *1936*

Nolini Heloïse Bonnerjee

OBITUARY

BONNERJEE, NOLINI HELOÏSE (MRS BLAIR): b. 16th July 1871, at Calcutta; elder daughter of W.C. Bonnerjee, barrister and politician of Calcutta, a pioneer of British education in India, and H. Muttylal; married in 1899, to George Blair, a Scottish barrister, later Colonel of Scottish Liverpool Regiment (died 1934).

EDUCATION: sent to England with small brother at the age of three to be educated in English family at Anerley; Croydon High School 1887–89; Girton 1889–92; Natural Sciences Tripos, Pt I, Cl. II

The Mistress and Fellows of Girton College, Cambridge in 1889. Miss Bonnerjee is seated in the front row, on the left.

1892; Studied medicine at the London School of Medicine for Women and Royal Free Hospital. First Indian woman to study at Girton and one of the first women to receive a London degree. Her younger sister Susila entered Newnham College in the same year and also qualified as a doctor. Nolini practised medicine in Liverpool and engaged in much welfare work between 1899 and 1922; worked for the Indian Famine Fund. Returning to India, she lived in Darjeeling where she did important social work, founding baby clinic, ante-natal clinic and Indian women's work centre, visiting prisoners in jail etc., 1922–1934. After the death of her husband she lived in Calcutta, continuing social work there until she died in 1936. She had no children.

THE GRAPHIC: *10th March 1888*

Cornelia Sorabji: The first girl-graduate in Western India

MISS CORNELIA SORABJI, a Parsee Christian lady, is the daughter of the Rev Sorabji Khursedji, Honorary Missionary of the Church Missionary Society in Poona, and Mrs Sorabji, who visited England in 1886 to plead the cause of female education in India. Miss Cornelia Sorabji was the first and only lady to enter the Deccan

Cornelia Sorabji was already a Fellow and Lecturer in English Literature and Professor of English at a Gujarat University when she came to Somerville College, Oxford in 1889 to read law.

College at Poona in 1884, and, as may easily be imagined, she had much to contend with. She felt keenly her isolated position among upwards of three hundred men, who, with the exception of two Englishmen and a few Parsees, were all Hindus, and who naturally looked with no kindly eye upon this *rara avis*. It is needless to dwell upon the annoyances to which she was subjected, or to the unfriendly criticisms among her own countrymen and women upon her unprecedented career, but with the goal of her ambition ever in view, she went bravely on, winning golden opinions from Principals and Professors alike. To all who have watched her course with interest, not unmixed with curiosity, it is no small gratification to find that she has, even at this early period of her life – for she is only just out of her teens – done her part in elevating the position of her own countrywomen. Her brave, high-souled, gentle behaviour and influence cannot fail to raise the character and ability of women in the estimation of the Parsee and Hindu young men with whom she daily came in contact. Among her own sex, her example has already borne fruit, two Parsee ladies and one Jewess having sought for admission into the Colleges in Bombay and Poona. In Miss Sorabji's case, no concessions were made. She studied Latin in common with the men. She was 'top of her year' in the previous examination, has held a scholarship each year of her course, was 'Hughlings Scholar' in 1885, having passed head of University in English, 'Havelock prizeman' the end of the same year, being top of the Deccan College in English, has taken honours each time, and in the final B A examination of the Bombay University, held in November, 1887, she was one of the four in the entire Presidency, and the only student from her own College who succeeded in gaining First Class honours.

THE GRAPHIC: *6th August 1904*

Miss Cornelia Sorabji has been appointed by the Bengal Government as legal adviser to the Purahnashin, or women kept in zenanas of the Court of Wards. The appointment is made in connection with the scheme proposed by Miss Cornelia Sorabji to the India Office for providing purdah ladies with qualified legal assistance in the administration of their estates.

Jawaharlal Nehru

IN MAY 1905, at the age of fifteen, Jawaharlal Nehru set sail for England with his father, Motilal Nehru, mother and his baby sister, Vijyalaxmi. The very first day after reaching London, which happened to be Derby day, they all went to the races. In his autobiography, Nehru writes:

I was a little fortunate in finding a vacancy at Harrow, for I was slightly above the age of entry. Never before had I been left among strangers all by myself and I felt lonely and homesick. I was put, to begin with, in a low form because of my small knowledge of Latin. In many subjects probably, and especially in general knowledge, I was in advance of those of my age. I remember writing to my father how dull most of the English boys were as, they could talk about nothing but their games

I was greatly interested in the General Election, which took place, as far as I remember, at the end of 1905 and which ended in a great Liberal victory. Early in 1906 our form master asked us about the new Government and, much to his surprise, I was the only boy in his form who could give him much information on the subject, including almost a complete list of members of Campbell-Bannerman's Cabinet. Apart from politics, another subject that fastinated me was the early growth of aviation.

There were four or five Indian boys at Harrow in my time. In our house we had one of the sons of the Gaekwar of Baroda. He was much senior to me and was popular because of his cricket. Later came the eldest son of the Maharaja of Kapurthala, Paramjit Singh, now the Tikka Sahab. He was a complete misfit.

Right through the years 1906 and 1907 news from India had been agitating me, big events were happening at home in Bengal, Punjab and the Maharashtra. There was the Lala Lajpat Rai's and S. Ajit Singh's deportation and Tilak's name was often flashed from Poona. All this stirred me tremendously; but there was not a soul in Harrow to whom I could talk about it.

A prize I got for good at work at school was one of G.M. Trevelyan's Garibaldi books. This fascinated me and I studied the whole Garibaldi story carefully. Visions of similar deeds in India came before me, of a gallant fight for freedom. Harrow seemed a rather small and restricted place for these ideas and I wanted to go to the wider sphere of university. So I induced father to agree to this and left Harrow after only two year's stay, which is much less than the usual period.

Cambridge, Trinity College, the beginning of October 1907, my age seventeen; I felt elated at being an undergraduate with a great deal of freedom. Three years I was at Cambridge. I took the Natural Sciences Tripos, my subjects being chemistry, geology and botany.

My general attitude to life at the time was a vague kind of cyrenaicism, partly natural to youth, partly the influence of Oscar Wilde and Walter Pater. Among the books that influenced me at Cambridge was Meredith Townsend's *Asia and Europe.*

From 1907 onwards for several years India was seething with unrest and trouble. For the first time since the Revolt of 1857 India was showing fight and not submitting tamely to foreign rule. News of Tilak's activities and his conviction, of Aravindo Ghose and the way the masses of Bengal were taking the swedeshi and boycott pledge stirred all of us Indians in England.

The Indians in Cambridge had a society called the 'Majlis'. We discussed political problems there often but in somewhat unreal debates. Frequently I went to the 'Majlis' but during my three years I hardly spoke there. I could not get over my shyness and diffidence. The same difficulty pursued me in my college debating society, 'The Magpie and Stump', where there was a rule that a member not speaking for a whole term had to pay a fine. Often I paid the fine.

I remember Edwin Montague, who later became Secretary of State for India, often visiting 'The Magpie and Stump'. He was an old Trinity man. It was from that I first heard the modern definition of faith: to believe in something which your reason tells you cannot be true, for if your reason approved of it there could be no question of blind faith.

The man who was to lead independent India was Jawaharlal Nehru, a politician of great experience, and a man the British authorities proved totally unable to subdue. It was not until he had reached the comparatively late age of fifteen years that Nehru's family brought him to Britain, securing him a place at Harrow public school.

Some of the noted Indian politicians of the day visited us at Cambridge. We respected them but there was a trace of superiority in our attitude. Among those who came to us were Bepin Chandra Pal, Lajpat Rai, and G.K. Gokhale. We met Bepin Pal in one of our sitting rooms with only a dozen of us present but he thundered at us as if he was addressing a mass meeting of ten thousand.

Among my contemporaries at Cambridge there were several who played a prominent part in the Indian Congress in later years, L.M. Sen Gupta, Saif-ud-Din Kitchlew, Syed Mahmud and Tasadduk Ahmed Sherwani. In London we used to hear of Shyamji Krishnavarma. Also, there was a student centre opened by the India office. This was universally regarded by Indians, with a great deal of justification, as a device to spy on Indian students.

Jawaharlal Nehru as a cadet in the Harrow School Corps in 1907.

I was twenty when I took my degree at Cambridge. In favour of the paternal profession, the Bar, I joined the Inner Temple. I left Cambridge after taking my degree in 1910. I was only moderately successful, obtaining second class honours. For the next two years, I hovered about London. I got through the Bar examination with neither glory nor ignominy. Ireland and the woman suffrage movement interested me especially.

Often I exceeded the handsome allowance that father made me. In the summer of 1912 I was called to the Bar and in the autumn returned to India after a stay of over seven years in England. Twice, in between, I had gone home during my holidays.

THE ILLUSTRATED LONDON NEWS: *24th June 1911*

Imperial statesmen who received the honorary LL D at Cambridge

ON WEDNESDAY last week, in the Senate House at Cambridge, a number of distinguished statesmen received the degree of LL D (Doctor of Laws), which was conferred upon them by the Chancellor of the University, Lord Rayleigh. While General Botha was receiving his degree, there was a thud on the floor as an object dropped like a bomb from the gallery. It turned out to be a parcel containing a calagash pipe and some tobacco as a present for the General.

The picture shows, left to right: The Aga Khan, The Maharajah of Bikaner, The Earl of Minto, Sir Edward Morris, The Duke of Devonshire, The Earl of Crewe, General Botha, and Sir Joseph Ward.

The Aga Khan and the Maharajah of Bikaner (*on the left of the group*) after receiving their degrees at Cambridge.

THE TIMES: *28th February 1921*

Lord Reading visits the Indian Students' Hostel

This 1903 photograph of the Mistress and Fellows of Girton College shows (*second from right, third row*) Isabel Tara Bhore who graduated in 1906 and died in the same year. She was born in 1871 in Ahmednager.

LORD READINGS YESTERDAY afternoon visited the Indian Students' Union and Hostel in Keppel Street. He received a cordial welcome from a large gathering of students, and, after listening to an address by Dr A.E. Garvie, of New College, London, on 'Political Idealism', and two speeches from Indians, he accepted a loudly-voiced invitation to say a few words.

The circumstances were interesting. Principal Garvie's lecture had been characterized by vigorous Radicalism, and Mrs Sarojini Naidu, who wore Indian costume, had taken the opportunity to speak before Lord Reading of India's aspirations. Liberty, justice, and love, she said, using a substitution of these words by Dr Garvie for the French principles of 'Liberty, equality and fraternity,' were the three things which summed up the whole of India's idea of politics. If he who was to be, for five years, the custodian of the Imperial honour in her country would remember what the lecturer had said, 'Be the other fellow', she thought there might be peace for India. India was setting out on the path to freedom. It was for the custodian of England's honour to see that that freedom was born of mutual understanding and respect for their liberty.

Lord Reading remarked that he was still Lord Chief Justice of England, and in the English judiciary they had no politics. (*Laughter*). Principal Garvie, however, when he claimed as his three leaders of thought Gladstone, Campbell-Bannerman, and Lord Morley, had stirred him for the moment to forget that he had nothing to do with politics. These three names stood among the great leaders of his political idealism. (*Cheers*). He placed justice above even so sacred a word as liberty, and for this reason, that he could not conceive real justice without real liberty. (*Cheers*).

Amy Behramjee Rustomjee

RUSTOMJEE, AMY BEHRAMJEE HORMUSJEE JAMSETJEE: b. 18th May 1896 at Poona; daughter of B.H.J. Rustomjee, merchant and Hilla J.M. Cursetjee.

EDUCATION: Cathedral Girls' High School and Elphinstone College Bombay; Girton College, Cambridge 1922–5; English Tripos Cl.II (a, b), 1925; Cambridge Teacher's Training 1926; took course but no examination for Bombay University Librarian's diploma; M.A.(Cantab) 1929. Senior French and Maths mistress at Cathedral Girl's School, Bombay, 1918–22; Lecturer and Master of Method in English, Secondary Training College, Bombay, 1927–31; Professor of English at Elphinstone College, Bombay, 1931–2; Inspector of Girl's Schools Bombay from 1932. Examiner in English for various examining Universities of Bombay, and examiner of Bachelor of Teaching examinations; as 'Daniel' reviewed books regularly every week and broadcast them from Bombay station, 1929–32; broadcast regularly, both school broadcasts and general talks for the All-India Radio from 1934; Member of All-India Radio 'Brains Trust'; organised children's Holiday Reading Rooms 1943–5. Vice-President of Maharashtra University Association, Member of Bombay Provincial Bodies of Adult Education, Primary Education and Physical Education, and Adult Education Committee for City of Bombay; Member of Managing Committee, National Council of Women; Member of Managing Committee, Bombay Presidency Women's Council and All-India Womens' Conference; Trustee of Lotus Trust; on managing committee, N.M. Petit Trust and J.N. Petit Institute Library.

PUBLICATIONS: *Seatwork* (Oxford University Press, 1931); *A New Way in Education* (Journal of Bombay University, 1933).

The Mistress and Fellows of Girton College with Amy Rustomjee seated on the left of the front row

THE TIMES: *30th December 1931*

Indian students in conference

THE TRAINING OF Indian lawyers in this country was deplored by Mr M.V. Gangadharan at the conference of Indian Students at London University Union Hall, Torrington Square, yesterday. He said that until now there were some advantages to be gained by English-trained lawyers, but now that those advantages had been withdrawn there was less justification than ever for Indians to be trained in this country for a legal career.

Mr M.S. Khanna said that, while in Germany Indian engineering students were encouraged to enter the factories there, they were discouraged from entering those in this country.

Mr A.P. Sinnah said that an English degree was of little value in present-day India. Many of his own friends possessing such degrees had failed to secure any good posts in India, and those who had obtained posts had been compelled to start on the same scale as graduates from Calcutta University. Mr Sinnah, referring to complaints of unfair treatment suffered by young Indian students in this country, said that a young medical student, training at one of the big London hospitals complained to him that when, with other students, he was waiting his turn to examine patients, he was constantly ignored by the lecturing surgeon. When he complained he was told that the patient disliked being touched by an Indian. That statement must have been untrue, because there were at least 300 Indian doctors practising in this country, and they were all doing well.

Mr M.A. Jinnah said that Indian engineering students could not expect British factory owners to welcome them into their concerns. The manufacturers were afraid that the Indian students might learn so much that they would be able to start such factories in India and take the trade from the British manufacturers. It was a natural fear and there was no need for young Indians to become bitter about it.

(*opposite*) The Mistress and Fellows of Girton College, showing, from the top:

1924, *third row, third from left:* DEVADOSS, Sita Vadivu: born 1906 in Palamcottah, Tirunelveli district; daughter of Hon. Sir D.M. Devadoss, Judge of High Court, Madras; Girton College 1924–8; called to Bar, Inner Temple, 1928; enrolled in Madras High Court 1928.

1928, *centre row, left:* BHATIA, Svarna Lata: born 1908 in Unao, United Provinces, daughter of Ram Narain Bhatia, surgeon. Girton College 1928–31.

1933, NANAVUTTY, Piloo is fifth from the right in the front row.

1936, DAS, Thakar, seated fifth from right in the front row.

Sushila Gauba (*in the centre of the front row*) at Girton College in 1921. She was born in Lahore in 1901.

(*left*) Miss Bharati Sarabhai, the daughter of Shree Ambalal Sarabhai of Ahmedabad, can be seen here, fourth from the left in the back row. Born in 1912, she was at Somerville from 1933 to 1936, Hons. PPE, and was a regular contributor to *The London Mercury* and *The Bookman*. She has not forgotten her old college and has only recently presented some of her books to the library.

Britain's first Youth Parliament was held at London's Seymour Hall in April 1939. Hundreds of young people took part, representing schools, universities, the Girl Guides, Junior League of Nations, and many other organisations.

Among the subjects under discussion were the Peace Bill, submitted by the League of Nations Union Youth Groups, and an Indian Independence Bill, submitted by the Federation of Indian Students. Miss Parvati Kumaramarjalam of St. Hugh's College, Oxford (*right*), moved the second reading of the Bill.

(*left and right*) One of the most famous Somervillians is, of course, Mrs Indira Gandhi, the Prime Minister of India and daughter of India's first Prime Minister, Pandit Jawaharlal Nehru. Indira Nehru, as she then was, attended the college between 1937 and 1938, and is seen here standing third from the left in the third row from the back. The photograph on the right shows her selling books on a Labour Party bookstall.

CHAPTER TWELVE

Indian nobility – the years before independence

(*left, above*) Indian students parade outside South Africa House, Trafalgar Square, in central London, to protest for the return of passports to the leaders of the South African non-Europeans, Dr Y.M. Dadoo and Dr G.M. Naicker, to enable them to place their case at the UNO meeting in Paris on 16th September 1946.

(*left, below*) The rock-like figure of Ernie Bevin in the centre symbolises the solidity of the educational bond which still existed between Britain and India. Here Labour's great statesman is pictured with a group of Indian trainees who had come to Britain under the scheme which bore his name.

IN THE YEARS before the second World War, the movement towards independence in India rapidly gathered momentum, and even the most heedless of the nobility finally had to face the writing on the wall. With the departure of the British, who had, traditionally, maintained them in power in return for their loyalty, the Indian princes were to find themselves in a new age.

Some entered into politics, or developed business interests, others, ostrich-like, enjoyed a hectic social life, the fore-runners of today's jet-set. Yet others educated their children abroad, or settled outside India themselves, often in England. Whatever their reactions, they could not ignore the fact that their familiar world was about to disappear for ever.

The Thakore of Morvi. His rule was typical of the kind of enlightened despotism encouraged by the British who ran India.

His Highness Shree Lakhadhiraj Bahadur (1876–1957) was educated privately in both India and England, coming to the throne in 1922. The 113,000 souls who lived in his domains enjoyed free primary and secondary education, a fine postal service, a state-owned railway and an extensive telephone network which linked his capital with some 40 per cent of the outlying villages. After twenty-six years on the gadi he abdicated in favour of his son in 1948, after India's independence. He contributed £37,000 towards the War.

The Maharajah of Mysore made his first aeroplane journey when he left Croydon with his retinue for Berlin. He stayed there for three days and then proceeded to Budapest, Vienna and Zurich. He is seen here talking to Captain Booth, the pilot, before leaving on 19th August 1936.

The Maharajah arriving at Dover.

The Maharajah of Mysore

HIS HIGHNESS SHREE KRISHNARAJA WADIYAR BAHADUR, Maharajah of Mysore (1884–1940), succeeded his father at the age of ten and during his minority his mother ruled the country as his Regent from behind the purdah. The Maharajah was installed with full powers in 1902. More than any other prince in India, he symbolised the ancient Hindu ideal of a king. A strictly orthodox Hindu, he did not share his table with Europeans. Only towards the end of his life, in 1926, did he visit Europe, bringing his own cooks for the journey and for his stay in London. His hotel suite had two rooms specially prepared, one as a temple and one as a kitchen. He could afford it, since his birthright came to £80m.

The Maharajah combined culture with perfect breeding. He encouraged and appreciated Indian music and, a violinist himself, loved the classical music of the West.

He married a princess from Kathiawad in his youth but had no children and was succeeded by his nephew, the son of his younger brother.

His Highness Shree Sir Krishnakumarsinhji Bavsinhji KCSI, the Maharajah of Bhavnagar, and the Maharanee with the two young princes disembarking at Plymouth on 11th October 1938. The Maharajah came to the throne in 1919 at the age of seven after the death of his father, His Highness Sir Bhavsinhji Takhtsinhji (1875–1915), who was a frequent visitor to Britain and who was one of the chief guests at the opening of the Imperial Institute in 1893.

The Maharajah of Jodhpur (1903–47). Air travel was close to the heart of the Maharajah, seen here dressed, as one might expect, in jodhpurs. He was the first Indian Prince to qualify as a pilot and was awarded the rank of Honorary Captain in the British Army in 1923. Flying was not his only passion for he was rated one of the finest polo players in India and was sponsor of the Jodhpur team.

In this 1932 photograph he is seen arriving at Croydon Airport with his two sons, his brother, and their entourage.

The Tikka Sahib, Crown Prince of Kapurthala, elder son of the reigning Maharajah, with his wife and secretary, on board a liner touring the world. The Crown Prince studied in London and his French-educated wife, Bindra Mathi, was a niece of the Raja of Jubal, whose estates were near Simla.

(*right*) Sayaji Rao, the Gaekwar of Baroda and the Maharani (*in the third row*) with some members of their family at the 1936 Olympic Games in Munich.

His Highness Sir Partab Singh, Gaekwar of Baroda, at his home in Epsom, Surrey, in 1946.

(*below*) Lt. Gen. H.H. the Maharajah Jam Saheb, Hon. ADC, at Jamnagar House, Staines, Middlesex, with his 1938 Humber Snipe.

The Maharajah of Rajpipla. Major His Highness Maharajah Vijayasinhji Chhatrasinhji (1890–1951), was educated at Rajkumar College in Rajkot and came to the throne of Rajpipla in 1915 at the age of 25. He is seen here with two society ladies on the eve of World War II.

Major His Highness Maharajah Shri Digvijaysinhji Ranjisinhji Jadeja, the Maharajah of Navanagar (1895–1966), presented his infant daughter Princess Harshad Kunvarba with this midget car in 1937, for use when she and her nurse took outings in the grounds of his Dorking home. The Maharajah was the adopted son of the great Ranji, and was himself a keen player of cricket, raquets and tennis, as well as being an enthusiastic marksman. He had a distinguished scholastic career at the Rajkumar College, Rajkot, Malvern College and University College London. In 1919 he received a commission in the 5th/6th Rajputana Rifles.

(*right*) The Maharajah of Burdwan, Sir Bijay Chand Mehtab (1881–1941), who succeeded to the title in 1887. He met both Edward VII and George V, and was awarded the Freedom of Manchester, Edinburgh and Stoke-on-Trent during his 1926 visit as a delegate to the Imperial Conference.

(*Opposite*) Gayatri Devi, the Maharani of Jaipur, was born in London in 1919, and was the daughter of the Maharajah of Cooch Behar and the granddaughter of the Gaekwar of Baroda. One of the best known members of the Indian nobility in the West and one of the world's most beautiful women, the Maharani went to a London school and later studied at the London College of Secretaries. She married the Maharajah of Jaipur in 1940. In her political career she achieved the distinction of winning the largest personal majority in an election that has ever been recorded, in the Indian General Election of 1962.

The thirty-ninth ruler of Jaipur and one of the best-known maharajahs in Britain, famous for his polo championships, His Highness Sir Sawai Mansinhji Bahadur (1911–70), in London with his two sons for the Victory parade in 1946.

CHAPTER THIRTEEN

Gandhi and the
Round Table Conferences

FIRST CONFERENCE: *16th November 1930 to 19th January 1931*
SECOND CONFERENCE: *1st September 1931 to 1st December 1931*
THIRD CONFERENCE: *17th November 1932 to 24th December 1932*

THE ROUND TABLE CONFERENCE, attended by Gandhi in 1931 in
London, was in fact the second of three held between November
1930 and December 1932. They showed that Britain recognised
that change had to come, and they led directly to the Government
of India Act of 1935, which was in many ways a blueprint for
independence.

The Act laid down a framework for the conservative development of India, which would have led to independence within
twenty years had the war not intervened.

The Act enshrined the federal principle in Indian Government,
and its other main provision was to set up the autonomous provincial government and the provincial structure was re-arranged.

It is not generally remembered that one of the principal reasons
for Churchill's years in the political wilderness in the mid-thirties
was his opposition to the Indian independence movement, which
was accompanied by great personal animosity towards Gandhi.

Just before he left India for the 1931 Conference, the Mahatma
had an interview with the Viceroy, Lord Irwin. It provoked

(*left*) The Maharao Raja of Bundi
in London in August 1946.

Churchill to fury, causing him to make a remark more remembered in Delhi than it is in London concerning 'the nauseating and humiliating spectacle of this one-time Inner Temple lawyer, now seditious fakir, standing half-naked on the steps of the Viceroy's Palace there to negotiate and parley on equal terms with the representative of the King-Emperor.'

GANDHI WAS A great favourite of the British, and in particular the Londoners of the East End. They liked his humour and saintly appearance. Though he had said 'I would bend the knee before the pooorest untouchable in India, I would not prostrate myself before the King, because he represents insolent might', he did, after all, go to Buckingham Palace to have tea with the King, dressed in his regular white dhoti and sandals. He made his famous remark that 'the King had enough on for both of us' when asked afterwards if he had enough and proper clothes to go to the Palace.

Gandhi

WHEN MOHANDAS KARAMCHAND GANDHI was born into the family of the hereditary Prime Ministers of Porbandar in 1869, no astrologer predicted that he would be both a great revolutionary leader and the first Indian to occupy the centre of the world stage. He was to accomplish his task with will-power rather than terror, with the

Three cheers and a warm welcome from the Lancashire mill workers during a visit there, which was described as a triumph that aroused an extraordinary curiosity and sympathy from the working-class population.

Gandhi meeting the Pearly King and the Prince and Princess in the East End.

spinning wheel rather than the machine gun, but his revolution was just as implacable, just as inevitable.

He was married as a young boy in Kathiawad and sent to London to qualify as a barrister, although many members of his family considered that he had broken caste by travelling abroad. His experiences in London made a lasting impression, for it was here that he met for the first time both racialism and the universalist teachings of Tolstoy, here that he imbibed both the Christian religion and the great Indian religious writings, here that he first realised that Western dress and manners left him still an Indian in his own and everyone else's eyes.

In 1891 Gandhi returned to practise at the Bar in Bombay, but ironically he failed completely because he was so poor at court-room oratory. In 1893 he set sail for South Africa, and a week after he arrived occurred one of those tiny events which shape the whole history of the world.

He was travelling first class on a train from Durban to Johannesburg and arrived in Pietermaritzburg at 9 p.m. At the station a white South African boarded and told a railway official to eject Gandhi because 'coolies' were not allowed to travel first class. Gandhi refused to move to the baggage car, and was ejected from the train by a policeman, who also locked away his overcoat and

The original caption in this *Punch* cartoon read as follows: FOR LAW AND ORDER. *Lord Willingdon*: 'And now to hear the *real* voice of India.'

baggage. He spent the night meditating in the freezing waiting-room and it was this experience, and other humiliations suffered in completing his journey, which made him realise that the only way his countrymen could attain equality was to fight for it.

During his later years in South Africa, Gandhi developed his concept of 'satyagraha' – soul force – which led to his advocacy of non-violence as a means of protest.

He put his principles into action in South Africa and succeeded in improving the lot of his fellow countrymen there, a victory which achieved widespread notice in India, and led to a huge welcome for him when he arrived at Bombay in 1915.

The poet Rabindranath Tagore dubbed Gandhi 'Mahatma' – great soul – and this title remained with him as both a blessing and a curse for the rest of his life. Wherever he went, multitudes turned out to see him in search of his 'darshan' the spiritual aura that Hindus believe emanates from great men, and after 1917 he could travel nowhere in India without being recognised and mobbed. 'The woes of Mahatmas,' he ruefully observed, 'are known to Mahatmas only.'

With supreme irony, it was only in the midst of his political opponents that Gandhi was relatively free to appear in public, as these photographs taken around the time of the Round Table Conference in 1931 demonstrate. The Mahatma eschewed Western dress from 1921, preferring a homespun dhoti and shawl, and it was then that he began his programme of civil disobedience against the British. He believed that the weaving of such cloth could solve India's poverty, leading to the second stage of his programme, economic self-sufficiency, and ultimately to the final stage, self-government.

In 1922 he was jailed for six years for 'exciting disaffection', a charge which he referred to disdainfully at his trial 'I am here to invite and cheerfully submit to the highest penalty that can be inflicted on me for what in law is a deliberate crime, and what appears to me the highest duty of a citizen.'

In March 1930 he led a 24-day march to the Arabian Sea with the aim of manufacturing salt, thus breaking a Government monopoly. The salt march led him to jail, and the independence issue to the centre of the world stage.

He went to London for the Round Table Conference, but it accomplished little, and soon after his return to India he was back in jail. His struggles as leader of the Congress party and the Indian people continued until 1947, when the British Labour Government finally extended freedom to the Indian masses.

Gandhi died a martyr. He was shot by a young Indian fanatic as he walked to his prayer meeting in Delhi on 30th January 1948, dying with the name of God on his lips.

This *Punch* cartoon, entitled A QUESTION OF CONTROL had India asking, 'What about changing places?', to which John Bull replied, 'Well, you're welcome to see what you can do at the wheel; but I think I'd better sit beside you – within reach of the brake.'

Models of sartorial excellence, three of the Indian delegates to the 1931 conference, standing in the rain in front of the Palace of Westminster.

THE TIMES: *12th December 1930*

The future of India: Mr Churchill on the Conference

THE INDIAN EMPIRE SOCIETY held a meeting at the Cannon Street Hotel yesterday, at which the principal speaker was Mr Churchill

The Chairman said they were no doubt fully alive to the fact that a conference, which was proceeding with great gravity, and in a most leisurely manner, at St James's Palace, was supposed to be determining, by the method of agreement, the destiny of India. The decision did not rest with any Round Table Conference; it rested with the people of this country.

Mr Churchill said they had thought it their duty to hold that meeting in order to draw the attention of the country to the altogether unwarranted change in the estimation of the facts and factors of the Indian problem which had marked the last disastrous twelve months. The extremists who were, and would remain, the dominant force among the Indian political classes, had moved their goal to absolute independence, and pictured to themselves an early date when they would obtain complete control of the whole of Hindustan, when the British would be no more to them than any other European nation, when white people would be in India only upon sufferance, when debts and obligations of all kinds would be repudiated and an army of white janissaries, officered, if necessary, from Germany, would be hired to secure the armed ascendancy of the Hindu.

The Indian gentlemen and notabilities who were attending the Round Table Conference were in no way representative of the real forces which challenged British rule in India. The truth was that Gandhism and all it stood for would, sooner or later, have to be grappled with and finally crushed. It was no use trying to satisfy a tiger by feeding him with cat's meat. The sooner this was realized the less trouble and misfortune would there be for all concerned.

The Chairman submitted to the meeting the following resolution, which was carried:

> That this meeting fully approves the aims and objects of the Indian Empire Society, and pledges itself to support the society in its efforts to awaken public opinion in this country to a sense of the grave danger with which our Empire in India is threatened, a danger which menaces the welfare and security of our fellow-subjects and is paralysing the commerce and industry of both Great Britain and India.

THE TIMES: *6th November 1930*

St James's Palace arrangements

THE PREPARATIONS at St James's Palace for the Indian Round Table Conference are now complete. The King will inaugurate the proceedings of the conference at a meeting in the Royal Gallery in the House of Lords. The secretariat of the conference has been housed at St James's Palace. One of the last furnishings to be completed is the 'round table' itself – specially made by the Office of Works. It is actually oval in shape, as Queen Anne's Drawing Room would not have been large enough for a round table for the 86 delegates, and yet with space outside for secretaries, advisers and others. The Banqueting Room will be available as a lounge. It will be connected with the Conference room by wires and the voices of the speakers will be carried by means of microphones to loudspeakers.

A photograph of the 1931 Round Table Conference on India showing the specially made oval table.

THE TIMES: *4th March 1931*

Viceroy and Mr Gandhi: an agreement

A REUTER MESSAGE from New Delhi states that an agreement between the Viceroy and Mr Gandhi was reached at a meeting which ended at 1.30 this (Wednesday) morning. The agreement will be reviewed and confirmed today.

From our special correspondent, New Delhi, 3rd March

MR GANDHI HAD another interview with the Viceroy this afternoon. He had spent most of the morning with Sir George Schuster, Finance Member of the Government of India, discussing essential points of the salt tax, and later had other talks with members of the Government. Mr Gandhi arrived at Viceroy's House at 2.30, and remained until nearly 7 o'clock. Mirabhai (Miss Slade) took along his evening meal, which consisted of 40 dates and one pint of goat's milk. On his return to Dr Ansari's house he promptly called the Congress Working Committee together. Simultaneously there was a meeting of the Viceroy's Executive Council, which is still sitting at the moment of writing. Mr Gandhi is returning to Viceroy's House this evening to continue the conversations, and another meeting is being arranged for to-morrow.

The utmost reticence is being observed in Government circles, which is all very well in its way, but has the unfortunate effect of driving foreign journalists into the Congress camp for news, which quite naturally goes overseas with the Congress interpretation thick upon it. The view expressed in Congress circles is decidedly optimistic, and the leaders are already discussing Congress representation at 'the next session of the Round Table Conference'.

For what it is worth, common gossip has it that the Government refuses to concede anything on the demand for an inquiry into alleged police excesses, and insists on the cessation of picketing on the form in which it is carried out at present. It is willing to concede certain compromises in other directions, but will not consent to an amnesty of prisoners unless a guarantee is provided that effective orders for the ending of the civil disobedience campaign are carried out in the letter as well as in the spirit. Apparently a stumbling-block to a quick settlement is the question of the confiscation of land from those who failed to comply with the law.

THE TIMES: *5th March 1931*

India and party politics

EDITORIAL

THE PROTRACTED CONVERSATIONS between the Viceroy and the Congress leader – far too protracted for the patience of some of us in England – came to an end in the early hours of yesterday. A brief message published in the morning papers recorded simply that they resulted in 'agreement'; and it is a singular illustration of the extent to which our party politics are encroaching on the Indian problem that within what must have been almost a matter of minutes this news was hailed on the one hand as a 'major surrender' and on the other hand as though it were the end of all our problems in India.

These rapid clear-cut conclusions had better be held in reserve. Whatever else may be true of Lord Irwin's long struggle for peace, there is certainly no prospect of complete tranquillity just because he has convinced Mr Gandhi that the way of co-operation is better than the way of conflict. Nor is there any sense in talking of surrender until it is clear that some vital concession has in fact been made to the forces of disorder. No doubt it may be argued that the meeting should never have taken place at all. They have certainly succeeded in placing Mr Gandhi in the very foreground of the picture – or was he there already? – and it is easy enough to make play with the 'seditious saint' (as Mr Churchill has called him in picturesque and conciliatory language) 'striding half-naked up the steps of the Viceregal Palace'.

There was never any question, of course, of 'negotiations' between Lord Irwin and Mr Gandhi over the future Constitution of India. Some credence seems to have been given to the suggestion that they were engaged behind closed doors in whittling down the safeguards which have been indicated here in London as the first and final condition of constitutional progress: but there is not a shadow of foundation for it. These conversations at Delhi were directed solely to the abandonment of that organized lawlessness which is known as civil disobedience; and no doubt their length is explained to some extent by the real difficulties on the side of the Congress in dealing with the vast numbers of ignorant people whom they have perverted during the progress of the campaign. It was not unnatural after all, when matters had reached this stage, that there should be discussion of the possibility that the Government, once civil disobedience was abandoned, would exercise its discretion in the case of proceedings still pending in the Courts. It was probably no more than a recognition of existing facts that villagers in the coastal belts – not, to be noted, in India generally – should be permitted henceforth to collect the salt of the sea-shore for their own domestic use.

At any rate the concession, such as it is, will remove an irritating restriction about which some of the wisest of the Indian officials have long had their doubts. If there is nothing worse to follow when the full official statement is published, it must be confessed that the 'surrender' of the Government begins to sound a little thin. On the other hand it is perfectly clear that attempts were repeatedly made in the course of the conversations to achieve what would have been a real surrender in the shape of an investigation into the conduct of the police. Those attempts, which were in the true manner of Oriental diplomacy, were flatly and very properly repelled by the Viceroy.

Their abandonment seems to be recorded in the formal document with which the conversations have been brought to a close, and that will perhaps turn out to be the most important clause in it. It was the rock, as our Correspondent at Delhi tells us this morning, on which the conversations were expected to founder, for there could be no question, as far as the Government of

India were concerned, of weakening the gallant and hardly tried forces who are responsible for the maintenance of law and order.

These of course, are the two main fields – the insistence on safeguards for Imperial interests and the maintenance of domestic law and order – where concession would be dangerous and is indeed unthinkable. Public opinion in England is right to be vigilant and sensitive in guarding them. No one doubts the complete sincerity with which Mr Churchill sets out to 'marshall British opinion' in support of a policy of repression. The use of force has always had an irresistible attraction for him, and his speeches may perhaps serve a useful purpose in reminding Indians that we have extremists as well as they.

THE TIMES: *9th September 1931*

Mr Gandhi's day of silence

THE AUTHORITIES HAVE been in consultations with Mr Gandhi's friends regarding the inconvenience to which he might be subjected by demonstrations and possible counter-demonstrations at Victoria Station on his arrival on Saturday. As a result they have sent to him an invitation to travel from Folkestone to London by road.

The problem presented by Mr Gandhi's outlook and habits are illustrated by his attitude towards the announcement that the Federal Structural Committee, of which he is a member, is to hold its first sitting for actual business on Monday. He has intimated that this will not suit him, as Monday is the day of complete silence. As Hinduism has no institution corresponding to the regular Christian observance of Sunday, there is nothing to prevent Mr Gandhi changing his twenty-four hours of silence to what is for the Conference a *dies non*, a Sunday or to Saturdays, when meetings are rarely held, instead of adhering to one of the five working days of the week. It may be pointed out that the Muslim delegates have never raised any obstacle to sittings of Committees or the Conferences on Friday, their day of prayer.

Mr Gandhi's arrival

MR GANDHI arrived in England on 12th September 1931 to attend the Round Table Conference, accompanied by his third son, Devdas, Mrs Sarojini Naidu, Pandit Madan Mohan Malaviya and Miraben. They landed at Folkestone and travelled to London by car and were welcomed at Friends House in Euston Road. In addressing the meeting, Mr Gandhi remained seated, apologising for his physical inability to stand and speak for any length of time.

Between 1,300 and 1,400 invitations are being issued to many MPs and peers, irrespective of party attachments or views on India, Indian residents and representatives of various societies.

Among the Social Secretaries of the Conference was Mr V.K. Krishna Menon (Commonwealth of India League) and the members included Mr Joseph Devlin, MP, Mr Ernest Bevin, Mr

(*right, above*) Gandhi recorded his spiritual world-message for the gramophone. A special Columbia recording outfit was taken to Kingsley Hall, Bow, for the purpose and the Mahatma made the record at 8 a.m. on 14th September 1931.

(*right, below*) Self-effacing he may have been, but wherever he went, he was news, and he knew it. Walking along the quayside at Boulogne with Sarojini Naidu, Gandhi is on the last leg of his voyage to England to attend the 1931 Round Table Conference.

A rare photograph of Gandhi at the Friends House, Euston Road, too tired after his journey to speak standing up.

A.F. Brockway, MP, Mrs Brijlal Nehru and Miss Dorothy Woodman. Afterwards, he left for the Kingsley Settlement at Bow as guest of warden Miss Muriel Lester. The next day he broadcast a message to America and afterwards preached at a Christian service in Kingsley Hall. In the evening he attended a dinner party at the Dorchester Hotel, where the Prime Minister called, on his way back from Chequers, for a short conversation with him.

On Mahatma Gandhi's arrival, *The Times* wrote on 14th September 1931:

GREAT PUBLIC INTEREST was taken in the arrival in this country on Saturday of more delegates to the Round Table Conference, among them Mr Gandhi. Although rain fell heavily all day, his comings and goings, clad in loin cloth and robe of white khaddar and with sandals on his feet, were watched by crowds at Folkestone Harbour where he landed.

The party drove to London to the Friend's Meeting House, where a crowd had assembled in pouring rain. Mr Gandhi's car drove to the quiet back entrance. When he entered the Hall the audience rose and cheered enthusiastically and he and Pandit Malaviya were garlanded.

Gandhi made a radio broadcast to America on 14th September 1931 and *The Times* reported:

Gandhi's broadcast: the world sick of blood spilling

Mr Gandhi broadcast a message from Kingsley Hall, Bow, to New York and other stations on the North American continent last night, in the course of which he said that in his opinion the Indian struggle and its consequences affected not merely India, but the whole world.

'We Indians,' he said, 'feel that the law that governs the brute creation is not the law that should guide the human race. That law is inconsistent with human dignity. I personally would wait, if need be, for ages rather than seek to attain freedom of my country through bloody means. I feel in the innermost recesses of my heart that the world is sick to death of blood spilling. I have therefore no hesitation whatsoever in inviting all great nations of the earth to give their hearty cooperation to India in her mighty struggle.'

THE TIMES: *3rd October 1931*

Mr Gandhi's birthday

The Times reported two very special functions of 2nd October 1931, celebrating Mahatma Gandhi's birthday:

Two celebrations in connexion with the sixty-third anniversary of Mr Gandhi's birthday were held yesterday. The first was a luncheon given by members of the ILP, the Gandhi Society and the Indian Congress league in the Westminster Palace Rooms. The luncheon was fruitarian, but Mr Gandhi took only goat's milk. About 300 persons were present, half of them Indians. Mr Gandhi

A visit to the Dairy Show at the Agricultural Hall in October 1931. While his companions Pandit Madan Mohan Malaviya and Miraben look on, Gandhi casts an eye over the prize-winning goats. He had returned from a journey to Canterbury, the purpose of which was to visit the Dean, Dr Hewlett Johnson. Another purpose was to pass by Tunbridge Wells, the home of Miraben, who was previously known as Miss Slade, the daughter of the late Admiral Slade. Miraben was one of the Mahatma's most devoted followers.

The official photograph of the Federal Structure Committee of the 1931 Round Table Conference, which met in St. James's Palace in London. Gandhi is flanked by Pandit Madan Mohan Malaviya, who helped put the Congress case. On the right of the Chairman, Lord Shankey, are two of the principal British representatives, Lord Peel, the Secretary of State for War and Sir Samuel Hoare. The official stenographers in the centre were to take down more than 200,000 words during the Conference.

Gandhi and Mrs Naidu setting off for Buckingham Palace from their Knightsbridge headquarters.

was presented with a spinning wheel by the Gandhi Society. He said in reply that he had experienced nothing but friendliness and genuine affection since coming to London.

An afternoon reception, organised by the London Committee of the Women's Indian Association and the Saroji Dutt Memorial Association was to have been held at Victoria House, Leicester Square, but it was not large enough for the purpose and the function took place in King George's Hall at the Central YMCA, Tottenham Court Road. Mr Gandhi, who arrived three-quarters of an hour later, explained that he had been attending the informal minorities conciliation committee. 'I have undertaken work of very considerable responsibility,' he said, 'and I could not tear myself away from a meeting that I was attending in connexion with the very mission that has brought me from India.'

Mrs Brijlal Nehru, who presided, spoke of the Mahatma as the incarnation of the spirit of India. Mrs Hannah Sen presented Mr Gandhi with a purse made of Indian handspun cloth containing £165, together with an illuminated scroll giving names of the subscribers.

Vote of Thanks by Mr M.K. Gandhi

Prime Minister and Friends, the privilege and the responsibility of moving a vote of thanks to the Chair have been entrusted to me, and I have taken up the responsibility and the privilege with the greatest pleasure. A chairman who conducts the proceedings of his meeting in a becoming and courteous manner is always entitled to a vote of thanks, whether those who compose the meeting agree with the decisions taken at the meeting or not. Brought up in your hardy Scotch climate, you have not known what rest is, and you have not allowed us, also, to know what rest is. With, shall I say, almost unexampled ferocity you worked everyone of us, including old men like my friend and revered brother Pandit Madan Mohan Malaviya and equally old men like me. You have worked almost to exhaustion, with a pitilessness worthy of a Scotsman like you, my friend and revered leader, Mr Sastri. You let us know yesterday

(*right, above*) Gandhi is mobbed by enthusiastic crowds on his way to meet Charlie Chaplin in 1931.

(*right, below*) Gandhi meets Charlie Chaplin at Dr Kantilal Shah's house in South London with Mrs Sarojini Naidu on extreme right.

Gandhi attends a fruitarian luncheon at Grosvenor House, London with Dr Joseph Oldfield and his daughter at the main table. Dr Oldfield, who died two days before his ninetieth birthday, had shared digs with the Mahatma in Bayswater, London, as a young man, during his student days.

that you knew his physical condition, but, before a sense of duty, you set aside all these personal considerations. All honour to you for that, and I shall treasure this amazing industry of yours.

Reply by the Chairman, Mr Ramsay MacDonald

I am so much obliged to Mahatma Gandhi for the very kind and friendly things he said in moving this resolution. There is only one thing I quarrel with him about. It is this. Why does he refer to himself, in relation to me, as an old man? I do not know which of us looks the older – but if you turn up the records that lie not, the records of 'Who's Who', and that sort of thing, you will discover that in the ordinary course of nature I am much nearer the end of my time than Mr Gandhi himself, and that if there is anybody who has got any grievance about prolonged sittings, it was the old man who presided over you and whom you kept out of bed until half-past two this morning and then made him get up at 6 o'clock this morning in order to come here with a prepared statement.

Gandhi is seen in the unlikely setting of the Ritz Hotel with the Aga Khan, spiritual leader of the Ismailis, a Muslim sect, and delegate to the Round Table Conference. With them is Mrs Sarojini Naidu (1879–1949), a talented politician who was also a poet, described as the nightingale of India, and a brilliant orator. Educated at Girton College, Cambridge, she was the first woman to be appointed a State Governor in the independent India.

CHAPTER FOURTEEN

Towards Independence

THE SOLID RELATIONSHIP between Britain and the jewel in her Empire was symbolised in stone in the centre of London with the construction of India House in Aldwych. It stands today, a grey majestic testimony to links which can never be forgotten.

The building not only set the seal on the relationship of two great cultures and provided a permanent showcase for India in the heart of the Empire's capital, it also had one side effect. For whenever Indian leaders came to London, it gave them a patch of home ground to confront their political opponents from, and allowed them to operate from familiar surroundings.

THE ILLUSTRATED LONDON NEWS: *6th October 1866*

The India House

THE STATELY PILE OF BUILDINGS which has for several years past been under construction at Westminster, adjoining the Government offices in Downing Street, and situated between King Street, which is to be merged in an enlargement of Parliament Street, and St. James's Park, near Storey's Gate, is now so far approaching completion that it will probably be ready for the accommodation of the Secretary of State for Foreign Affairs and the Secretary of State for India early in the next Session.

An engraving by Jackson of the impressive grounds and offices of India House.

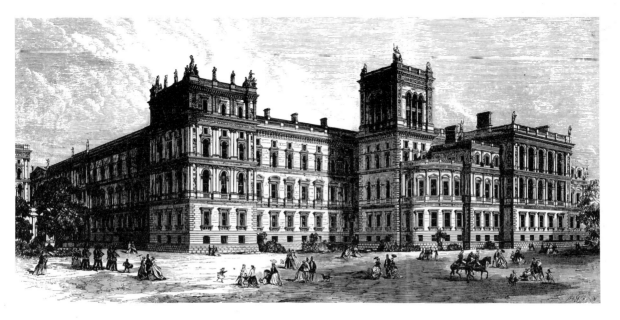

We now present two views of the new office as it will soon appear; one view representing the quadrangle, with the sculptured figures, which are to adorn the outside of the topmost storey; the other showing the park front as seen on approaching it from the parade behind the Horse Guards; the principal features on this side being the lofty tower of the India Office and the grand semi-circular sweep which rounds off the angle of the building towards the park. The niches on this side will also be adourned with statues of Indian statesmen. The tower on the Foreign Office side is not so lofty, but more massive than that of the India Office. The exterior of the whole group of buildings was designed by Mr George Gilbert Scott, RA, who is the architect of the Foreign Office throughout; while the interior of the India Office, with the external work of the inner court belonging to that range of buildings, is in the hands of Mr D. Wyatt. The carving for the Foreign Office, both inside and out, is executed by Mr Farmer; while for the India Office Mr Earp is intrusted with it for the inside and Mr Philip for the outside. The series of sculptured figures on the India Office represent the Indian tribes, an Afghan, a Ghoorka, a Malay, a Mahratta, and so on. In the inner court of the India Office where the most elaborate ornamentation external is displayed, some of the panels in relief are being carved by Mr Phyffers. Some of the ceilings of rooms on this side will show handsome work in plaster, partly modelled from Indian fruit and flowers. On the India Office side there are four great staircases.

THE TIMES: *21st February 1930*

India House, Aldwych

THE NEW OFFICES of the High Commissioner for India in Aldwych, to be known as India House, built and equipped at a total estimated cost of £324,000, are now being rapidly prepared for occupation,

An artist puts the finishing touches to the exquisitely detailed decorations of India House.

A view of the main entrance hall with the internal dome which is one of the most important architectural features of the building. Elaborate filigree combines with elegant clean lines to produce an airy, light effect.

The spacious library and reading room of India House. The panelling, floor and furnishings are all of Indian timber.

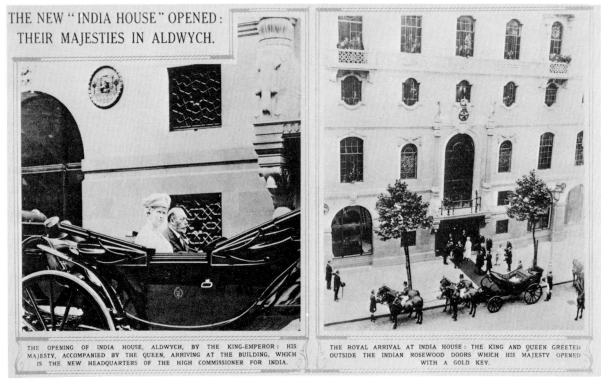

THE NEW "INDIA HOUSE" OPENED: THEIR MAJESTIES IN ALDWYCH.

THE OPENING OF INDIA HOUSE, ALDWYCH, BY THE KING-EMPEROR: HIS MAJESTY, ACCOMPANIED BY THE QUEEN, ARRIVING AT THE BUILDING, WHICH IS THE NEW HEADQUARTERS OF THE HIGH COMMISSIONER FOR INDIA.

THE ROYAL ARRIVAL AT INDIA HOUSE: THE KING AND QUEEN GREETED OUTSIDE THE INDIAN ROSEWOOD DOORS WHICH HIS MAJESTY OPENED WITH A GOLD KEY.

and arrangements have been made for the transfer of all branches and records from Grosvenor Gardens to be begun on 5th March and completed not later than 16th March.

Now that the hoarding in Aldwych has been removed, a better idea can be gained of the distinctively Indian features of the external decoration. The plaques running from the main entrance are now filled in with the respective arms, richly coloured, of the various Indian provinces. The telephone number of India House will be Temple Bar 8484.

THE TIMES: *9th July 1930*

Opening by the King: 'a happy augury'

AT NOON YESTERDAY the King-Emperor, who was accompanied by the Queen-Empress, unlocked with a golden key the great rosewood doors of India House, Aldwych, and after listening to an address from the High Commissioner, Sir Atul Chatterjee, in the library, formally declared open a building worthy of the direct representative of the Government of India in the capital city of the British Commonwealth of Nations.

His Majesty, speaking before a distinguished company which embodied a remarkable accumulation of experience and knowledge of India, rejoiced that through many changes and some dark days India had steadily advanced to an assured place among the great peoples of earth and expressed the wish that India House, by

The cameras were rolling on the 9th July 1930 to record the historic opening of India House by the King and Queen.

spreading sound knowledge, might foster between the peoples of India and Great Britain the 'wider sympathy' for which he pleaded many years ago and pleaded again, today.

A large crowd had gathered in Aldwych to see the arrival of the King and Queen. The High Commissioner stepped forward to receive them and presented the architect, Sir Herbert Baker, who offered to the King a gold key. When the door had been unlocked, their Majesties, attended by the Secretary of State for India, entered the hall, where a detachment of Indian Gentlemen Cadets from Sandhurst were stationed, and Lady Chatterjee presented a bouquet of carnations to the Queen. The Royal Party, which included the Duke of Connaught, then proceeded to the library.

For an hour before the ceremony, the scene in the library had been one of exceptional interest and animation. Half the company was Indian. Ruling Princes in Durbar robes and with brightly coloured turbans had places immediately to the right of the dais, and while some of the other Indians wore Western morning-coats, many were in the dress of their own country. Women in vivid saris gave splashes of orange, green, yellow and pink to the gathering. The Prime Minister and many members of the Cabinet were present. Mr Baldwin, Mr Lloyd George sat together. Three former Viceroys, Lord Reading, Lord Hardinge and Lord Chelmsford, and also Lord Goschen and Lord Lytton, who have acted as Viceroys, were noticed in the throng and former Secretaries of State for India included Lord Middleton, Lord Peel, Lord Crewe and Sir Austen Chamberlain. The Simon Commission was also presented and a large attendance of Peers was grouped beyond the Ruling Princes and in the body of the library. Among them were Lord Salisbury, Lord Hailsham and Lord Linlithgow.

It was a few minutes after noon when the King and Queen took seats at the front of the dais. At either side of the platform stood two of the King's Indian orderly officers in their effective uniforms.

THE HIGH COMMISSIONER

The High Commissioner at once moved to the steps of the dais and read an address to the King-Emperor:

'In welcoming your Majesty and her Majesty the Queen-Empress on behalf of his Excellency the Viceroy and the Indian Government I thank you most humbly and respectfully for the signal honour you have today conferred on my country and my people. It is ten years since your Majesty was graciously pleased to create by Order in Council the post of a High Commissioner for India in London. The premises in Grosvenor Gardens, where the Office has hitherto been housed were soon found to be inadequate and unsuitable for the steadily increasing duties devolving on the High Commissioner as the official representative of India in this country. The Indian Government and Legislature therefore decided to provide the new accommodation, where the various functions of the Office could be discharged in an appropriate manner and in a building worthy both of India and of the capital of the British Empire. Our architect had the difficult duty of designing a building which, while harmonising with surroundings, would at the same time express its Indian purpose and association. Though it was not possible to obtain all materials from India, the timber used in the building for joinery, panelling and furniture is of

Indian origin and some of the marble and stone work was carried out in Delhi by Indian craftsmen. The sculptures and carvings are the work of Mr Joseph Armitage and Mr Charles Wheeler.

I have now the honour to request that your Majesty may be graciously pleased to declare India House open.'

THE KING'S SPEECH

'It gives me great pleasure to come here today to open this imposing and beautiful building. At this critical period of India's history, I regard it as a happy augury that we are able to open a building which marks the end of one period of advancement and the beginning of a new. The position of India House, among those of the sister nations, here in the centre of my capital, further symbolises the unity of the greater Commonwealth of which she is a part.

I now have pleasure in declaring India House open; and trust that it may not only serve the material progress of that country but, by spreading sound knowledge, may foster links between the peoples of India and Great Britain.'

After the ceremony, the King and Queen shook hands with many of those present, and made a tour of the India House. They visited the High Commissioner's room where the King accepted a replica of the key with which he had opened the building and a specially bound copy of the souvenir book of the occasion. The King and Queen also proceeded to the roof. Their Majesties left India House at 12.45 p.m.

Among those who had accepted invitations to be present at India House were: The Maharajah of Kapurthala and the Tikka Rajah, the Maharajah of Rajpipla, the Maharajah of Tripura, the Chief of Bhor and the Yuvaraj, the Maharajah of Pithapuram, Sir Padamji and Lady Ginwala, Sir Manokji and Lady Dadabhoy, Mrs M.C. Ghose, Mr K.P. and Mrs Mehta and many others.

At the reception given by the Indian High Commissioner at India House, Lady Runganadhan, his wife, is striking in an embroidered sari, and Mr F. J. Bellinger, the Minister of War, is shaking hands with Pandit Nehru, with Lord Pethick-Lawrence looking on attentively.

(*left, above*) Indian leaders in London for vital talks on the future of India. The picture shows the Secretary of State for India, Lord Pethick-Lawrence, receiving Mr Jinnah and Baldev Singh with Jawaharlal Nehru in December 1946.

(*left, below*) Indians in London had the opportunity to greet Pandit Nehru, Vice-President of the interim Indian Government, during the reception given at Kingsway Hall by the India League. He is seen here surrounded by officials at the reception on 5th December 1946.

INDIA OFFICE LIBRARY & RECORD OFFICE

Independence

VITAL TALKS on the future of India were held in London in December 1946 and invitations were sent to Pandit Nehru, Mr M.A. Jinnah, Mr Liaquat Ali Khan (Mr Jinnah's number two), Mr Baldev Singh, the Sikh leader and the Viceroy. Pandit Nehru declined the invitation but later agreed to come to London when Mr Attlee, the Prime Minister, sent a personal request for his presence. Mr Jinnah, who had agreed to come, heard of the Prime Minister's special invitation to Nehru, backed out, complaining that he too deserved a personal invitation from Mr Attlee. Eventually the talks began on 3rd December with a warning from the Viceroy, Lord Wavell, to the Cabinet that the aim of the Congress was to get rid of the British influence as soon as possible.

The talks were fruitless and Nehru returned to India demanding Independence, saying, 'We are not going to have an external monarchy and have stopped looking to London.' Mr Jinnah, once private secretary to Dadabhai Naoroji, stayed on in London. Later at a public meeting in Kingsway Hall, he too demanded Independence saying, 'Give Muslims their homeland and give Hindus Hindustan'.

THE TIMES: *16th August 1947*

V. K. Krishna Menon addressing a student meeting in 1939.

Independence ceremonies: historic scenes in London

THE BIRTH of the two new Dominions was celebrated yesterday in London by large gatherings of Indians. One scene of rejoicing was India House, Aldwych, headquarters of the High Commissioner for India: the second was Lancaster House, lent by the British Government for the occasion as a meeting-place for the well-wishers of Pakistan, which has not yet had time to set up its own offices in London. Many non-Indians were present by invitation at both ceremonies. Among them were Mr Alexander, Minister of Defence, Mr Herbert Morrison, Lord Pethick-Lawrence, members of the Diplomatic Corps. Great number of Indians not only attended and cheered the first unfurling of their own flag, but also before and after their own celebrations shared as guests in the other.

By mutual arrangement the events at India House began at 11 a.m. and those at Lancaster House at 12.15 p.m. traffic in Aldwych was stopped and crowds filled the pavements. Inside India House the principal guests were received in the domed library by the acting High Commissioner, Mr M. K. Vellodi. Mr V. K. Krishna Menon, who was to succeed him as High Commissioner an hour later was also present, with the High Commissioner for Pakistan, Habib Ibrahim Rahimtoola.

Behind the platform was a full-length painting of Mr Gandhi. The crowded scene was brightened by some white suits and the saris worn by many Indian women.

Mr Vellodi began his speech by welcoming the High Commissioner for Pakistan as an old friend.

It was a matter of deep thankfulness that India's freedom was by consent and in comparative peacefulness. In a speech punctuated by repeated applause, he paid homage to the leaders in the struggle for Indian independence beginning with 'one whose name is imperishable, Mahatma Gandhi, the greatest Indian of all time, and one of the world's greatest men, who led us with unfaltering steps into the domain of independence'. He then read the King's message which was also being given to the Indian Constitutent Assembly, and a message from Mr Nehru. After a speech by Mr Alexander, who read a message from Lord Addison, Secretary of State for Commonwealth Relations, regretting his absence, Mr Vellodi led the company outside the building to the west corner where a guard of honour of Indian soldiers and airmen was drawn up and he hoisted the flag of India beside a Union flag. Before and after the unfurling of the flag two students, Miss Vijaya Patwardhan and Mr Pandya sang the 'Salutation to the Motherland' and the 'Salutation to the flag'.

Celebrations outside India House on the historic occasion of India achieving her independence. The Indian flag flies beside the Union flag, a symbol of the passage of power into India's own hands.

A personal postscript

MY PURPOSE in putting together this book has been to present contemporary evidence, in words and pictures, of the gentle, respectful relationship which existed between the Indians and the British in this country. Since independence, numbers of Indians have come to settle in Mother England, but the links between the two nations date back for generations. I am particularly aware of this because my own family's links with Britain extend back over many years, and, in the shape of my young nephew and niece, will reach out into the future. Having read these accounts, the reader will, I hope, appreciate the mutual generosity and affection experienced at a personal level between individuals from India and Britain. Nation speaks to nation most effectively when one individual meets another.

Mathuradas Pitamber Gajjar, 1872–1930

Mathuradas Pitamber Gajjar.

MATHURDAS PITAMBER GAJJAR, my maternal grandfather, born in Amreli, Gujarat, was last in line of a family of gold- and silver-smiths, whose clients included most of the princely families of Gujarat and Rajasthan, and in particular, the Gaekwars of Baroda, the Thakores of Morvi, the Maharajahs of Bhavnagar, Porbandar, Rajkot, Gondal and the Nawabs of Junagadh, as well as members of the British and French companies in India. The family specialised in making hand-made, decorative, engraved tea services, perfume holders, incense burners, goblets, picture frames, cigarette cases, holders, lighters and items of luxury of the period. Not surprisingly, some of their creations also came to Britain by way of gifts and souvenirs which had been chosen to represent Indian art.

The craftsmanship was handed down by Vaghji Anand Gajjar, who lived in a small town called Sirdhar c. 1820. The then Gaekwar of Baroda's, Diwan and chief of Army, Vithal Rao, was having difficulty in finding someone to repair a timepiece, presented to him by his French opposite number; his search led him to Vaghji Gajjar, who put it right immediately. So impressed was Vithal Rao that he requested the family to move to Amreli, a Baroda State town, where such talent would enhance the prestige of the State. As a goodwill gesture, the family was presented with a plot of land on which stood the ancestral home and workshop for more than a century, before being destroyed by storms only recently.

The Gajjars were for ever being rewarded with money, medals and certificates of merits for their superb craftsmanship. A gold

Narayan Vaghji, my great-great grandfather, to whom the gold medal was presented in 1881 and (*left*) his son Pitamber, wearing the medal.

medal, presented to Narayan Vaghji at the 1881 Art and Industrial Exhibition at Baroda, is among the prizes treasured by the family.

With the death of my grandfather, a keen student of British history and literature, a link which had endured for more than a century with the princes and noble families of India came to an end, his own sons being too young to learn the craft. Of course, the princes, too, are no more and all that remains in Amreli today of the Gajjars is a wooden sign with the name of the last of them, Mathurdas Pitamber, engraved, appropriately, in gold.

Maganlal Premji Vadgama, 1895–1963

My FATHER, MAGANLAL PREMJI VADGAMA came to London as a young student of automobile engineering and ever since Britain has been a source of interest and influence in the family. The British system of education and way of life impressed him deeply and he promised himself to give all his children a British education – a promise he fulfilled with care and enthusiasm during the following three decades.

Born in Jamnagar, Kathiawad, he went to Kenya, then a British Colony, to join his father, who worked for the British, laying the railway line between the capital Nairobi and the seaport of Mombasa. He was conscripted in the 1914–18 war in East Africa. As soon as the war ended he decided to come to Britain, a decision that was to change our lives. He lived in France and Germany for some time, but it was in Britain that he spent most of his student days.

My father's return to Jamnagar was quite traumatic: coming

Premji Vishram Vadgama, (1867–1938) who worked in Africa, laying the railway line between Nairobi and Mombasa.

Maganlal Premji Vadgama

My father's passport photograph, 1921, which defined his national status as: a subject to the state of Kathiawar a native state in India and as such entitled to His Majesty's Protection.

from a caste-ridden society as he did, he had to go through a compulsory body and soul purification ritual in order to wash away the 'evils' of the Western world. He agreed most reluctantly but refused to have his head shaved. The incident provoked him to write a book in Gujarati in 1930, *Andh Rudhee Cheetar*, attacking what he called blind faiths. He opposed child marriages, child brides for old men: he advocated rights of women, family planning, education for boys and girls and a boycott of all British goods. He became a social reformer and freedom fighter, writing pamphlets on the subjects and issues that disturbed him most.

In 1957 my father established two educational institutes in Jamnagar. Vadgama Vidya Pracharak Mandal provides text books and school and college fees for over seven hundred boys and girls annually and Champaben Vikas Grah, named after my mother, trains women for a three-year diploma course in dress-making. It is now twenty-seven years since these institutes were established. They are a testimony to my father's determination to help the community – a determination fired by the passion and respect for the British system of education which he acquired during his student days in Britain.

The new generation, Reena and Rooshin.

All the members of my family, except one brother, have made their home in Britain. For my niece Reena, aged six, and nephew Rooshin, aged four, born in Britain, the children of my youngest brother Pankaj and his wife Dixa, Britain is the only home they know.

Britain is also my home but my homeland is India.

Index

Page numbers in *italic* refer to the illustrations and captions.

Abdullah (royal servant), 25
Adcock, W., 143
Addison, Lord, 250
Afzal, R., 149
Aga Khan, 76, 90, 205; *82, 106, 205, 240*
Aga Khan, Begum, 90
Ahmed, F.A., 149
Ahmed, N.A., 149
Ajit Singh, S., 202
Albani, Madame, 71
Albany, Duke of, *195*
Albert, Prince Consort, 18, 55
Alexander, Mr, 249, 250
Alexander, Prince, Marquis of Carisbrooke, *29*
Alexandra, Queen, *112*
Ali, Rahim, *88*
All-India Women's Conference, 111
Allen, G.O.B., 136
Allen, Colonel Sir James, 163
Allen, R., 149
Amar Singh, L., 133, 136; *29*
Amarnath, L., 139,141
Ambedkar, Dr Bhimrao Ramji, 109–10
Ameer Ali, Waris, 155, 160
Amery, Leo, 163; *174*
Ames, L.E.G., 133
Ansari, Dr, 232
Arcot, Prince of, 40
Arjan Singh, 105
Armitage, Joseph, 247
Atkinson, Captain E.G., 144
Attlee, Clement, 249
Australian Field Force, 105

Bagshot Park, 185
Bahadurji, Dr, 158
Baig, A.A., 149
Baig, Ali, 116
Bailey, Lt-Col., 131
Bajpai, G.S., 163
Baker, Sir Herbert, 246
Baksh, Mohammed, *28, 30*
Baktawar Singh, Thakur, *142*
Baldev Singh, Jinnah, 249; *248*
Baldwin, H.G., 139
Baldwin, Stanley, 166, 246
Baluch Regiment, 87
Banerjee, *140*
Banerji, Albion R., 190
Banerji, Comolata, 190–3
Banoo Khan, 181–2
Baroda, Maharanis of, 31, 111; *110, 219*
Baroda, Sir Partab Singh, Gaekwar of, *220*
Baroda, Pratapsinhji, Gaekwar of, 90, 111
Baroda, Sayaji Rao, Gaekwar of, 14, 31, 41, 109–11, 115-16, 123; *110, 147, 219*
Baroda, Vithal Rao, Gaekwar of, 251
Bayley, Lt-Col. S.F., *85*
Beatrice, Princess of Battenberg, 31, 35; *29*
Bedford, Duchess of, 64
Bedser, A.V., 139, 140
Beet, G., 141
Beg, M.A. 149
Bellinger, F.J., *247*
Belper, Lord, *128*
Bennett, C.T., 131
Berry, Graham, 66

Besant, Annie, 198
Bevin, Ernest, 234; 212
Bhagat, Lt. Premindra Singh, 171
Bhagat Singh, 166–7
Bhatit, Ram Narain, 208
Bhatia, Svarna Lata, *209*
Bhavnagar, Sir Bhavsinhji Takhtsinhji, Maharajah of, *215*
Bhavnagar, Sir Krishnakumarsinhji Bavsinhji, Maharajah of, *215*
Bhavnagar, Sir Takhtsinhji Jaswantsinhji, Thakore of, 14, 56–7, 71–2; *57*
Bhawalpur, Nawab of, 90
Bhola Nath, Lt-Col., 105
Bhopal, Begum of, *85, 112*
Bhopal, Nawab of, 90
Bhor, Rajah of, 90, 247
Bhore, Isabel Tara, *206*
Bhownagree, Lady, 158
Bhownagree, Sir Mancherjee, 15, 66, 157-8; *110, 157*
Bhurtpore, Rajah of, 22
Bhyrowal, treaty of 55
Bikaner, Major-General Sir Ganga Singh Bahadur, Maharajah of, *93*
Bingham, Sir Cecil Edward, *84*
Blair, George, 199
Bombay Grenadiers, 87
Bombay University, 56, 201
Bonnerjee, Nolini Heloîse, 199–200; *199*
Bonnerjee, Susila, 200
Bonnerjee, W. C., 199
Booth, Captain, *214*
Botha, General, 205
Bowes, W.E. 'Bill', 133, 139
Bowles, Colonel C.W., 118
Bowring, Lewin, 46
Boys, A.H., 149
Brahma Samaj of India, 181
Bright, John, 20
Brighton Corn Exchange, *99*
Brighton Hospital, 96–103; *96, 98, 100*
British Army, 57
British Empire Exhibition (1924), 72; *72*
British Expeditionary Force, *117*
British Legion, 104
British Socialist Party, 159
Brockway, A.F., 235
Brooke, Rupert, *96*
Brougham, Lord, 179
Brown, F.R., 133; *132*
Brown, John, 20
Brown, W.A., 149
Buccleuch, Louisa, Duchess of, 35
Bundi, Maharao Rajah of, *224*
Burdwan, Maharajah of, *223*
Burma Rifles, 87
Burnham, Lord, 155

Calcutta, Tagore, Maharajah of, *77*
Calcutta Cricket Club, 123
Calcutta University, 208
Cama family, *153*
Cambridge University, 56, 84, 128, 131, 148, 202–5; *112, 129, 205*
Campbell-Bannerman, H.C., 202, 206
Canning, Lord, 19
Chamberlain, Sir Austen, 99, 103, 246
Chamberlain, Neville, 165
Chambers, Thomas, 179
Champaben Vikas Grah Mandal, 253
Chand, Dhyan, 149, 150
Chaplin, Charlie, *239*
Chapman, Percy, *132*

Chatterjee, Sir Atul, 244–7
Chatterjee, Lady, 246
Cheals Stores, Pimlico, *88*
Chelmsford, Lord, 246
Chester, F., 133, 136, 141
Chhatri, Brighton, 103–4; *103*
Chopin, Frédéric, 84
Chrimes, Mrs M., 163
Christian, Prince of Denmark, 128
Chunda Singh, 144
Chunder Sen, Keshub, 15, 52, 119, 180–1; *180*
Church of Scotland, 76
Churchill, Sir Winston, 155–6, 166, 225–6, 230–1, 233, 234; *173*
Clayton, 150
Clive, Lord, *111*
Colah, S.H.M., 133
Colcutt, T.E., *69*
Collings, Jesse, *188*
Colonial and Indian Exhibition (1886), 15, 60–6, 68, 69; *60-4, 66*
Commonwealth Institute, 15
Communist Party of Great Britain, 159
Compton, D.C.S., 139, 140
Congress Party, 165–6, 229
Connaught, Prince Arthur, Duke of, 35, 36, 184–5, 246; *78*
Conservative Party, 166
Cooch Behar, Indira, Maharani of, 111, 115–16; *114, 147, 196*
Cooch Behar, Kumar Narayan, Maharajah of, 115–16; *114, 115, 196*
Cooch Behar, Maharani of (19th century), 35, 50–2, 69, 76, 116; *50*
Cooch Behar, Narendra Narayan, Maharajah of, 114
Cooch Behar, Sir Nripendra Narayan, Maharajah of, 14, 35, 50–2, 69, 76, 114–15, 119; *51*
Coorg, Rajah of, 43–4
Coronation Durbar (1911), *109*
Coronation Exhibition (1911), 85
Crewe, Earl of, 205, 246
Cross, Lord, 35
Crystal Palace, 18
Cubborn, Sir Mark, 46
Cursetjee, Hilla J.M., 207
Cursetjee, Sir Manockjee, 179–80
Curzon, Lord, 18
Cutch, Rao of, 14, 35, 69, 90; *48, 120*

Dadabhoy, Lady, 247
Dadabhoy, Sir Manekji, 90, 247
Dadoo, Dr Y.M.,*213*
Dale, J.B., 142
Dalhousie, Lord, 46, 55
Daniell, Thomas, 18
Daniell, William, 18
Darbhanga, Maharajah of, 40
Das, Thakar, *209*
Das Gupta, Monica, 171; *171*
Davar, J.S., 149
Davidson, Ian, *193*
Davidson, Mary, *193*
Dawson, Lt-Col., *78*
Decca, Nawab of, 40
Deccan, Nizam of the, 46
Deccan College, Poona, 201
Deen, Nawab Wali Ud, *196*
D'Egville, Sir Howard, 164
Devadoss, Sir D.M., *208*
Devadoss, Sita Vadivu, *209*
Devlin, Joseph, 234
Devonshire, Duke of, 205
Dhuleep Singh, Maharajah, 53–6; *53, 54*

Diamond Jubilee (1897), 32, 37–40; *38, 196*
Digvijaysinhji, K.S., *131*
Disraeli, Benjamin, 17, 21, 32; *21*
di Veroli, Signor, 190
Doulat Singh, 76
Drummond, Major, 43
Drummond, Mrs, 43, 44
Duckworth, G., 136
Duke, Lady, 163
Duke, Sir William, 163
Duleepsinhji, K.S., 131; *130, 131*

Earp, Mr, 242
East India Association, 152, 158
East India Company, 7, 18, 21, 23, 43, 44, 105, 179, 185
Edinburgh, Alfred, Duke of, 70
Edinburgh University, 57
Edward VII, King of England, 26, 31, 34, 35, 39, 55, 59, 60–1, 68–71, 73–81, 95, 107, 109, 111, 121; *53, 54, 109*
Edward VIII, King of England (Duke of Windsor), 73, 86, 103–4; *25, 103*
Egerton, Colonel, 78
Elizabeth, Queen, consort of George VI, *91, 174*
Ellenborough, Lord, 185
Elvedon Hall, Suffolk, 55, 56, Ely, T.H., 149
Empire Parliamentary Association, 163
Escombe, W. 179
Eton, *196*

Fagg, A.E., 136
Farmer, Mr, 242
Federation of Indian Students, *211*
Fenton, Roger, *42*
Fernandez, J.A., 149
Feroze Khan, 149
First World War, 14, 92–106, 107, 117, 120
Fisher, Lieutenant J.D., 149
Fishlock, L.B., 136
Fitzgerald, Mr, 36
FitzRoy, Mrs, 90
Frederick, Empress, *40*
Freeman, *134*
Fremantle, Admiral Sir Edmund, 163
Frogmore, 20; *18*
Fry, C.B., 126, 127, 128; *127*

Gajjar, Mathuradas Pitamber, 251–2; *252*
Gajjar, Narayan Vaghji, 251; *252*
Gajjar, Vaghji Anand, 251
Gandhi, Devdas, 234
Gandhi, Mahatma, 156, 159, 165, 166, 167, 195, 197–8, 225–9, 232–40, 249–50; *16, 197, 226, 227, 234-40*
Gandhi Society, 236, 238
Ganga Singh, Havildar, 101–2
Gangadharan, M.V., 208
Garibaldi, Giuseppe, 202
Garvie, Dr A.E., 206–7
Gaselee, General Sir Alfred, 84–5
Gateley, M., 149
Gauba, Sushila, 208
General Strike (1926), 158
George V, King of England, 14, 73, 81, 82, 84, 85, 95, 101, 102, 107, 111, 121, 157, 231, 244–7; *81, 91, 109, 120, 133, 244, 245*
George VI, King of England, 73, 86–90, 250; *25, 91, 120, 174, 187*
Ghanshyamsinhji, K.S., 133
Ghose, Mrs M.C., 247

Gian Singh, Naik, *176*
Gibb, P.A., 139, 140
Giffen (cricketer), 126
Gilbert Scott, T., *133*
Gilbey, Guy, 142
Gillam, 150
Gilligan, Arthur, *128*
Gimblett, H., 136
Ginwala, Lady, 247
Ginwala, Sir Padamji, 247
Girdhari Singh, Kunwar, *142*
Girton College, Cambridge, *199, 206–9*
Gladstone, W.E., 154, 190, 206
Glasgow Exhibition (1888), 67; *67*
Gloucester, Duchess of, 173
Gokhale, G.K., 203
Golden Jubilee (1887), 32, 34–6, 197; *32–5*
Golders Green Crematorium, 115
Gondal, Thakore Sahib of, 14, 36, 40, 57, 69, 71, 72; *57, 82*
Goodise Cullen, J., 149
Gordon, George, *30*
Gouramma, Princess, 43–4; *42*
Gover, A.R., 136
Government of India Act (1919), 94
Government of India Act (1935), 225
Grace, W.G., 126; *125*
Great Exhibition (1851), 18
Gretton, Colonel John, 155
Gujarat, Gaekwar of, 44; *44*
Gujarat State Education Board, 253
Gul Mahomed, 139
Gunga Singh, Maharajah, 63
Gungahmah, Princess, 44
Gurbuchan Singh, 104–5
Gurung, Lance Naik Dhanbhakta, *176*
Gwalior, Baji Rao Scindia, Maharajah of, 14, 22, 47–8, 63; *47*
Gwalior, Daulat Rao, Rajah of, 47
Gwalior, Jeewaji Rao Scindia, Maharajah of, 85
Gwalior, Sir Madho Rao Scindia Bahadur, Maharajah of, 76, 84–5, 116; *84, 113*
Gwalior Imperial Service Troops, 85

Hailsham, Lord, 126, 246
Haksar, K.N., 194
Hall, Sidney Prior, *48, 49, 51, 119*
Hamidullah Khan, Sahibzada, *112*
Hamilton, Lord George, 81
Hammond, L., 149
Hammond, W.R., 133, 136, 139, 140
Hampton Court, 83, 106; *87, 89*
Hanut Singh, Captain Rajah, 144
Hardinge, Sir Henry, 55
Hardinge, Lord, 246
Hardinge, Viscountess, 43
Hardstaff, J. jr., 133, 136, 139, 140
Harman Singh, Kunwar, 69
Harmsworth, Esmond, 155
Harrow School, 201–2; *204*
Harshad Kunwarba, Princess, *221*
Hastings, Warren, 7
Hatton, 150
Hawke, Lord, 143
Hazare, V.S., 139, 141
Henriques, E.C., 103
Henry, Prince of Battenberg, 35; *29*
Hewlett Johnson, Dr, *236*
Himatsinhji, K.S., *131*
Hindlekar, D.D., 139, 141
Hindu Muslim Association, *111*
Hitler, Adolf, *173*
Hoare, Sir Samuel, *237*

Hochte, Captain W., 22
Holkar, Maharajah of Indore, 34, 35, 46, 47, 48; *46*
Holmes, P., 132, 133
House of Commons, 151–5, 157–9, 163
House of Lords, 160–2, 231
Housman, Laurence, *16*
Hussain, Nawab Mir Ekram, *196*
Hussein, Mohammed, *65*
Hutton, L., 139, 140
Hyder Ali, Maharajah of Mysore, 45–6
Hyderabad, Nizam of, *52*
Hyderabad Regiment, 87

Ikin, J.T., 139, 140
Imperial Institute, 15, 26, 60, 68–71, 158, 185, 193; *68, 69*
Imperial War Cabinet, 160; *93*
Imperial War Conference, 118, 160; *93*
Independent Labour Party (ILP), 236
India Act (1858), 21; *17*
India Club, 52
India House, 241–7, 249; *241–5, 250*
India Office, 53, 55–6, 81, 160, 201, 203, 242
India Society, 194
Indian Air Force Squadron, 87
Indian Army, 74–5, 82, 83, 87, 105–6, 169–71; *74, 78, 83, 93*
Indian Civil Service, 70
Indian Congress League, 236
Indian Empire Society, 155–6, 230–1
Indian Gymkhana Club, 143
indian Medical Service, 198–9
Indian Military Service, 105
Indian Mutiny (1857), 7, 18–19, 22–4; *23*
Indian National Congress, 152, 156, 159, 203
Indian Police, 87
Indian Polo Association, 144
Indian Social Club, London, 158
Indian Volunteer Ambulance Corps, 99
Indore, Jeswunt Rao, Maharajah of, 46
Iqbal, Sir Muhammad, 15
Irwin, Lord, 156, 166, 167, 225–6, 232–3
Islington, Lord, 160–2
Ismail, Mohamed, *30*

Jacob, Sir Swinton, 103
Jahangir Khan, M., 133, 136; *129*
Jaipal Singh, I., 148, 149; *148, 149*
Jaipur, Gayatri Devi, Maharani of, 116; *222*
Jaipur, Maharajahs of, 62, 76, 90; *146, 223*
Jamkhandi, Rajah of, 90
Jamnagar, Maharajah of, *220*
Jang Rana, Bahadur, Sir Bir Shamsher, 40
Jardine, D.R., 133; *132*
Jareja, Kumar Shri, *196*
Jaswant Singh, 144
Jassawalla, Khan Saheb Aspindiar Coverjee, *187*
Jaswant Singh, 144
Jat Regiment, 87
Jayakar, Lt-Col. Atmaram Sadasiva Grovindin, 158–9
Jehangir, Sir Cowassee, 185
Jehangir, Jahangier Cowassee, 185
Jejeebhoy, Sir Jamsetjee, 39; *188*
Jeoomal, Naoomal, 133
Jerome, Sydney, 90

Jessop, G.L., *125*
Jinnah, M.A., 208, 249
Jivan Singh, Lt-Col., 105
Jodhpur, Maharajahs of, 37, 90, 144; *106, 144, 145, 216–17*
Jogindra Singh, 144
John, Augustus, *107*
Jones (cricketer), 126
Jowitt, Sir William, 166
Junagad, Nawab of, *58*
Jung Bahadoor, Prince of Nepal, 44

Kalooba, Kumar Shri, 69
Kanta Prasad, Colonel, 105
Kapurthala, Maharajah of, 40, 90, 247; *91*
Kapurthala, Rajah of, 71, 72
Kapurthala, Tikka Sahib of, *218*
Kardar, A.H., 139, 141
Karim, Abdul (the Munshi), 20, 26, 31; *27, 30*
Karuli, Maharajah of, 40
Kashmir, Maharajahs of, 41; *106, 172*
Kerr, Deborah, *141*
Keshar Singh, 149
Khairpur, Mir of, 40
Khan, A.A., 155
Khan, R.M., 149
Khanna, M.S., 208
Khem Singh, Sir Baba, *75*
Khetri, Raja Ajit Singh Bahadur of, 39
Killick (cricketer), 127
King's College, London, 69–70
Kipling, John Lockwood, 184
Kipling, Rudyard, 41, 184
Kishore Singh, Thakur, *142*
Kitchener, Lord, 83; *83*
Kitchener Hospital, Brighton, 97, *100*
Kitchlew, Saif-ud-Din, 203
Knox, Major-General Sir Alfred, 155
Koh-i-Noor diamond, 53, 55, 56
Kolhapur, Maharajah of, 76, 121; *121*
Koonjhar, Rajah of, 90
Krishna Gokhale, Gopal, 15
Krishna Gupta, Sir, 116
Krishna Menon, V.K., 15, 234, 249; *16, 249*
Krishnamachari, Lady, 90
Krishnamachari, Sir V.T., 90
Krishnamchari, Shyamji, 203
Kuch Behar, *see* Cooch Behar
Kumar, Y., 150; *150*
Kumaramarjalam, Parvati, *211*
Kutch, *see* Cutch

Labour Party (Britain), 229
Lagden, Sir Godfrey, 162
Lahore, treaty of, 55
Lake, Lord, 46, 109
Lal, Jawahir, 164
Lal, Pandit Moti, 164
Lall Singh, 133
Lancaster, Captain, 7
Lawley, Sir Arthur, 163
Lawley, Lady, 163
Lawrence, Sir Henry, 22
Lawrence, Lord, 181
Lawson, Sir Charles, *36*
League of Nations, 94, 118, 126
League of Nations Union Youth Groups, *211*
Lester, Muriel, 235
Liaquat Ali Khan, 249
Liberal Party, 152, 202
Life Guards, 90
Limri, Thakore Sahib of, 36, 69; *49*

Linlithgow, Lord, 246
Little, C.W., 149
Lloyd George, David, 160, 246
Loharu, Nawab Amir-un-din-Ahmed-Khan Bahadur, chief of, 40
London Committee of Women's Indian Association, 238
London Indian Society, 152, 154–5
London School of Tropical Medicine, 188
London University, 150
London Zoo, 129
Lytton, Lord, 143, 246

McCormack, W., 163
MacDonald, Ramsay, 156, 240
McLeod, Sir Charles, 163
'The Magpie and Stump', 202
Mahmood, W., 149
Mahmoud, Sultan, 185
Mahmud, Syed, 203
'Majlis', 202
Malaviya, Pandit Madan, Mohan, 92, 234, 235, 238; *236, 237*
Mandi, Rajah of, 90
Mankad, V.M.H., 139, 141
Maratta Light Infantry, 87
Marie, Queen of the Belgians, 34
Marlborough, Duke of, 155
Marsh, Henry, 159
Marsh, Sheri, 159
Marthins, G., 149
Mary, Princess Royal, 101; *25, 170*
Mary, Queen, consort of George V, 85, 101, 102, 120, 244–6, 247; *91, 109, 157, 244, 245*
Marylebone Cricket Club, *134*
Mathi, Bindra, *218*
Maurice, Prince of Battenberg, *29*
Mayo School of Art, Lahore, 184
Mayurbhanj, Dowager Maharani of, 119
Mayurbhanj, Maharajah of, 119–20
Maywar, Rajputs of, 39
Meer Jafur Khan, Bahadoor of Surat, 24
Meherhomji, K.R., 136
Mehta, K.P., 247
Mehta, Mrs, 247
Merchant, V.M., 136, 139, 141; *137, 141*
Merwanjee, Benzonjee, 57
Middleton, Lord, 246
Minto, Earl of, 205
Mir Dast, Jamadar, 101
Mir Jaffar, *111*
Mirza, Captain Mohammed Ali, 83
Mirza Beg, Captain Shah, 83
Mirza Mahmed Bahadur, 24
Modi, R.S., 139, 141
Montague, Edwin, 202
Morley, Henry, 190
Morley, Lord, 206
Morley Brown, C., 149
Morris, Sir Edward, 205
Morrison, Herbert, 249
Morvi, Lakhadhiraj Bahadur, Thakore of, *213*
Morvi, Sir Waghji, Thakore of, 14, 36, 69; *36, 119*
Mountbatten, Lord, 86
Murari, T., 149
Murshidabad, Nawab Bahadur of, *111*
Mushtaq Ali, 136, 141
Mysore, Maharajahs of, 45–6, 90, 215; *45, 214*

Naicker, Dr G.M., *213*

Naidu, Sarojini, 206, 234; *235, 237, 240*
Nanavutty, Piloo, *209*
Naorji, Dadabhai, 14–15, 152–5, 156–7, 198, 249; *151, 153*
Narayan, Jitendra, 115
Narayan, Rajendra, 115; *196*
National Association for the Promotion of Social Science, 179–80
National Council of Women, 111
Native Unitarian Christians, 181
Natural History Museum, 199
Navangar, Jam Sahib of, *see* Ranjitsinhji, Prince
Navanagar, Maharajah of, 90; *221*
Navle, J.G., 133
Nayudu, C.K., 133, 136; *129*
Nayudu, C.S., 136, 139
Nazir Ali, S., 133
Nehru, Brijlal, 235, 238
Nehru, Indira, *211*
Nehru, Jawaharlal, 156, 167, 195, 201–5, 249, 250; *203, 204, 247, 248*
Nehru, Motilal, 201
Nihal Singh, Sidar, 93; 143
Nilgiri, Rajah of, 90
Nissar, Mahomed, 133, 136; *129*
Nobel Prize, 178, 189, 195; *189*
Noon, Sir Firoz Khan, *172*
Northbrook Society, 158

O'Dwyer, M.F., 164
Ogilvy, A.D., 149
Oldfield, Dr Joseph, *238*
Oldfield, Thomas, Mr, 199
Ormsby-Gore, W., 163
Orr, Messrs P. & Sons, *36*
Osborne House, 178, 184–5
Oxford University, 111, 121, 148

P and O, 61
Pal, Bepin Chandra, 203
Palenpur, Maharajah of, 90
Palia, P.E., 133
Pandya, Mr, 250
Paramjit Singh, 202
Parsee Association of Europe, 158
Parsee Cricket Club of Bombay, *122*
Pataudi, Nawab of, 15, 137, 138–9, 141, 150; *138, 139, 145*
Patel, V.J., 163–4
Patel, Vallabh Bhai, 15
Pater, Walter, 202
Patiala, Maharajah of, 117–18, 123, 143; *103, 106, 117, 118, 123, 134*
Patwardhan, Vijaya, 250
Pavlova, Anna, 192–3; *192*
Pavri, Dr M.E., *122*
Paynter, E., 133
Peel, Lord, 246; *237*
Penniger, E., 149
People's Russian Information Bureau, 159
Pethick-Lawrence, Lord, 249; *247, 248*
Petit, Bomanjee Dinshaw, 188–9
Petit, Sir Dinshaw Maneckjee, 188
Philip, Mr, 242
Phyffers, Mr, 242
Pithapuram, Maharajah of, 247
Pollard, R., 140
Ponsonby, Sir H., 65
Porbander, Maharajah Rana of, 133; *132*
Pratapsinhji, K.S., 131; *131*
Prestonji, Khan Bahadur M., 163
Pretiva, Princess, 115
Prickett (cricketer), *131*

Prithi Singh, Thakur, 144
Privy Council, 160, 167
Purneah, Prime Minister of Mysore, 46
Putteeallah, Rajah of, 22

Rahimtoola, Habib Ibrahim, 249–50
Rai, Gagan Chandra, *77*
Rai, Lala Lajpat, 202, 203
Raisinhji, K.S., *131*
Rajendrasinhji, K.S., *131*
Rajpipla, Maharajah of, 247; *147, 221*
Rajputana, Kisham Singh, Maharajah of, 107–9; *108*
Ram Singh, Bai, 184–5; *184*
Ram Singh, Thakore, 144
Ramaswami, C., 136
Ranelagh Club, 142
Rangachariar, Mr, 166–7
Ranjeet Singh, Maharajah, 53, 54–5
Ranjitsinhji, Prince, 14, 15, 39, 123, 125–9, 131; *124, 125, 127, 128, 134, 221*
Rapson, E.J., 194
Ratcliffe, Alan, 138
Ratlam, Maharajah of, 90
Rayleigh, Lord, 205
Raymond Electric Company, *141*
Reading, Lord, 206–7, 246
Rewa, Vyankatesh Raman Singh, Maharajah of, 40
Roberts, Field-Marshal Lord, 95
Robins, R.W.V., 133, 136
Rocque, M.E., 149
Rodrigues, Captain B.E., 171; *71*
Ross, Sir Denison, 193–4
Ross, Lady, 193
Round Table Conferences, 15, 118, 166, 225, 229, 230–2, 234; *225, 231, 237*
Roxburgh, Duchess of, *30*
Roy, Rajah Rammohun, 181
Royal Albert Hall, London, 63–5
Royal Colonial Institute, 162
Royal Commission on Indian Expenditure, 152
Royal Garhwal Rifles, 87
Royal Indian Navy, 87
Runganadhan, Lady, *247*
Rustomjee, Amy Behramjee, 207; *207*
Rustomjee, B.H.J., 207
Rustumjee, A., 24
Ruxton, Buck, *186*

Saklatvala, Dorabji, 158
Saklatvala, Jerbai, 158
Saklatvala, Shapurji, 158–9; *159*
Salisbury, 3rd Marquis of, 20, 155, 156
Salisbury, 5th Marquis of, 246
Salmon, Edward, 163
Sapru, Sir Tej Bahadur, 15
Sarabhai, Bharati, *211*
Sarbjit Singh, Major, *168*
Sardar Khan, *88*
Saroji Dutt Memorial Association, 238
Sarve, Sardar Bahadur Kashi Rao, 40
Sarwate, C.T., 141; *140*
Sastri, V.S. Srinivasa, 15, 162–3
Saunders, Mr, 167
School of Modern Oriental Studies, 69–70, 193
Schuster, Sir George, 232
Scott, Dr, 190
Scott, George Gilbert, 242
Scott, Mrs, 190

Scott Freeman, R., 149
Seaman, F.S., 149
Seaman's Hospital Society, 189
Second World War, 169–76
Sen, Hannah, 238
Sen, Mr, 116
Sen, N.C., 163
Sen Gupta, L.M., 203
Shah, Kantilal, *238*
Shahpura, Rajah Dhiraj of, 39
Shankar, Pandit Shyam, 194
Shankar, Uday, 15, 192–3; *192*
Shankey, Lord, *237*
Sharpe, A.W., 149
Sharpley, A.W., 149
Shaukat Ali, 150
Shaw, Bernard, 190
Shelly, L.H., 149
Sher Singh, Sergeant-Major, *175*
Sherwani, Tasadduk Ahmed, 203
Shinde, S.G., 139
Sikh Regiment, 87
Sikh wars, 55
Simon Commission, 164, 246
Singh, Sir Partab, 35, 36, 37–9, 40, 69, 76, 94–5; *78, 95, 142*
Singh, Raj Kumar Sardar, 39
Singh, Raj Kumar Umaid, 39
Singh, Sir Sajjan, *120*
Sinha, Sir Satyendra Prassano (Lord Sinha), 160–2; *161*
Sinnah, A.P., 208
Slade, Miss (Miraben), 232, 234; *236*
Smailes, T.F., 139
Smart, J., 139
Smith-Carrington, N.W., 163
Sociological Society, 193
Sohoni, S.W., *141*
Sorabji, Cornelia, 200–1; *200*
Sorabji Khursedji, Rev., 200
South Kensington Museum, *59*
Spy, *95*
Stanley, Dean, 181
Stockton, Sir Edwin, *128*
Stoddart, A.E., 126
Sueter, Rear-Admiral, 155
Sullivan, Sir Arthur, 71
Summer, G.F., 149
Sutcliffe, H., 132, 133
Swaraj party, 164
Swoboda, Rudolf, *65, 91, 184*
Sydenham, Lord, 160

Tagore, Prince Dwarkanath, 189
Tagore, Maharshi Debendranath, 189, 190
Tagore, Rabindranath, 15, 178, 189–90, 195, 228; *189, 191*
Tagore, Sarda Devi, 190
Tata, Jamsetji Nasarwanji, 15, 158
Tehri Garhwal, Rajah of, 90
Tilak, 202
Tippoo Sahib, Maharajah of Mysore, 45–6
Tirvana, Malata Umar Hayat Khan, 83
Tolstoy, Count Leo, 227
Townsend, Meredith, 202
Trevelyan, G.M., 202
Trinity College, Cambridge, 128, 202–5
Tripura, Maharajah of, 247
Trott (cricketer), 126
Tupper, Sir Charles, 66
Turnbull, W., 163

Umrao, Singh, Havaldar, *176*
University College, London, 69–70
Urs, Lieutenant Krishna, 83

Vadgama, Dixa, 253
Vadgama, Maganlal Premji, 252–3
Vadgama, Pankaj, 253
Vadgama, Reena, 253; *253*
Vadgama, Rooshin, 253; *253*
Vadgama, Vidya Pracharak Mandal, 253
Vellodi, M.K., 249–50
Verity, H., 136
Versailles Treaty (1919), 94
Victoria, Queen of England, 7, 14, 15, 17–20, 24, 25–40, 43–4, 52, 55, 60–1, 64–6, 68–72, 73, 94–5, 114, 178, 182–5; 197; *18, 19, 21, 27, 29, 30, 38, 40, 54, 68, 71, 196*
Victoria College, Kuch Behar, 52
Victoria Eugénie, Princess, *29*
Vivekananda, Swami, 15
Vizianagram, Sir Vijaya, 136; *135*
Voce, W., 133, 140

Wade, F.C., 163
Walden, F., 136
War Office, 93, 155
Ward, Sir Joseph, 205
Warlekar, Colonel, 105
Warwick, Lady, 75
Warwick, Lord, 75
Warwick Castle, 75; *75*
Washbrook, C., 139, 140
Wavell, Lord, 249
Wazir Ali, S., 133, 136; *129*
Wedderburn, Sir William, 157
Weir Hogg, Sir James, 43
Wellesley, Marquis of, 46
Westminster, Duke of, *145*
Westminster Abbey, 73, 76
Wheeler, Charles, 247
Wilde, Oscar, 84, 202
Williams, Captain A.H., 144
Williams, Mr, *88*
Willington, Lord, 157
Wilson, Dr John, 198
Windsor Castle, 20, 64
Woodman, Dorothy, 235
Woolley, F.E., 132, 133, 138
Workers' Welfare League of India, 159
Worthington, T.S., 136
Wright, D.V.P., 139, 140
Wyatt, D., 242

Yasut, S.M., 149
Yates, Colonel, *77*
Younghusband, Colonel Sir Francis, 194
Youth Parliament (1939), *211*

Zinda, Maharanee, 54–5

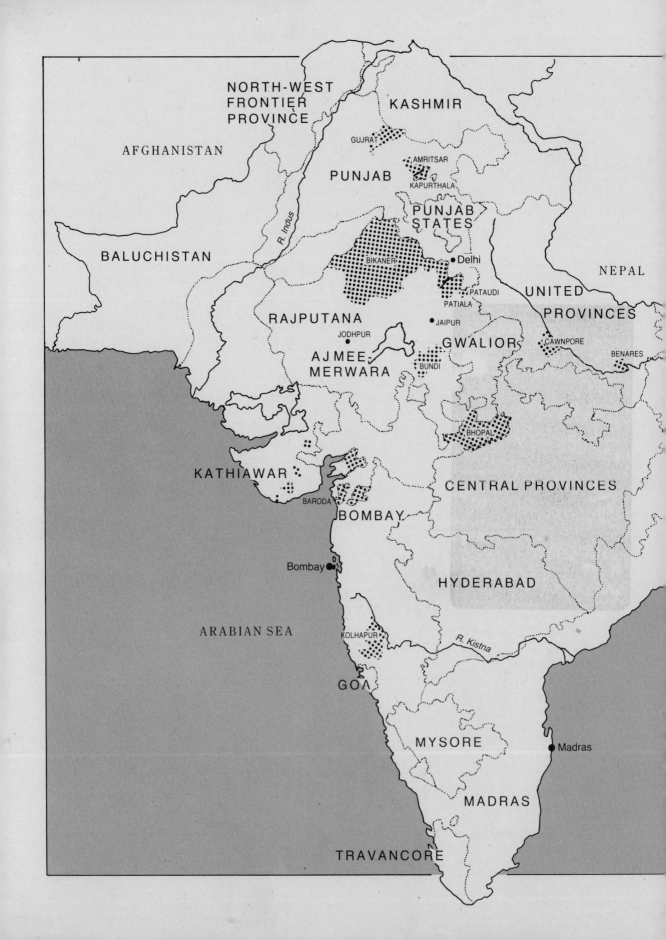